Workers and the Global Informal Economy

The global financial crisis and the subsequent increase in social inequality have led in many cases to a redrawing of the boundaries between formal and informal work. This interdisciplinary volume explores the role of informal work in today's global economy, presenting economic, legal, sociological, historical, anthropological, political and cultural perspectives on the topic.

Workers and the Global Informal Economy explores varying definitions of informality against the backdrop of neo-liberal market logic, exploring how it manifests itself in different regions around the world, and its relationship with formal work. This volume demonstrates how neo-liberalism has been instrumental in accelerating informality and has resulted in the increasingly precarious position of the informal worker. Using different methodological approaches and regional focuses, this book considers key questions such as whether workers exercise choice over their work; how constrained such choices are; how social norms shape such choices; how work affects their well-being and agency; and what role culture plays in the determination of informality.

This interdisciplinary collection will be of interest to policy-makers and researchers engaging with informality from different disciplinary and regional perspectives.

Supriya Routh is assistant professor at the Faculty of Law, University of Victoria, Canada.

Vando Borghi is associate professor at the School of Political Sciences, University of Bologna, Italy.

Routledge studies in labour economics

1 Youth and the Crisis
Unemployment, education and health in Europe
Edited by Gianluigi Coppola and Niall O'Higgins

2 Workers and the Global Informal Economy
Interdisciplinary perspectives
Edited by Supriya Routh and Vando Borghi

Workers and the Global Informal Economy

Interdisciplinary perspectives

Edited by
Supriya Routh and Vando Borghi

LONDON AND NEW YORK

First published 2016
by Routledge

2 Park Square, Milton Park, Abingdon, Oxfordshire OX14 4RN
52 Vanderbilt Avenue, New York, NY 10017

Routledge is an imprint of the Taylor & Francis Group, an informa business

First issued in paperback 2020

British Library Cataloguing in Publication Data
A catalogue record for this book is available from the British Library

Library of Congress Cataloging in Publication Data
Names: Routh, Supriya, editor. | Borghi, Vando, editor.
Title: Workers and the global informal economy: interdisciplinary
perspectives/edited by Supriya Routh and Vando Borghi.
Description: Abingdon, Oxon; New York, NY: Routledge, 2016.
Identifiers: LCCN 2015044018| ISBN 9781138904729 (hardbook) |
ISBN 9781315696201 (ebook)Subjects: LCSH: Informal sector
(Economics) | Labor. | Under-the-table employment.Classification: LCC
HD2341. W664 2016 | DDC 331–dc23LC record available at
http://lccn.loc.gov/2015044018

ISBN: 978-1-138-90472-9 (hbk)
ISBN: 978-0-367-66842-6 (pbk)

Typeset in Times New Roman
by Deanta Global Publishing Services, Chennai, India

For Martin and Emma
– Supriya

and

For Silvia, Dante and Sergio
– Vando

Contents

Figures

Tables

Contributors

Petr Bizyukov is senior expert at the Centre for Social and Labour Rights, Moscow, Russia. From 1995 to 2006, he was director of the Kemerovo branch of the Institute of Comparative Labour Studies (ICLS-ISITO). As leader of the research team and director of the research projects, he participated in many Russian and international projects. He is the author of books and articles on labour relations, the trade union movement, labour disputes and employment issues.

Vando Borghi is associate professor of Sociology at the School of Political Sciences, University of Bologna. His main research interests – pursued in different empirical fields such as labour and work, unemployment and vulnerability, active policies, urban cultural policies, metamorphoses of public realm, critique and social emancipation – can be summarised in terms of a general interest in the "social bases of democracy".

Sandra V. Constantin is PhD candidate in sociology at the Institute of Gender Studies, University of Geneva, Switzerland. She holds a master's degree in International Relations from the Graduate Institute of International and Development Studies in Geneva, and another in Social and Economic History from the University of Geneva. Her current research focuses on the individualisation of Chinese society.

Claudia Danani is professor and researcher in the field of Social Policy at the National University of General Sarmiento and at the University of Buenos Aires. Her research interests include social policies – especially their political content – and living and employment conditions, unionism and social economy. During the last few years, she has been working on research projects related to the political and social inheritance from neo-liberalism in Argentina, lack of social and labour protection, and increasing social inegalitarianism.

P. Martin Dumas is associate professor of Labour Law at Laval University and holder of the Marcelle-Mallet Research Chair on Philanthropy, Law, and Development. His research interests mainly lie in the fields of labour and social law, legal theory, child labour economics, consumocratic regulation, philanthropy and cosmopolitanism.

Marisa N. Fassi is "Renato Treves" PhD candidate in the International PhD Program in Law and Society, Università degli studi di Milano, in consortium with University of Antwerp, University of Bologna, Carlos III University of Madrid, University of Lund, University of the Basque Country, International Institute for the Sociology of Law of Oñati, Carlo Bo University of Urbino, University of Insubria, University of Milan-Bicocca and Italy's Centro nazionale di prevenzione e difesa sociale.

Roberto Fragale Filho teaches courses in Labour Law and Sociology of Law at the Programa de Pós-Graduação em Sociologia e Direito (PPGSD) at the Universidade Federal Fluminense (UFF), where he coordinates a research group on juridical practices and institutions (Núcleo de Pesquisa sobre Práticas e Instituições Jurídicas). He also acts as a labour judge in the State of Rio de Janeiro. Since 2004, he has been the appointed judge for the 1ª Vara do Trabalho from São João de Meriti and has closely collaborated with the Judicial Labour School from the State of Rio de Janeiro.

Alioum Idrissou is senior lecturer in the History Department at the University of Yaounde I (Cameroon). His current research interests are related to the discourses and practices of taking care of social diseases; the history, memories and legacies of slavery and the slave trade; and the impact of migrants and refugees, especially in Africa.

Claire La Hovary is Lord Kelvin Adam Smith Fellow at the University of Glasgow, United Kingdom. She holds a PhD in Public International Law from the Graduate Institute of International Studies, Switzerland, and she is a member of the Bar of Québec, Canada.

Javier Lindenboim is professor on National Accounts at the University of Buenos Aires; he is also a researcher at the National Scientific and Technical Research Council (CONICET). He is the director of the Centro de Estudios de Población, Empleo y Desarrollo (CEPED), a research institute specialising on employment, development and social issues studies. His current work focuses mainly on employment, income distribution and national accounts.

Alvaro Martinez is lecturer in the Department of Sociological Studies at the University of Sheffield, working on the informal economy, undeclared work and informal entrepreneurship. His research interests also include social stratification and inequalities and the use of advanced quantitative methods for social sciences research.

Supriya Routh is assistant professor at the Faculty of Law, University of Victoria, Canada. Supriya's research interests include atypical and informal workers in the Global South, theoretical conceptualisations of work and labour law, workers' organisation initiatives, international labour law, and human rights and human development.

Zoran Slavnic is associate professor at the Institute for Research in Migration, Ethnicity and Society, Department of Social and Welfare Studies, University of Linkoping, Sweden.

Colin C. Williams is professor of Public Policy at the Sheffield University Management School. His research interests lie in the determinants and consequences of informal economy, undeclared work and informal entrepreneurship. He has published widely on these topics.

Aiqing Zheng is associate professor of Labor and Social Security Law and member of the Foreign Affairs Committee of Law School of Renmin University, China.

Preface

This volume explores two interrelated themes: the relation between the neo-liberal market order, regulation and informality; and the possibilities and limitations of informal workers in realising their aspirations within this order. These two themes are pursued through interdisciplinary engagement, with reflections from scholars from the disciplines of law, sociology, economics, anthropology and history. Even though one of the thematic focuses of this collective effort is to analyse informality against the backdrop of the neo-liberal market logic, we do acknowledge that the so-called informal practices extend beyond their causal relation to neo-liberalism. However, the fact that the neo-liberal justifications have been instrumental in accelerating informality and precariousness is brought out through the different contributions in this volume. That neo-liberalism has also made it difficult for informal workers to improve their conditions is also manifest through this collection of chapters.

This volume particularly emphasises informal workers, their agency, and their engagement with law, policy and sociocultural practices. Our focus on informal workers is directly related to how we understand the very concept of informality. The contributions in this volume are concerned with the promotion of the aspirations of informal workers – in the sense of whether or not workers are able to live the life they have reason to value – in determining whether informality is a constrained necessity or a free choice; a trap or a buffer. Such a reflective space allows the contributors in this volume to look at workers from two points of view: first, whether policies, laws and sociocultural practices facilitate informal workers' aspirations; and second, whether it has been possible for workers to employ (innovative) means to engage with policies, laws and sociocultural practices so that they can realise their own aspirations. Both of these points of view, articulated through different methodological approaches and regional focuses, are worker-centric specific concerns that follow on from the general discussion of neo-liberalism and informality.

While the basic terms of reference for this volume were discussed with all the authors, authors were also given complete freedom as to how they wished to engage with the two thematic issues mentioned here. It is not envisaged that every contribution needs to analyse neo-liberal policies and their influence on informality, and place workers against that backdrop. The idea of this collection is, first, to set the stage with the discussions around neo-liberalism and informality; second, to analyse the role of law and regulation against this backdrop; and then, finally, to situate informal workers within this overall context. We do so by drawing on evidence from the different regions of the globe – the South as well as the North, and others in between. While our representation of the different regions is not comprehensive, it is certainly indicative of how the two themes interact with each other in specific country contexts that differ in their respective levels of industrialisation, nature of capitalism, and politics.

Since contributors were free to decide the scope of their individual chapters within the framework of the overall theme of the book, we relaxed the consistency requirement between the different chapters. This is not to say that specific chapters do not follow a common thread and link together fluently; what it means is that the different chapters do not adopt a common hypothesis. Authors in the volume have disagreed with each other on characterisation of the problem, identification of the solutions, and articulation of the cause–effect relationship. Additionally, the chapters also represent different writing styles originating in the different regions, disciplines and languages (in which authors are primarily proficient) represented in this volume. In order to clearly articulate the intended meaning (and also to indicate the diversity in understanding informality) by the respective authors, we have consciously kept the writing styles and expressions used out of the purview of the editorial work. We expect readers to take account of these diversities in engaging with this collected volume. We hope that this volume will be an interesting and worthwhile contribution to the debate on informality and policy as far as workers are concerned, and will generate further debates around the issues raised here. However, we leave it to the readers to deliver the final judgement on the volume's worth.

Supriya Routh, Victoria, Canada,
Vando Borghi, Modena, Italy,
10 October 2015.

Acknowledgements

The project of this book was conceptualised during a fellowship stay spent by the editors and some of the authors of the book at the Institute of Advanced Studies in Nantes, France. The Institute offered us an extremely stimulating environment, from a scientific and, more generally, intellectual and human point of view, and an effective opportunity to discuss and exchange our perspectives of research, possible collaborations, and other research agendas. We are twice indebted to the Institute, as one year later it generously sponsored and hosted an international seminar at which the different topics and the first draft of the book's chapters could be discussed. For this generous help, and also for his active participation in the seminar, we wish to warmly thank the director of the Institute, Samuel Jubé, and for organising the international seminar, we thank the secretary general, Aspasia Nanaki. We also acknowledge the help and encouragement offered by Alain Supiot during the conceptualisation of the project. Additionally, the whole of the Institute's staff were particularly helpful, and we share with them the success of realising this book.

Beyond the participating authors, many other experts had a key role in improving the quality of our interpretation of the issues the book analyses, and particularly of the different chapters, through their discussion at the seminar and later during the publication process: Nicolas Dumas (DAEI – Bureau International Travail, Emploi, Affaires sociales et Droits de l'Homme, Ministère du travail, de l'emploi et du dialogue social, Ministère des affaires sociales, France); Jyotsna Jalan (Professor of Economics at the Centre for Studies in Social Sciences in Calcutta); Nandan Nawn (Associate Professor of Economics at TERI University, New Delhi, India); Judy Fudge (Professor of Law at the Kent Law School, University of Kent, United Kingdom); Nicole Maggi-Germain (Associate Professor of Law and Director of the Labour Studies Institute at Paris I-Panthéon-Sorbonne/ISST University); Moussa Samb (Associate Professor of Private Law-Business Law at the University Cheikh Anta Diop, Senegal). We take this opportunity to acknowledge their role in the publication and thank them sincerely.

Additionally, we also thank the two anonymous referees, who gave us fruitful suggestions and comments in order to strengthen the book's structure and its general line of reasoning. We also thank Emily Kindleysides, the commissioning editor at Routledge, for her enthusiasm and support for our project, and Michelle van Kampen and her editorial team for their excellent editorial assistance during the publication of the book.

The idea of form, informality and aspirations of workers

Supriya Routh and Vando Borghi

Introduction[1]

The interactions between formal and informal activities constitute a key field of research for understanding the evolution of our contemporary societies. Contrary to some influential conceptions of modernisation, informal work remains a relevant feature all over the world. "Most of the world's workers" – as stressed by the Organisation for Economic Co-operation and Development (OECD) – "are informally employed" (Jütting, de Laiglesia, 2009, p. 20). According to the latest available data, while in many countries over 55 per cent of non-agricultural employment is informal, the actual size of informality varies depending on the region. The Global South has traditionally experienced a higher level of informality: in sub-Saharan African or South Asian countries, proportions of non-agricultural workers involved in the informal economy are close to 80 per cent. For example, 83 per cent of Indian non-agricultural workers and 95 per cent of non-agricultural workers in Chad are informally employed (Jütting, de Laiglesia, 2009, p. 18). However, the size and role of the informality phenomenon are significant in other regions too: according to current estimates, the size of the informal economy as a percentage of the gross domestic product (GDP) (2012) in Europe, for instance, varies from Austria's 7.6 per cent to Sweden's 14.3 per cent, Italy's 21.6 per cent, Greece's 24 per cent and Bulgaria's 31.9 per cent, with the EU average at 18.4 per cent (Williams, 2014, p. 11; Packard *et al.*, 2012).

In spite of the pervasiveness of informality, the concept of informality is variously defined and conceptualised. These different definitions and conceptualisations are not always compatible with each other. The idea of informality becomes confusing and, therefore, variously contested, because it is sometimes understood as enterprises (i.e. the informal sector), sometimes as the nature of an activity (informal employment), and sometimes as a section of the economy (the informal economy). Accordingly, the concept of informality often appears to be a subjective opinion of a scholar's understanding of the concept at a definite point of time (Guha-Khasnobis *et al.*, 2006, p. 3).

Even though there are different conceptualisations surrounding informality, we can assume, as an initial point of reference, that it can be defined as activities that are not adequately regulated, monitored or controlled, directly or indirectly, by the institutions of the state. Based on the report on *Decent Work and the Informal Economy* (2002), the International Labour Organization (ILO) defined the informal economy as "all economic activities by workers [informal employment] and economic units [informal sector] that are not covered or insufficiently covered by formal arrangements" (ILO, 2002, p. 2). Informal employment was further clarified as: "[e]mployment includes paid employment as well as self-employment, including unpaid work in an enterprise owned and operated by another member of the household or family, and the production of goods for own final use by households. The production of services (e.g. housework, caring for family members) for own final consumption by households is excluded" (ILO, 2002, p. 126).

The phenomenon of informality, manifesting itself in different forms and experiences, is more or less omnipresent, differently combined with formal activities. However, since the emphasis of the policies pertaining to informality is on the economy and not on workers, legal policy has fallen short of addressing the concerns of informal workers. Studies in the Global South, for instance, allege that law has generally failed to attune itself to the requirements of informal workers (de Soto, 1989; Perry *et al.*, 2007). More particularly, scholars identify the failure of law in furthering amelioration of conditions of informal workers. In the African and the South Asian context, scholars note that since the idea of labour law is based on the juridical concept of the employment relationship, it excludes the majority of informal workers, who are primarily self-employed, apart from being in different varieties of (open or hidden) dependence relationships (Tekle, 2010). Accordingly, it is no surprise that legal scholars are in search of ideas of labour law that can address the concerns of informal and atypical workers who are not part of a neat employment relationship.

At the same time, while informality is not as predominant in the Northern countries as it is in the countries of the Global South,[2] the post-Fordist "working arrangements" (such as subcontract workers, homeworkers and self-employed workers) have given rise to situations in which workers are falling outside the scope of safeguarding afforded by the employment relationship-based traditional idea of labour law (Supiot, 2001, pp. 13–15; Portes *et al.*, 1989). While informality in Northern countries is more visible now, we should be mindful that in many Northern territories (for example Southern Europe, New York, Miami) the informal economy has, for some time now, maintained a relevant role – as a trap and as a buffer – within the folds of the formal economy (Portes *et al.*, 1989).

While law is increasingly found to be incapable of addressing the concerns of informal workers – both in the regions of the South and in the North – neo-liberal capitalist logic holds law to be the *raison d'être* for the prominence of the informal economy (De Soto, 1989; Perry *et al.*, 2007). Peruvian economist Hernando de Soto notes that laws make it costly and complicated for entrepreneurs to operate formally and remain competitive, and, accordingly, force them into informality. Relying on de Soto's analytical lens, a World Bank report holds laws responsible for increasing the cost of competition for firms (Perry *et al.*, 2007). The ILO, too, regards the rising cost of formality as the reason for increasing informality (ILO, 2002, pp. 4–5, 29–32; Portes *et al.*, 1989; Portes, Benton, 1984, pp. 595–598). The ILO's proposal for the formalisation of the informal economy pertains to cutting down on laws (such as labour laws and tax laws), promoting property rights of entrepreneurs, and the integration of national markets into the world economy (de Soto, 1989, 2001; Perry *et al.*, 2007; Bacchetta *et al.*, 2009, pp. 127–128, 140).

These studies (and policy proposals), thus, analyse the role of the law in informality from the logic of the neo-liberal competitive market (Harvey, 2005, p. 98, 2006, pp. 11–25), with a view to promoting higher growth and macroeconomic stability, and strengthening government finances (Bacchetta *et al.*, 2009, p. 127). These studies are not concerned about how law might be attuned to suit the actual necessities of informal workers, many of whom do not directly participate in the market. Moreover, the principal focus of both the World Bank's report and de Soto's study is on informal entrepreneurs.[3] Even though informal entrepreneurs are an important subcategory of informal workers, there are a plethora of other informal workers who engage in activities that do not amount to entrepreneurship.

In view of the diverse range of informal economic activities, it is necessary to analyse the role of law from the point of view of the lived experiences of workers rather than the sole point of view of the informal entrepreneurs engaged in profitable ventures. In so doing, we need to contextualise informal workers' experiences against the backdrop of the dual role – as a trap and a buffer – of the informal economy, rather than accepting the neo-liberal market economy as the point of reference, which seeks to formalise informality. We need to ask what advantages informality brings to workers so that they operate informally. We also need to ask, on the other hand, why workers are involuntarily falling into the trap of informality.

However, while conceptualising informality, scholars pay less attention to this two-pronged role (i.e. as a buffer and a trap) of informality. While initially, with the discovery of the concept of informality, the ILO positively evaluated informal economic activities and, accordingly, sought to encourage such activities in the Global South, of late, the ILO has been more suspicious and negative about such activities. This initial enthusiasm of a new discovery and later disillusionment is also reflected in the scholarly literature. The very term "informal" suggests negativity – something that is *not* formal. While this term is useful in pointing out the precarious activities that informal workers are engaged in and the deplorable conditions in which they work and live, some scholars argue that the very idea of informality is a misnomer – they note that what are being termed "informal" are actually activities that workers around the globe have traditionally engaged in (Guha-Khasnobis *et al.*, 2006; Chen, 2005, p. 29).

This reflection indicates an even deeper proposition on individual autonomy and choice, that is, how the (informal) workers themselves perceive their work. While conceptualising informal activities, one needs to be mindful of the experiences of workers themselves. One needs to inquire whether workers exercise choice over their work; how constrained such choices are; how social norms shape such choices; what are their own experiences of their work lives; whether their work opens up opportunities to them or restricts their well-being and agency; and what role culture plays in the formulation of the informality problem. Unless these aspects are brought centrally into the debates on informality, the idea associated with the term will remain obscure. Accordingly, in this collection of chapters, we initiate a dialogue among scholars from different disciplines, including law, anthropology, sociology, economics, and history, to explore these multidimensional issues of informality from a cross-national point of view, integrating the perspectives of both the Global South and the North into the debate. However, we do not undertake a comprehensive review of either the North or the South; our attempt is only indicative of how the *informality* phenomenon plays out in different jurisdictions that are predominantly formal and predominantly informal.

The perspective of the study

The literature on informality is rich and diverse. Two of the dominant analytical themes are the conceptual analysis of the idea of the informal, and the role of the informal economy in the overall productivity and growth of the economy. Additionally, there is literature on organisations and trade unionisms of informal workers, case studies of specific informal entrepreneurships, and interactions between informal entrepreneurs and workers with the government and the civil society. We briefly discuss some of these analytical approaches that are closer to our agenda in the present volume.

In the context of neo-liberal economic policies, Neema Kudva and Lourdes Beneria (2005) lead the debate on economic informality and its relationship to the ownership and factors of production, on the one hand, and distribution of resources, on the other (Kudva, 2005, pp. 166–168; Beneria, Floro, 2005, pp. 11–12, 17–18, 24). They are interested in an economic analysis wherein issues of distribution and equity are centrally emphasised, taking into account the actors and processes engaged in the informal economy. However, Kudva, Beneria and their colleagues are concerned only with neo-liberal policy-induced informality (Beneria, Floro, 2005, p. 10; Heintz, Pollin, 2005, pp. 50–52, 64).

The studies guided by their analytical lens adopt two perspectives in explaining informality: first, that there is an increase in informality because of over-regulation, and second, that firms increasingly informalise because of the profit motive (Heintz, Pollin, 2005, pp. 48–50). From this point of view, informality is a result of the changing economic structures. The informal *economy* being the point of reference (Beneria, 2005, pp. 6–7), contributions in the volume analyse increasing informalisation of the labour market, resultant deterioration of workers' bargaining power, feminisation of the informal workforce, and inadequacy of existing policies and (labour) laws in promoting workers' interests (Beneria, Floro, 2005, pp. 15–16, 18; Chen, 2005, pp. 38–39). Their objective is to envisage ways to reverse the process of informalisation, thereby formalising the informal economy (Heintz, Pollin, 2005, p. 45). This agenda of formalising the informal economy is in keeping with the neo-liberal way of perceiving the informal, as we mention at the outset.

The agenda of formalising the informal economy underlies the World Bank's approach to informality. The World Bank report in this respect perceives informality as the relation between economic agents and the state (Perry, 2007, p. 1).

The report offers an overview of the reasons for the inception, heterogeneity and socio-economic ramifications of informality in order to facilitate efficient macroeconomic policy-making, in the context of the informality phenomenon in the Latin American and Caribbean regions. It understands informality as a result of both compulsion and choice (Perry, 2007, pp. 1–2). As we indicate earlier, it argues that, on the one hand, because of over-monitoring and over-regulation by the state, actors (mainly entrepreneurs) are compelled to work informally; on the other, actors choose to operate informally after a cost–benefit analysis in order to enhance their benefit (Perry, 2007, pp. 1–4, 6–10). Like the approach adopted by Kudva and Beneria, their (i.e. Perry *et al.*'s) understanding of informality is based primarily on the economic significance of the idea of informality.

In this report, there is a bias against the idea of informality, in the sense that informality is not only understood as negativity; the analytical approach is attuned to avoiding informality and embracing formality, or one specific *form* of formality, as we will discuss – an approach that the ILO is presently engaged with – and an approach that we question in this book (Perry, 2007, pp. 1, 13, 17–18). The report, in its ultimate analysis, is concerned with economic growth of the Latin American and Caribbean regions by devising an appropriate macroeconomic policy (Perry, 2007, pp. 11, 13). In this report, law is seen as one of the reasons that induce informality (Perry, 2007, pp. 12, 14–15, 17–18; Kucera, Roncolato, 2008). Analysis of a more nuanced role of law in ameliorating conditions of workers engaged in informal activities is absent from this study. We distance ourselves from such an economy-centric understanding of the informal. Our position is that macroeconomic policies *per se* cannot be effective for informal workers unless such policies centrally locate the concerns of workers as experienced by themselves into policy-making initiatives.

Our approach is more in tune with the one offered by Guha-Khasnobis, Kanbur and Ostrom, in so far as they avoid the dichotomy between the formal and the informal (2006, p. 2). Their agenda is to demonstrate the continuum between the formal and the informal rather than the divide between the two concepts (Guha-Khasnobis *et al.*, 2006, p. 16; Chen, 2006). In thus establishing the linkage, they too, nonetheless, emphasise an economic analysis of informality. Focusing on the *economic activities in poor countries* of the Global South, their work offers policy reflections that can benefit the poor, rather than workers, engaged in myriads of economic activities (Guha-Khasnobis *et al.*, 2006, p. 7). In conformity with their approach of seeing formal/informal as a continuum, Hart reflects that the idea of informality and the formal/informal dichotomy should be taken as an abstract concept rather than signifying the diverse range of concrete situations (Hart, 2006, pp. 22, 27, 29). That abstraction itself, it is claimed, is the usefulness of the concept of informality.

We defer to Hart, Guha-Khasnobis, Kanbur and Ostrom on the point that the abstractness of the idea of the informal is one of the virtues of the concept. However, contrary to some of the works mentioned earlier, our objective is not to develop an analytical framework for *formalising the informal economy*; we are concerned with critically looking at the conceptual, social, cultural and legal issues surrounding informality with a view to bringing workers into the centre of the law and policy debates. Kudva and Beneria excessively focus on neo-liberal policy-induced informalisation, thereby ignoring the myriads of so-called non-formal ways of work that workers around the globe – primarily in the Global South – were (and are) engaged in both before and after the advance of neo-liberalism.

We, on the other hand, do not take informality as a neo-liberalism-induced aberration *per se*; we attempt to look at informality from a wider perspective that does not hold *only* neo-liberal globalisation responsible for informal activities. However, we understand that neo-liberalism has aggravated precarious conditions associated with informality and has narrowed down the possible responses to informality as far as the interests of workers are concerned. Unlike some scholars' preoccupations, we are also not concerned only with the re-emergence of informalisation; we are concerned about the idea of informality and its relation to the workers, albeit with a focus on workers' own experience of working informally. Moreover, the abovementioned works principally focus on countries in the Global South, an orientation we hope to overcome in this book by integrating perspectives from both the Global South and the North, albeit illustratively. However, a caveat must be added that since the informality phenomenon is much more pervasive in the South, our collection, too, has more contributions from this region, reflecting this pervasiveness.

While the analytical perspective of viewing informal and formal as a continuum, as pursued by Guha-Khasnobis, Kanbur and Ostrom, is an important conceptual development, the relation between formal and informal remains underexplored (with few exceptions; see, for instance, Gibson-Graham, 1996; Glucksmann, 1995, 2005; Ram *et al.*, 2001; Nadin, Williams, 2012; Slavnic, 2010; Williams, 2009, 2014; McLain *et al.*, 2008). Moreover, the legal and sociocultural analysis that forms the core of our contribution is absent from the present scholarship on informality. Whenever reference to law is made, it is analytically seen as a negative factor giving rise to informality. Informality as a cultural or social phenomenon is absent from the present understanding on the subject. Furthermore, the experiences of workers working informally do not constitute a central frame of reference for the authors. Their concern is economic growth, and their focus is primarily on the poor, not on workers (Guha-Khasnobis *et al.*, 2006, pp. 2, 7).

In fact, what are largely absent in the existing literature are analyses of law in the context of informal activities; an analysis of informality in the jurisdictions of both the Global South and the North; an interdisciplinary analysis of the potentialities and problems of informality; and an analysis of the cultural underpinning of the concept, putting workers at the centre of such an analysis. While the idea of culture is important in determining the contours of informality, the idea of culture is sometimes perceived as merely concerning the past: customs, heritages, shared beliefs, traditions. For different reasons, economics became the *science of the future*, and its vocabulary is a strong hegemonic source for any social discourse about human needs and wants. "In a word, the cultural actor is a person of and from the past, and the economic actor a person of the future" (Appadurai, 2013, p. 184). This vision has to be profoundly revised. As we will insist later, only if we assume cultural capacity as a relevant factor for any social and economic action – in the formal as well as in the informal dimension – can we have a full understanding of the issues we are dealing with.

Accordingly, an overwhelming emphasis on the economy defines the existing scholarship on informality. Our collective contribution seeks to overcome this narrow frame of economic reference and places the experiences of workers engaged in informal (economic or not) activities into the centre of our analytical framework. We seek to evaluate informality from legal, sociocultural and political points of view, putting workers at the centre of the debate.

Underlying themes of the book

Since the beginning of this century, there has been a resurgence of interest in the informal economy (after the 1970s bout of interest on the subject) by academics and policy-makers equally. The ILO and some governments, such as the government of India, are at the forefront of this renewed interest in the informal. While the ILO's initial enthusiasm about informal economic activities during the early 1970s (ILO, 1972) had turned into a more cautious approach by the early 2000s (ILO, 2002), India, peculiar for the enormity of its informality, arrived at the problem quite late, through the constitution of the National Commission for Enterprises in the Unorganised Sector in 2004.

This late beginning notwithstanding, countries such as India have enacted social security law for the majority of their workforce who are informal workers. While India enacted the Unorganised Workers' Social Security Act, 2008, in order to ameliorate the living conditions of the informal workers in the country, the ILO has recently formulated a policy (analysed in La Hovary's contribution in this volume) on *transitioning from the informal to the formal economy*. While this emphasis concerning the majority of the workers globally (who are primarily based in the Global South), and in India's case, more than 90 percent of the work force, is important, one must be careful about one's context and objectives when attempting to convert informal to formal.

A good starting point towards a contextual understanding of the informal could be the idea of the informal itself. We analyse the theoretical and policy-related usefulness of the idea of the informal, and argue for a worker-centric understanding of the concept, thereby indicating a way to overcome a neo-liberalism-dominated economy-centric conceptualisation of the informal. Pushing the boundaries of the idea of the informal, we also propose the recognition of unremunerated work as socially valuable and a category of informal work. However, for policy purposes, we argue that we need to focus on each specific category of informal work and put workers at the centre of the policy-making process. We elaborate on these aspects in the following.

The idea of form and informality

The ILO was particularly quick in picking up (and, one might add, popularising) the idea of the informal sector from the British anthropologist Keith Hart's study in Ghana (1973). Coming from the United Kingdom, where industry was bureaucratically controlled and monitored, and was subject to well-developed legal and institutional frameworks, the range of economic activities undertaken in Ghana were novel to Hart. When he termed the activities of the street vendors, manual workers and odd jobbers in urban Ghana *informal*, he had the industry in the United Kingdom and other industrial capitalist countries as his frame of reference. According to him, since the Ghanaian economic activities did not have a specific form akin to that of the industry model in the industrial capitalist countries, the economic activities were informal (Hart, 2006, pp. 22–23).

Thus, the idea of the informal germinates from the concept of form, albeit one specific form. The specific form on the basis of which the idea of the informal developed is just that – *a* form, or *a* model. The economic arrangement on the basis of a clearly identifiable employer–employee relationship, based on a definite workplace, regulated through determinate rights and duties and government supervision, is a model that developed at a specific point of time in the context of a specific society. A significant number of economic activities, then as well as now, did not and do not conform to that model of organisation of work. That model (did not and) does not resonate with the experiences of the majority of workers globally today (ILO, 2013). Should we, then, conclude that the idea of the informal has become meaningless and does not serve any conceptual and, consequently, policy purpose?

In spite of the preconceived bias and negativity (i.e. *not* formal) loaded in the concept, it would be unwise to discard the idea of the informal from academic or policy circles. The idea of the informal serves useful purposes. One of the foremost useful purposes that the concept serves, in fact, relates to its negativity. Rhetorically, when something is determined as being *not* formal or unusual, it carries a tremendous power of mobilisation. The statement that more than 90 per cent of the working population in India are informal sounds an alarm. Such rhetoric prompts urgent responses. The concept of informal is extremely useful in this respect. Second, the idea of the informal also indicates the gap between the privileged and the precarious workers. Third, the concept projects an ideal – a form – to aim for (even though that form itself might need rethinking). Fourth, it offers a language to a movement, in both its academic and its activist sense. Finally, the concept of the informal helps frame broad policy agendas.

Some scholars argue that informality could also be a driving force for development, but the agenda of formalising the informal stunts the possibility of any such trajectory. In this respect, looking at historical experience, we can see the contradiction inherent in the Northern bureaucratic perspective, according to which the informal economy represents only an obstacle to development. "The irony", as Hart writes (2010, p. 147), "is that these regions took full advantage of the flexibility afforded by informal arrangements in their own drive for development a century or two ago, but deny it to those who would develop from behind today."

In spite of the advantages, the problem with accepting the idea of the informal as determinative of policy is that the concept hides as much as it reveals.

Informal activities are as diverse as one could imagine. For example, for a country of India's size, the heterogeneity of informal activities is endless.[4] The problem of capturing the varieties of these activities through the concept of the informal is further complicated by the fact that even formal undertakings engage in informal transactions and relations. For policy purposes, it is necessary for the veil of the informal to be lifted and the heterogeneity of the range of activities to be recognised. The idea of the informal is not appropriately suited for the recognition of this heterogeneity.

In this sense, a plausible, tentative approach to analytically organising the field[5] of informality consists of distinguishing processes of informalisation *from above* and processes of informalisation *from below* (Slavnic, 2010; Theron, 2010). The former case (from above) concerns workers' conditions produced by:

1 the different processes of post-Fordist economic restructuring (corporate strategies of externalising, downsizing, outsourcing and subcontracting), which multiplies employment conditions in which – despite the fact that they are formally regulated – labour standards (rights, protections, etc.) are either minimal or completely inapplicable;
2 a combination of welfare restructuring and subordination of the state and public realm to the imperatives of economic competition, which results in a progressive weakening of workers' access to the "social property", that is, collective goods and services with the social purpose of reducing insecurity and promoting equality (Castel, Haroche, 2001; Castel, 2002).

The second case (i.e. from below) is about the diverse range of actors who commonly experience lack of legal status and protection, and different degrees of vulnerability, instability and dependence. Informality from below involves many and different conditions: legal or illegal migrants working in agriculture or construction; self-employed or small business owners in a vast range of sectors; low-income employees or working poor trying to improve their earnings; and slum/shack dwellers or "citizens without a city" (Appadurai, 2013, p. 158). All these heterogeneous actors differently (and in different contexts) enter into and experience the informal economy as they look for tentative, temporary, differently successful ways of coping with their own generally difficult and vulnerable conditions.

Studies concerning different regions confirm this vast range of conditions. For instance, in Southern European countries, where there is a high percentage of informal employment,[6] it is possible to identify the range of abovementioned working arrangements (Borghi, Kieselbach, 2012). First, one can identify a condition of *permanent irregular employment*, that is, when employment is precarious and insecure but is still a permanent, full-time and long-lasting condition of work; second, a condition of *irregular seasonal employment*, which is characterised by intense periods of work concentrated during a limited period of time (usually in the touristic or agricultural sectors); and finally, *casual irregular employment*, that is, a category that includes the different, fragmented and casual working opportunities that workers undertake in their survival strategies, and which are available usually for a very short period of time and without any possibility of training and education of workers. These conditions suggest that informality can act as a trap in vulnerability, and/or as a buffer against it, at the same time.

These abovementioned conditions are now globally visible. In general, we are observing a change in the forms of the formal/informal interaction and in its territorialisation. While in the past, informality was associated with less rationalised economies and societies, markedly separated from formal activities, located in the Global South, and in conditions of backwardness, currently we have to investigate a different landscape. On the one hand, as a result of the structural adjustment policies of neo-liberalism aiming to modernise the economies of the Global South, the informality phenomenon, far from being residual (if ever it was), is now reinvigorated in its direct relation with formality (Hart, 2010; Aksikas, 2007). On the other hand, the neo-liberal turn affected the whole world, and to the extent that this turn "has succeeded in reducing state controls, the world economy itself has become largely an informal zone" (Hart, 2010, p. 152). That is why Western economies, too, are clearly experiencing a "strong trend towards informalization" (Breman, van der Linden, 2014, p. 926).

A second problem with the idea of the informal is the nature of understanding of the term: what does one understand when one uses the term "informal" – is it sector, economy or employment? For a long time, the ILO's understanding of the informal was shaped by the concept of the sector, which means informal enterprises. Over the years, the ILO developed the parameters of the informal economy and informal employment. While the idea of the informal economy is juxtaposed with the formal economy with a view to ascertaining the productivity of the informal part of the economy and calculating its contribution to the economic development of a country, the idea of informal employment permeates both the formal and the informal sector and economy.

The idea of informal employment is devised in order to conceptualise the diverse range of economic activities performed by (informal) workers, irrespective of their engagement in the formal or the informal economy (or sector). From a policy point of view, the analytical focus of informality ought to be informal workers and their working conditions, if, instead of getting at the problem of informality through the conceptual idea of the term, we analyse informality from the point of view of the experiences of workers. Our focus then shifts from the *idea* of the informal to the *reality* of the varieties of work performed by workers, largely unmonitored by the state. It is the overall development of workers – their working conditions, health, safety, education, nutrition and income (among others) – that policy initiatives need to facilitate. From such a point of view, the concept of informal employment becomes important. However, the idea of informal *employment* is restrictive at the same time. The idea articulates the varieties of *economic* activities that are not formal, the emphasis being economic. Such an understanding obscures the fact that informality is not only a problem of the economy; it is a much larger problem of society and culture, a perspective that we discuss below.

Informality is not solely an economic concern; it is a social concern

As we already mentioned, the idea of the informal has its origins in the basis of comparison with a specific form; a form that was a result of the Industrial Revolution and bureaucratic control over industries, and, hence, pertained to profitable economic activities. Unsurprisingly, therefore, the idea of the informal came to be associated with productive (or profitable) economic activities. However, if the *activities* of (informal) workers *per se* are the centre of our attention, it does not always hold that their activities are economic. Prominent non-economic activities are care work, subsistence agriculture, (certain) domestic work, and unpaid family labour. While there is debate over whether or not these activities qualify as informal work, neo-liberalism-induced policy initiatives generally exclude them from being considered as informal employment.

In the absence of a better phrase and for the sake of prompt comprehension, even though we use the phrase "informal economic activities" to suggest the varieties of activities that informal workers engage in (in the previous section), the idea of the informal is not limited to the economy; it is a larger phenomenon of society, which of course, includes the economy. We must be careful not to subsume the idea of society into the concept of the economy; a society is a much larger domain, the economy being one component of it (Polanyi, 2001, pp. 60, 71–79; Hart, Hann, 2009). If the economy becomes the sole reference point for all social, political, cultural and environmental concerns, our policy lens becomes substantially narrower (Stiglitz, 2001). Analytically, much is gained and a larger policy space is created if the economy is perceived as one of the components of society and not the only reference point for human interactions (Polanyi, 2001, pp. 74, 116; Parry, 2009).

If we are able to adopt such an analytical lens, it is easier to see why activities such as care work and unpaid domestic work need to be recognised as important informal activities, as we presently discuss. There are two issues in this context that call for answers. First, why should one term these unpaid activities informal? And second, why must these activities be recognised as work? It is difficult to imagine that Hart had these categories of workers in mind when he coined the terminology "informal sector". However, his idea of the informal was *contra* a specific form. If that specific form is absent, an activity could possibly be termed informal. In this sense, it might be possible to argue that types of unpaid work that are presently not recognised as work are, in fact, other categories of informal work.

While it is not necessary to encompass unremunerated work with the idea of the informal, doing so could help visualise such work as requiring specific policy attention, different from that required for formal work. Even if unpaid work is broadly categorised as informal, one must not lose sight of the typical nature of such work, and formulate policy responses accordingly. The category of the informal, as we mention, is only an overarching concept, which should group together socially valuable work that falls outside the formal monitoring and regulatory framework.

That brings us to the next question – why must unpaid work be recognised as work? Unpaid work such as care work and domestic work positively contributes to society, which cannot be, and, we want to add, need not be, measured in terms of direct economic contribution. Unremunerated work contributes to social sustenance and evolution. And if the very idea of society signifies togetherness and solidarity, which it does, then it is the responsibility of society as a whole to see that the unremunerated contributors do not go unrecognised. This recognition of unpaid work is, thus, based on reciprocity between social contributors and society.

Our polity should find a way to recognise socially valuable contributions made by unremunerated workers. One of the bases of such recognition, as Alain Supiot and his colleagues propose in the European context, could be the obligatory nature of unremunerated work performed by workers (Supiot, 2001). Supiot *et al.* note that if an activity is performed as an obligation, it should be recognised as work. Such a conceptual lens, we propose, is equally efficacious for other jurisdictions, particularly in the context of informal activities. However, the policy challenge remains as to how to recognise such work and promote the interests of such workers. We address this issue in the following section.

Aspirations of workers and the idea of informality

Whether or not we recognise informal economic activities and informal non-economic activities as work is an ideological and, hence, a political challenge. Conceptually, both of these categories of work are socially valuable. However, we must be careful not to conflate socially *valuable* work with socially *productive* or *economically* contributory work. Once the ideological challenge to recognising these unremunerated categories of informal work is overcome, we encounter several proposals articulating ways to practically recognise these works. The proposals range from a claim to wages for care and domestic work to the provisioning of an *en masse* basic income irrespective of other economic or employment considerations (Weeks, 2011; Fudge, 2011).

However, there is reason to argue that monetary payment or economic remuneration need not be the only basis through which unremunerated informal work could be recognised.[7] It is possible to envisage other pragmatic non-monetary ways of recognising unremunerated informal work. In order to conceptualise different policy-based mechanisms in furtherance of recognising these diverse categories of informal work, the experiences and aspirations of workers need to be taken into account. On the one hand, workers' own experiences are valuable policy resources that help identify the nature and challenges of work they undertake. Their aspirations, on the other hand, offer an important normative direction for policy formulation. An appropriate understanding of the aspirations of informal workers could suggest ways – including non-monetary ways – to recognise the different categories of informal workers and promote their well-being.

In this context, a crucial question concerning the cognitive bases of policies emerges. Public decisions and actions need classifications, categorisations and criteria of selection in order to structure categories and schemes of assessment. In other words, collectively relevant decisions and actions incorporate and use, putting it in Amartya Sen's language, *informational basis of judgement for justice* (IBJJ): "In each evaluative structure, some types of factual matters are taken to be important in themselves [...]. The former variables, which reflect the basic ends in that specific evaluative system, constitute the 'informational basis' of evaluative judgements in that system" (Sen, 1991, p. 16). In this sense, the IBJJ is at the very core of any process of evaluation, whether it is exercised in the context of social policy, labour policy, or others. This question of informational basis is also at the core of the (existing and possible) policies addressing the relationship between formality and informality in working lives: what counts as information when the formalisation of informal working arrangements has to be undertaken? How do workers' experiences become (or not become) part of the informational basis on which policies are designed and delivered? And what does not count, that is, what does the prevailing mode of policy-making/delivering determine marginal or irrelevant, and, accordingly, what kinds of cognitive gaps and ignorance become politically and bureaucratically transformed in legitimated "areas of indifference"?[8]

According to Sen, it should be stressed that "[e]ach evaluative approach can, to a great extent, be characterized by its informational basis: the information that is needed for making judgments using that approach and – no less important – the information that is 'excluded' from a direct evaluative role in that approach. Informational exclusions are important constituents of an evaluative approach. The excluded information is not permitted to have any direct influence on evaluative judgments, and while this is usually done in an implicit way, the character of the approach may be strongly influenced by insensitivity to the excluded information [...]. In fact, the real 'bite' of a theory of justice can, to a great extent, be understood from its informational base: what information is – or is not – taken to be directly relevant" (1999, pp. 56, 57). The concrete relevance of these informational bases becomes evident when we consider that they "embody definitions of problems and targets, categorisations of individuals and social groups, as well as complex systems for assessing actions against objectives" (de Leonardis, Negrelli, 2012, p. 17).

According to our perspective in this volume, the informational basis of any policy addressing the field of informal work should take into account workers' *aspirations* and *agency*, which means moving towards a research and policy approach relying on "a broader informational base, focusing particularly on people's capability to choose the lives they have reason to value" (Sen, 1999, p. 63). The freedom of individuals, "seen in the form of individual capabilities to do things that a person has reason to value" (Sen, 1999, p. 56), constitutes, in this perspective, a key criterion for fully understanding the meaning of informal practices and for drawing any conclusion about it.

Of course, freedom is not to be confused with mere (utilitarian) freedom of choice, in which individual decision is a selection among already given preferences, produced by an individual conceived as an independent and isolated atom

(Bonvin, Favarque, 2005). In the perspective that we are trying to sketch here, there is a fundamental relationship among freedom, the public realm, and culture. On the one hand, this relationship has strong participatory roots, as "the exercise of freedom is mediated by values, but the values in turn are influenced by public discussions and social interactions, which are themselves influenced by participatory freedoms" (Sen, 1999, p. 9). In this sense, capability is significantly connected to what Hirschman (1970) focused on in terms of *voice*, which is the "capacity for voice", that is, the capacity to express one's own thought and to make it count in the public realm (Bifulco, 2013; de Leonardis, Negrelli, 2012). Democratic institutions have the responsibility to promote the capacity for voice, and the public sphere should encourage such capacity.

On the other hand, this perspective underlines the relationship between voice and culture, where culture means the *capacity to aspire* (Appadurai, 2013) – a specific cultural capability, not equally distributed in society, which enables individuals to imagine a future different from and better than their own current condition. Arjun Appadurai developed this concept while collaborating with associations and organisations of some of the most humble informal workers – shack and slum dwellers in Mumbai – studying the concrete strategies through which these "citizens without city" enhance their own capacity to aspire. Appadurai indicated how the slum dwellers and workers, facing regular problems of humiliation and safety during the management of sanitation, are transformed into experts and creative designers of toilets and toilet festivals; and how they themselves become their own officers of registry, collecting data and information otherwise ignored by the political authorities. According to this analytical framework, the capacity to aspire is a cultural precondition of capability, and the capability for voice is the way through which the former (i.e. the capacity to aspire) approaches the latter (i.e. capability).

The significance of Appadurai's research about *capacity to aspire* and the way it is concretely practised by grassroots associations in Mumbai is that it shows that the capacity to aspire and voice act together and reinforce each other (Bifulco, 2013, p. 183). His definition of a "politics of shit" – "When a World Bank official has to examine the virtues of a public toilet and discuss the merits of this form of shit management with the shitters themselves, the condition of poverty moves from abjection to subjectivation" (ibid., p. 170) – clearly demonstrates the way in which a strong repositioning of the starting point of the knowledge-making process can affect its transformation into relevant information for a decision. Analyses and research have widely recognised that durable and more equitable development needs the poor's capability for voice. But what "has not been adequately recognised is that for 'voice' to be regularly and effectively exercised by the poor, in conditions of radical inequalities in power and dignity, requires permanent enhancements of their collective capacity to aspire" (Appadurai, 2013, p. 213).

In this sense, any revaluation of the formal/informal relationship should be inspired by "cosmopolitanism from below" (Appadurai, 2013). We need to avoid being trapped in the dilemma between a passive and ethnocentric reproduction of the imperial project of European cosmopolitanism and modernisation, on the one hand, and the simplistic assertion of the local and particular experience, which is as much ethnocentric as the first alternative, on the other. A *cosmopolitanism from below* represents a perspective according to which we have to explore and promote the frameworks of "deep democracy" (ibid., p. 212), that is, an ideal of social organisation based on universalist rights and duties (as assumed in a cosmopolitan view), revised by according full regard to the concrete, situated voices of the weak, the very poor, the women and the workers that are coming from below.

If ideological challenges and political conservatism are overcome, one of the principal tasks of the policy-makers should be locating informal workers at the centre of the policy-making process. Informal workers should become participants in determining their own policy regime. Workers need to be engaged in a social dialogue process. Depending on the category of work and the nature of the workers engaged in such work, the social dialogue process could be devised in such a way as to allow the maximum meaningful participation from the workers.

One further challenge needs to be met in integrating informal workers in a social dialogue process. As we discuss, the idea of informal work is only an umbrella concept; in reality, there are several categories of workers engaged in activities that do not conform to the *form* in contrast to which the idea of the informal is developed. In order to understand the nuances of the specific categories of work and workers, each of the specific categories needs to be treated as a *sui generis* phenomenon. The diversified nature of informal work, therefore, mandates that policy-making be decentralised. These issues will be re-emphasised in the different chapters of the present volume, albeit from varying points of view. We discuss the aim of the book and the methods employed in the following section.

Aims of the book and methods

The two-pronged objective of the book is to analyse the link between neo-liberalism and informality, and to locate workers within this relation. We are interested in an analysis of informality that places workers at the centre of the debate. Accordingly, we hope to address the following questions. What relationship exists, in different contexts, between individual engagement in informal activities and freedom to pursue the life individuals have reason to value? How has this relationship been reframed in the process of expansion and hegemony of the neo-liberal capitalism? How does informal work affect the terms of recognition for the workers involved in the informal activities? How have different jurisdictions dealt with the problem of this recognition? What kinds of social processes emerge at the crossroads of local forms of life, abstract logics of neo-liberal capitalism, and the formal and informal economy? In which ways do situated individuals, social groups and communities locally combine formal and informal dimensions in order to pursue their own self-determination? How could law intervene, in different contexts and situations, to ameliorate the conditions of workers? What about the role of different institutions and public action?

While we cannot possibly offer any conclusive answer to the questions we ask, we think that asking these questions is itself an important endeavour. Our aim in this volume is to initiate an interdisciplinary debate on informality that looks at the issue in a more open and embracing manner, and in the process, to distance ourselves from an overwhelmingly economy-focused understanding of informality, as is presently predominant. The book is aimed at an interdisciplinary readership, and accordingly, we refrain from focusing too narrowly on any specific issue pertaining to informal workers or the informal economy. We want to identify the relationship between deregulated neo-liberalism and informality; but our agenda is not limited only to this exploration.

What we hope to achieve through the different contributions of the volume is to indicate how the dominant neo-liberal economic policies and laws ignore informal workers' own experiences in determining policy priorities, and whether it is possible to adopt other, more worker-sensitive approaches to policy-making with respect to informality. While we cannot offer a conclusive answer to these questions, through the different chapters, we hope to indicate possibilities of a worker-sensitive approach to informality.

As we mentioned, human beings, in different social and political contexts, always experience different conditions in terms of their own capacity to aspire, that is, in terms of their situated cultural capability, which is not equally distributed in society, and which enables individuals to imagine a better future than their present condition. We aim to explore the multidimensional aspects of these abovementioned issues in different social, cultural, economic and political contexts, in pursuance of the idea that social and cultural sciences need to experiment with and elaborate post-colonial and world analytical categories more and more, while at the same time testing their strength in the concrete circumstances of local daily life experiences.

Since we are concerned with how neo-liberalism influences policy and law related to informality, we wanted to see how informality plays out in countries that are characterised predominantly by the formal economy and countries that are characterised predominantly by the informal economy, and others in between. In pursuance with that strategy, we analyse informality in the context of diverse countries located in different regions.

In furtherance of the abovementioned objective, we do not envisage that every chapter needs to reiterate how informal workers could exercise choice over their working conditions and living situations. We think that the dialectic between the different formal/informal ways of integrating the economy and society is structurally at the core of our different societies and of their development. At a general level, the book represents an understanding of the contemporary metamorphosis of social organisation, albeit in different contexts, by looking at a specific but crucial aspect: the tensions and interactions between the informal and the formal dimensions in the field of working life. Beginning from an exploration of the broader effects and consequences of the neo-liberal deregulatory perspective, we plan to gradually focus on state policies and laws, and then locate informal workers within this larger discourse. We hope that concerns pertaining to the workers and the exclusion of their aspirations from law and policy will emerge from the entire contribution taken as a whole.

The book develops through three thematic parts. In the first part, we engage with the debate on neo-liberal capitalism and its influence on policy formulation, and how such policy orientation, in turn, influences or is influenced by informality in its different variations. In the second part, we analyse the relationship between law and informal economic activities. In this part, we engage with the role of the ILO and its understanding of the problem of informality. We also look at how and to what extent the legal understanding of informality pertains to the lived experiences of informal workers. In the third and final part of the book, we group together studies analysing the lived experiences of the informal workers and how such workers strategise in order to improve their condition even in the face of hostile socio-political circumstances. Each of these parts builds on the previous parts of the book. While the role of law in informality flows from the overall neo-liberal outlook of the economy, the actual lived experiences of the workers are shaped by such laws and policies. In this sense, our attempt is to locate workers within the larger discourse of the neo-liberal economic policies and their legal instruments and, at the same time, challenge the neo-liberal formulation of informality from the point of view of the workers. There follows a chapter outline of the different contributions to the book.

Chapter outline

In furtherance of the two-pronged objective of this book, we do not envisage that every chapter needs to formulate the relation between neo-liberalism and informality, and reiterate whether or not informal workers could exercise choice over their working conditions and living situations. Instead, beginning from a broader neo-liberal deregulatory perspective (involving cross-national comparative data from 116 countries from the North and the South), we plan to gradually focus on state policies and laws, and then situate informal workers within this larger discourse. In order to follow this plan, apart from this introductory chapter and the concluding chapter, the other contributions in this volume are divided into three parts. The first part, titled *Neo-liberalism, State, and Regulation in Formulating Informality* engages with the relation between neo-liberal logic of the market, the role of the state, and regulatory intervention in constituting informality.

In Chapter 1, Colin C. Williams and Alvaro Martinez challenge the neo-liberal notion that enterprises operate in the informal sector due to high taxes, public sector corruption and too much state interference in the free market. According to this neo-liberal interpretation, reductions in taxation and corruption, along with deregulation in order to minimise state interference in the market, would formalise informality. Using data generated by the World Bank and the International Monetary Fund in assessing cross-national variations in informal undertakings in 116 economies, the authors come to the conclusion that the contrary is true: more, rather than less, state intervention is necessary in order to safeguard workers' interests and reduce the level of informality among enterprises. According to Williams and Martinez, "the current neo-liberal explanation has little or no evidence for its promulgation of lower taxes and reduced public spending as a remedy for tackling informality."

Continuing the discussion initiated in this introductory chapter on the conceptual issues pertaining to informality, Zoran Slavnic, in Chapter 2, objects to the tendency to disregard the unity of the economic system by dividing it into several separate economies, such as the formal and the informal. Slavnic draws our attention to an alternative view on these issues, which includes informal economic *actors* that conventional research in this field has had trouble comprehending as participants in the informal economy, namely, big businesses and the state. Through an empirical study of the Swedish taxi industry as an illustration of informalisation, he charts the complex nature of policy engagement with the multifaceted challenges of economic informality, particularly when the state is involved in the informal economy. On the basis of this illustration, recalling Max Weber, Slavnic weighs several policy directions to engage with informality, which, he argues, will determine how informality is seen vis-à-vis the economy and how informal actors engage with the political economy.

Sandra V. Constantin continues the conversation in Chapter 3 by documenting how political economy responds to state policy, albeit in the specific context of China. Constantin notes that Chinese society has moved from being generically collective (i.e. on the basis of kinship, community, etc.), to work unit-based collective, to individualistic, shaped primarily by the party-state's priorities. Her case study in urban Beijing reconstructs the life-course of 916 respondents in order to ascertain how they encountered and engaged with informal employment – one of the socio-economic uncertainties that have shaped their lives – in the process of becoming "responsible for their destinies", as mandated by the party-state during the reform period. On the basis of her case study, she notes that informal employment is an involuntary choice and is shaped by several factors, such as education, skill, migration, locality and overall insecurity, that constrain the choices of an individual in reaching their aspirations. Constantin's case study corroborates the argument that informal employment has been, to a large extent, used by the party-state in order to pass on the negative effects of the market reform to the citizens.

The second part of the book – *Law in Formalising Informal Workers* – focuses on the international legal standards and other regulatory possibilities – and problems – in ameliorating the conditions of informal workers. In Chapter 4, Claire La Hovary looks at the concept of informality from a legal point of view and contextualises the ILO's recent Recommendation No. 204, on *Transition from the Informal to the Formal Economy*, against this backdrop. La Hovary asserts that the term "informal" is very imprecise and becomes a cumbersome concept if defined from a legal point of view. Therefore, she argues that, instead of focusing on the generic concept of the informal, legal policy should concern itself with ameliorating the conditions of specific categories of workers with a more nuanced attention to their typical needs and concerns. She criticises the ILO's Recommendation No. 204 on these grounds. Looking at the geopolitics behind the adoption of the

ILO Recommendation, she notes that the biggest thrust for the adoption of the Recommendation came from the Employers' group at the ILO, because they were concerned with the uneven competition between formal and informal enterprises, rather than having any real concern for the improvement of workers' conditions. This being the backdrop of the Recommendation, La Hovary contends that it does little for amelioration of workers' conditions.

In Chapter 5, based on three vignettes drawing on his courtroom experience in the state of Rio de Janeiro in Brazil, Roberto Fragale Filho, a labour court judge, analyses how the idea of informality is shaped by the different actors in the courtroom and what it means for the workers in concrete terms. Indicating the complexity of courtroom interpretation, he notes that straitjacket legal concepts – often necessary for formulating legal claims – turn the formal/informal debate into a legal/illegal dichotomy, thereby ignoring the continuum between formal and informal and, accordingly, stunting a judicially creative approach to informal workers' claims. Even though informal workers present their cases in terms of their concrete situations, the only vocabulary at the disposal of the court officials (lawyers and judges) through which to ascertain the rights of the workers seems to be the *formal employment contract*. Fragale Filho concludes that while judging informality in labour courts, if the focus should be on workers, judges need to overcome the limited and strict legal notion of *formality* in deciding remedies for precarious workers. Relatedly, he asserts that what workers are interested in are their rights; the loci of such rights – formal or informal – are irrelevant to them.

As an evidence of China's economic prominence, we have two chapters focusing on the Chinese informality scenario. While Constantin offers an outsider's account of the Chinese informality scenario, Aiqing Zheng provides an insider's reflection in Chapter 6, albeit from a legal perspective. Even though Zheng generally agrees with Constantin's overall thesis, she differs from her on the nature and influence of the labour law reforms on informality in post-reform China. Zheng indicates that the rise of informal employment in China is the result of three factors – the market-reform policies of the party-state, the actual process of marketisation, and urbanisation. In contrast to Constantin, Zheng notes that increasing informal employment in China is actually evidence of the choice exercised by workers in a more economically and socially open society that allows "people to choose their own profession". Zheng argues that since the Labour Law of 1994 was China's first nationwide labour law initiative, there were certain problems inherent in it, which allowed workers to be exploited in the market regime. One form of such exploitation was informal employment without social security. However, Zheng points out that the defects of the 1994 Labour Law were amended through the Labour Contract Law of 2007 in order to ensure better safeguards for informal workers, albeit to a limited extent.

P. Martin Dumas's chapter (Chapter 7) builds on the exclusion of informal workers from legislative safeguards, as pointed out by others, prominently Constantin, Zhang, and Routh and Fassi, in this volume. Dumas indicates that since the state-enacted laws are failing to address the concerns of informal workers, the idea of *consumocratic law* might be more useful in addressing the vulnerabilities of such workers. Contrasting consumocracy with a more self-centred concept of consumerism, he conceptualises a regulatory regime wherein consumers have a broader notion of *desirable goods and services*, which includes concerns about the treatment of workers in the production (or service delivery) process, and use this notion of desirability in order to compel corporations to develop policies and norms that promote the abovementioned desirable conditions. Dumas shows the effectiveness of the consumocratic private regulatory form by looking at the regulation of child labour by RugMark/GoodWeave in the Indian carpet belt in the state of Uttar Pradesh. Consumocratic law, Dumas argues, has "a degree of directness the state could hardly approach", and since it is a market-based regime, it is better attuned to promote conditions of workers through the formal/informal continuum.

The third part of the book, entitled *Informal Workers and their Multidimensional Interactions*, explores how informal workers engage with state policy, law and the neo-liberal market, and what role their agency plays in their continuous face-off with these and other institutions in society. This part begins with Claudia Danani and Javier Lindenboim's chapter (Chapter 8), wherein the authors chart the evolution of the Argentinian labour force from a lower level of informality and universalisation of labour rights, to the naturalisation of inequality brought in through the neo-liberal transformation, to the post-2001–2002 regime, wherein precariousness has become more and more socially and culturally hegemonic. The authors' hypothesis is that in the context of the "Argentine history of labour", the neo-liberal attack on wage labour introduced a more general worsening of social and labour conditions, wherein workers are deprived of social protection and labour security. They also make the point that holding the complexity of (labour) laws *per se* responsible for instigating informality is myopic. They note that the analytical focus should be on the content of law, and the endeavour should be the improvement of legislative instruments so as to address the concerns of informal workers. Their assertion resonates well with both Zheng's and Constantin's chapters, which show that in China, while the Labour Law of 1994 inadvertently promoted precarious informal employment, the Labour Law of 2007, in fact, promoted better conditions for informal workers. There is, thus, nothing wrong in regulation *per se*; what is important is the use of regulation in furtherance of promoting the aspirations of workers so that their choice of living a valuable life is maintained.

Chapter 9, by Petr Bizyukov, is structured in two parts. In the first part, he discusses the Russian post-socialist evolution of informality, the contemporary situation of the growing level of informality, and the border between informality and precariousness. In the second part of the chapter, Bizyukov presents the principal results of his empirical research on "the practices of regulation of labour relations in the conditions of precarious employment" in Russia, with particular attention to hiring (i.e. standard or arbitrary ways of hiring); occupational path (i.e. descending labour mobility or an adaptive path); working hours regulation (i.e. extremely rigid regulation to control the output, instead of the working time); wage system (i.e. one characterised by the strict control of employers, who do not tolerate any workers' initiative); benefits package and sick leave (i.e. discriminatory practices); and labour relations regulation (i.e. workers have no effective mecha-nisms for control and counteraction). The results indicate that precarious labour relations, unilaterally generated by the employer, appear to be widespread, and the border between these and informality (with virtually no rights) is very thin, if it exists at all, in Russia.

In Chapter 10, Alioum Idrissou reports part of his empirical research among informal workers in Yaounde, Cameroon. Idrissou locates two specific categories of informal economic activities – commercial motorcycle riders and call boxers – one of which is regulated by law (if only partially) and the other is not, in the urban economic landscape of Yaounde. He notes that, even though specific cat-egories of informal workers are seen as political resources in the limited sense of vote-banks by political parties of all dispensations, these workers receive no state-formulated support towards the promotion of their livelihoods. In view of such exclusion, informal workers develop their own solidarity-based social secu-rity frameworks and sometimes integrate formal financial institutions (banks and microfinance institutions) into their endeavour. Furthermore, Idrissou's study shows that in spite of the continuous struggle for the urban space, informal work-ers have developed a more accommodative strategy towards coexistence for mutual advantage. In spite of their everyday struggle, Idrissou indicates that con-trary to some accounts, the majority of informal workers in Yaounde pay some simplified income tax to the authorities. Informal workers' agency in Yaounde is, therefore, not only instrumental for the improvement of their own livelihoods, but also directly contributory to the state exchequer.

Following up on Idrissou's chapter on informal workers' agency, Chapter 11 deals with informal workers' agency and collective action. Supriya Routh and Marisa Fassi engage in a South–South dialogue on the experiences of waste pick-ers' organisation initiatives in Córdoba, Argentina and Kolkata, India. Arguing that an overly state-focused rights-based strategy for the improvement of condi-tions of informal workers cannot be successful in view of the marginalisation, deprivation and vulnerability of such workers, indicated by others in this book, they emphasise that in furtherance of promoting a dignified life for informal workers, what is necessary is collective action on behalf of such workers. Such collective action, they note, should pursue a multidimensional approach in fur-thering informal workers' agenda, which need not be limited only to political activism pertaining to the realisation of their labour rights. According to Routh and Fassi, workers' collective action – as Idrissou, too, points out in the context of Cameroon – also needs to further their social security concerns, integrating formal financial institutions into the process. By bringing together concrete examples of collective action of informal workers from India and Argentina, the authors suggest that a broadly conceptualised collective agency involving networking and multidimensional action is capable of pursuing strategies aimed at promoting a dignified life for informal workers, and could serve as a model for collective initiative by informal workers across the globe.

Finally, Vando Borghi concludes this collected volume by bringing together the different threads of neo-liberalism, the role of the state, regulation and workers' agency and contextualising these into the overall capitalist productive process and workers' choice, thereby offering a holistic perspective to the debate this book hoped to generate.

Notes

1 Some parts of this chapter have been published in Routh, S. (2014). An Ambitious Interpretation of the Informal for Policy-Makers. *Yojana*, 58 (October), pp. 41–44.
2 We use North and South as shorthand to signify countries and regions that are predominantly industrialised capitalist countries with comparatively less informal economic activity, and others that industrialised late and are characterised by significant informal economic activity, respectively. We do recognise that these distinctions are not clearly marked and regimented, and there are regions that need not conform to our North/South binary (such as Russia and China, discussed in this volume). However, for the sake of clarity at a general level, we use these terms.
3 The relationship between informality and entrepreneurial activities is also explored by Bruton et al. (2012), Godfrey (2011) and Webb et al. (2009).
4 For example, grazing someone's goats constitutes wage employment for some informal workers. It is an activity that is generally outside the policy reference with respect to informality and is grouped with agricultural activities. See "70-year-old does three jobs to support his family", 17 August 2014, *The Hindu*, available at http://www.thehindu.com/news/national/andhra-pradesh/70yearold-from-lakshmipuram-village-of-ramannapet-mandal-does-three-jobs-to-support-his-family/article6324637.ece?homepage=true (Accessed 17 August 2014).
5 According to the perspective defined by Bourdieu, a field works as a sort of magnetic field, which is structured by a system of objective forces, characterised by its own relational configuration and specific gravity, affecting all the agents or the objects that join it. In this sense, as Bourdieu underlines, "to think in terms of field is to *think relationally*" (Bourdieu, Wacquant, 1992, p. 96).
6 As a report published by the World Bank stressed, all Southern European countries show a strong degree of informality, with proportions from 37 per cent to 53 per cent of the economically active but weakly socio-economically integrated population working informally in Greece, Israel and Cyprus. In other Southern European countries, such as Spain, Italy and Portugal, this proportion is between 19 per cent and 22 per cent. The informal part of the working population in Europe is, indeed, constituted by this group of six countries, together with Ireland (33 per cent), the United Kingdom and Poland (22 per cent each) and Austria (20 per cent) (Hazans, 2011, p. 12).
7 Again, to take another example from India, a number of workers in rural as well as in urban areas still receive non-monetary wages for their work. While this practice is not the same thing as undertaking unremunerated work, it indicates that monetary wage payment is not the only way to recognise and compensate work. See, generally, National Sample Survey Organisation, Wages in Kind, Exchange of Gifts and Expenditure on Ceremonies & Insurance in India, 1993–94, 5th quinquennial survey of consumer expenditure, NSS 50th Round, July 1993–June 1994 (New Delhi: Department of Statistics, Government of India, 1998), pp. 11–15.
8 Herzfeld (1992) has clearly shown that the cultivation of indifference is first of all a process of social production, which is based on crucial mediation of the bureaucracy. It is a process through which parts of the social reality is emphasised (and bureaucratically administered), while the other parts of it is (politically, bureaucratically, and socially) ignored. The role of bureaucracy is crucial in this respect, because it transforms a political issue (such as what has to be highlighted and what could be disregarded or completely neglected) into a technical matter. The contemporary process of "bureaucratization of

the world", in which the informational bases of public action are increasingly becoming abstract, quantified, and objectified (Lampland, Leigh Star, 2009; Espeland, Stevens, 2008) is significantly expanding the production of indifference (Hibou, 2012).

References

Aksikas, J. (2007). Prisoners of Globalization: Marginality, Community and the New Informal Economy in Morocco, *Mediterranean politics*, 12(2), pp. 249–262.

Appadurai, A. (2013). *The Future as Cultural Fact*. London, New York: Verso.

Bacchetta, M., Ekkehard, E., Bustamante, J.P. (2009) *Globalization and Informal Jobs in Developing Countries*. Geneva: WTO and ILO.

Bifulco, L. (2013). Citizen Participation, Agency and Voice. *European journal of social theory*, 16(2), pp. 174–187.

Bonvin, J.-M., Favarque, N. (2005). What Informational Basis for Assessing Job-Seekers? Capabilities vs. Preferences. *Review of social economy*, 63(2), pp. 269–289.

Borghi, V., Kieselbach, T. (2012). The Submerged Economy as a Trap and a Buffer: Comparative Evidence on Long-Term Youth Unemployment and the Risk of Social Exclusion in Southern and Northern Europe. In T. Kieselbach, S. Mannila (Eds), *Unemployment, Precarious Work and Health. Research and Policy Issues*. Heidelberg: Verlag VS.

Bourdieu, P., Wacquant, L. (1992). *An Invitation to Reflexive Sociology*. Chicago: The University of Chicago Press.

Breman, J., van der Linden, M. (2014). Informalizing the Economy: The Return of the Social Question at the Global Level. *Development and change*, 45(5), pp. 920–940.

Bruton, G.D., Ireland, R.D., Ketchen, D.J. Jr. (2012). Toward a Research Agenda on the Informal Economy. *Academy of management perspectives*, 26(3), pp. 1–11.

Castel, R. (2002). Emergence and Transformations of Social Property. *Constellations*, 9(3), pp. 318–334.

Castel, R., Haroche, C. (2001). *Propriété privée, propriété sociale, propriété de soi*. Paris: Fayard.

de Leonardis, O., Negrelli, S. (2012). A New Perspective on Welfare Policies: Why and How the Capability for Voice Matters. In O. de Leonardis, S. Negrelli, R. Salais (Eds), *Democracy and Capabilities for Voice: Welfare, Work and Public Deliberation in Europe*. Bruxelles: Lang.

de Soto, Hernando F. (1989). *The Other Path – The Invisible Revolution in the Third World*. New York: Harper & Row.

de Soto, Hernando F. (2001). *The Mystery of Capital – Why Capitalism Triumphs in the West and Fails Everywhere Else*. London: Black Swan.

Espeland, W.N., Stevens, M. (2008). A Sociology of Quantification. *Journal of European sociology*, XLIX(3), pp. 401–436.

Fudge, J. (2011). Labour as a "Fictive Commodity": Radically Reconceptualizing Labour Law. In G. Davidov, B. Langille (Eds), *The Idea of Labour Law*. Oxford and New York: Oxford University Press.

Gibson-Graham, J.K. (1996). *The End of Capitalism as We Knew It? A Feminist Critique of Political Economy*. Oxford: Blackwell.

Glucksmann, M. (1995). Why Work? Gender and the Total Social Organization of Labor. *Gender, work and organization*, 2(2), pp. 63–75.

Glucksmann, M. (2005). Shifting Boundaries and Interconnections: Extending the "Total Social Organization of Labor", *The sociological review*, 53(2), pp. 19–36.

Godfrey, P.C. (2011). Toward a Theory of the Informal Economy. *Academy of management annals*, 5(1), pp. 231–277.

Guha-Khasnobis, B., Kanbur, R., Ostrom, E. (Eds). (2006). *Linking the Formal and Informal Economy: Concepts and Policies*. Oxford and New York: Oxford University Press.

Hart, K. (1973). Informal Income Opportunities and Urban Employment in Ghana. *Journal of modern African studies*, 11(1), pp. 61–89.

Hart, K. (2006). Bureaucratic Form and the Informal Economy. In B. Guha-Khasnobis, R. Kanbur, E. Ostrom (Eds), *Linking the Formal and Informal Economy: Concepts and Policies*. Oxford and New York: Oxford University Press.

Hart, K. (2010). Informal Economy. In K. Hart, J.L. Laville, A.D. Cattani (Eds), *The Human Economy*. Cambridge-Malden: Polity Press.

Hart, K., Hann, C. (2009). Introduction: Learning from Polanyi 1. In C. Hann, K. Hart (Eds), *Market and Society – The Great Transformation Today*. Cambridge and New York: Cambridge University Press.

Harvey, D. (2005). From Globalization to the New Imperialism. In R. Appelbaum, W.I. Robinson (Eds), *Critical Globalization Studies*. New York: Routledge.

Harvey, D. (2006). Neo-Liberalism and the Restoration of Class Power. In D. Harvey, *Spaces of Global Capitalism: Towards a Theory of Uneven Geographical Development*. London: Verso.

Hazans, M. (2011). *Informal Workers across Europe: Evidence from 30 European Countries*, World Bank, Working Paper Series, Policy Research Working Papers. http://elibrary.worldbank.org/doi/book/10.1596/1813-9450-5912 (Accessed 20 January 2016).

Herzfeld, M. (1992). *The Social Production of Indifference. Exploring the Symbolic Roots of Western Bureaucracy*. Chicago: The University of Chicago Press.

Hibou, B. (2012). *La bureaucratization du monde*. Paris: La Découverte.

Hirschman, A. (1970). *Exit, Voice, Loyalty: Responses to the Decline in Firms, Organizations, and States*. Cambridge, MA: Harvard University Press.

ILO (1972). *Incomes, Employment and Equality in Kenya*. Geneva: ILO.

ILO (2002). *Decent Work and the Informal Economy*. International Labour Conference, 90th Session. Geneva: ILO.

ILO (2013). *Women and Men in the Informal Economy: A Statistical Picture*, 2nd Ed. Geneva: ILO.

Jütting, J., de Laiglesia, J.R. (Eds). (2009). *Is Informal Normal? Towards More and Better Jobs in Developing Countries*. OECD: Publishing.

Kucera, D., Roncolato, L. (2008). Informal Employment: Two Contested Policy Issues. *International labour review*, 147(4), pp. 321–348.

Kudva, N., Beneria, L. (Eds). (2005). *Rethinking Informalization: Poverty, Precarious Jobs and Social Protection*. Cornell, USA: Cornell University Open Access Repository.

Lampland, M., Leigh Star, S. (Eds). (2009). *Standards and their Stories. How Quantifying, Classifying and Formalizing Practices Shape Everyday Life*. Ithaca: Cornell University Press.

McLain, R.J., Alexander, S.J., Jones, E.T. (2008). *Incorporating Understanding of Informal Economic Activity in Natural Resource and Economic Policy*. United States Department of Agriculture.

Nadin, S., Williams, C. (2012). Blurring the Formal/Informal Economy Divide: Beyond a Dual Economies Approach. *Journal of economy and its applications*, 2(2), pp. 1–19.

Packard, T., Koettl, J., Montenegro, E.S. (2012). *In from the Shadow. Integrating Europe's Informal Work*. Washington, DC: The World Bank.

Parry, J. (2009). "Sociological Marxism" in Central India: Polanyi, Gramsci, and the Case of the Unions. In C. Hann, K. Hart (Eds), *Market and Society – The Great Transformation Today*. Cambridge and New York: Cambridge University Press.

Perry, G.E., Maloney, W.F., Arias, O.S., Fajnzylber, P., Mason, A.D., Saavedra-Chanduvi, J. (2007). *Informality: Exit and Exclusion*. Washington, DC: The World Bank.

Polanyi, K. (2001). *The Great Transformation – The Political and Economic Origins of Our Time*. Massachusetts: Beacon Press.

Portes, A., Benton, L. (1984). Industrial Development and Labor Absorption: A Reinterpretation. *Population and Development Review,* 10(4), pp. 589–611.

Portes, A., Castells, M., Benton, L. (Eds) (1989). *The Informal Economy – Studies in Advanced and Less Developed Countries*. Baltimore and London: The Johns Hopkins University Press.

Ram, M., Edwards, P., Gilman, M., Arrowsmith, J. (2001). The Dynamics of Informality: Employment Relations in Small Firms and the Effects of Regulatory Change. *Work, employment & society*, 15(4), pp. 845–861.

Sen, A.K. (1991). Welfare, Preferences and Freedom. *Journal of econometrics*, 50, pp. 15–29.

Sen, A.K. (1999). *Development as Freedom*. Oxford: Oxford University Press.

Slavnic, Z. (2010). Political Economy of Informalization. *European societies*, 12(1), pp. 3–23.

Stiglitz, J.E. (2001). Foreword. In K. Polanyi, *The Great Transformation – The Political and Economic Origins of Our Time*. Massachusetts: Beacon Press.

Supiot, A. (2001). *Beyond Employment*. Oxford: Oxford University Press.

Tekle, T. (Ed.) (2010). *Labour Law and Worker Protection in Developing Countries*. Oxford: Hart Publishing.

Theron, J. (2010). Informalization from Above, Informalization from Below: The Options for Organization. *African studies quarterly*, 11(2/3), pp. 87–105.

Webb, W.W., Tihanyi, L., Ireland, R.D., Sirmon, D.G. (2009). You Say Illegal, I Say Legitimate: Entrepreneurship in the Informal Economy. *Academy of management review*, 34(3), pp. 492–510.

Weeks, Kathi. (2011). *The Problem with Work – Feminism, Marxism, Antiwork Politics, and Postwork Imaginaries*. Durham and London: Duke University Press.

Williams, C. (2009). Formal and Informal Employment in Europe: Beyond Dualistic Representations. *European urban and regional studies*, 16(2), pp. 147–159.

Williams, C. (2014). *The Informal Economy and Poverty: Evidence and Policy Review*. London: Joseph Rowntree Foundation.

Part I

Neo-liberalism, state, and regulation in formulating informality

1 Tackling the informal economy

A critical evaluation of the neo-liberal policy deregulatory perspective

Colin C. Williams and Alvaro Martinez

Introduction

Over the past decade or so, there has been growing recognition that enterprises operating in the informal sector are not some minor residue leftover from a pre-modern mode of production existing in just a few marginal enclaves of the global economy (Geertz, 1963; Lewis, 1959) but a pervasive and expanding feature of the global economy employing some one-third of the global non-agricultural work-force (Williams, 2013). To explain this large and growing share of the workforce in informal sector enterprise, a neo-liberal school of thought has emerged which transcends the traditional modernisation perspective depicting such enterprise as pre-modern and a sign of under-development and argues, instead, that enterprises operate in the informal sector due to high taxes, public sector corruption and too much state interference in the free market, and that reductions in taxation and corruption along with deregulation in order to minimise state interference in the market are therefore required (Becker, 2004; De Soto, 1989, 2001; London and Hart, 2004; Nwabuzor, 2005). The aim of this chapter is to evaluate critically the validity of this neo-liberal perspective.

To achieve this, the first section briefly reviews the neo-liberal explanation for the prevalence of informal sector enterprise and its policy approach for tackling the informal sector, along with the other competing explanations. Revealing that there have been no evaluations of the validity of this neo-liberal approach in relation to developing and transition economies, the second section then introduces the methodology here employed to do so. This investigates whether there is an association between the cross-national variations in the share of enterprises starting their operations without formal registration and cross-national variations in tax rates, corruption and state interference in the market, while controlling for firm-level characteristics as well as key facets of the business environment in which these enterprises operate. To do this, the World Bank Enterprise Survey (WBES) is used to examine the prevalence of informality across 116 developing and transition economies, and this is enriched with various World Bank and International Monetary Fund (IMF) development indicators on tax rates and state intervention, as well as the well-known country-level index on perceptions of public sector corruption developed by Transparency International. To report the findings, the third section provides descriptive statistics on the cross-national variations in the share of enterprises starting their business informally across the 116 economies analysed for the period 2002–2014. This is then followed by a multilevel analysis to test the validity of various tenets of the neo-liberal approach. The fourth and final section then draws conclusions regarding the validity of the neo-liberal approach, and the outcome is a tentative call for greater rather than less state intervention to protect workers in order to reduce the level of informality.

At the outset, however, what is meant by an informal sector enterprise needs to be clarified. Here, the definition of an informal sector enterprise is that adopted by the 15th International Conference of Labour Statisticians (ICLS) in 1993 (Hussmanns, 2005; ILO, 2011, 2012). This defines enterprises in the informal sector as "private unincorporated enterprises that are unregistered or small in terms of the number of employed persons" (ILO, 2012, p. 1). Informal sector enterprises are thus "unincorporated" enterprises that are also either "small" or "unregistered". "Unincorporated" means that they are not constituted as a separate legal entity independent of the individual (or group of individuals) who own them, and no complete set of accounts is kept for them. "Unregistered" means that they are not registered under specific forms of national legislation (e.g. factories' or commercial acts, tax or social security laws, professional groups' regulatory acts). Holding a trade licence or business permit under local regulations does not qualify as registration. An enterprise is "small", moreover, when its size in terms of employment levels is below a specific threshold (e.g. five employees) determined according to national circumstances (Hussmanns, 2005; ILO, 2011, 2012). Throughout this chapter, therefore, informal sector enterprises are defined as private enterprises that are unincorporated as separate legal entities and do not keep a complete set of accounts for tax and social security purposes, and are also either unregistered or small.

Explanations for the persistence of the informal economy

During the twentieth century, the common belief was that the modern formal sector was expanding and that the informal sector was a leftover from a pre-modern mode of production and was gradually disappearing (Boeke, 1942; Geertz, 1963; Lewis, 1959). From this modernisation perspective, the prevalence of informal sector enterprises in any economy was seen to signal its "backwardness" and "underdevelopment". As such, there was little reason to pay much attention to the informal sector, since such enterprises would naturally and inevitably disappear with economic advancement and modernisation as the formal sector became hegemonic.

Over the past few decades, however, this conventional modernisation perspective has come under heavy criticism, as it has been recognised that the informal sector remains a pervasive feature of the global economic landscape (Buehn, Schneider, 2012; Feld, Schneider, 2010; ILO, 2011, 2012, 2013; Jütting, Laiglesia, 2009; OECD, 2012; Rodgers, Williams, 2009; Schneider, Williams, 2013; Williams, 2014). Given this, informal sector enterprises are no longer seen as some remnant, relic or residue from a pre-modern period, and new explanations have emerged to explain the persistence, prevalence and pervasiveness of informality.

Since the 1980s, a political economy perspective has argued that enterprises operating in the informal sector are not prior to and discrete from, but are an integral aspect of, modern-day capitalism, providing a channel for flexible production, profit and cost reduction. Informal sector enterprises are, therefore, seen as a core component of the new subcontracting and outsourcing arrangements emerging under deregulated global capitalism, as well as a means of livelihood for marginalised populations confronted by no alternative sources of support (Castells, Portes, 1989; Davis, 2006; Gallin, 2001; Sassen, 1996; Slavnic, 2010; Taiwo, 2013). Viewed through this lens, employment in informal sector enterprises is a direct result of a lack of state intervention in work and welfare to protect workers, and those working in such enterprises are viewed as being engaged in "sweatshop-like" dependent employment and/or "false" self-employment and as working in such enterprises out of necessity (Ahmad, 2008; Geetz, O'Grady, 2002; Ghezzi, 2010).

Since the turn of the millennium, however, the dominance of this political economy perspective has waned, and a new way of viewing the relationship between neo-liberal deregulated globalisation and informality has emerged. Resulting from the recognition that a large proportion of work in the informal sector is conducted on a self-employed basis, often as a matter of choice (Cross, 2000; Cross, Morales, 2007; De Soto, 1989, 2001; ILO, 2002; Neuwirth, 2011; OECD, 2012; Small Business Council, 2004; Snyder, 2004; Venkatesh, 2006; Williams, 2007a, 2007b, 2009a, 2009b, 2010; Williams, Gurtoo, 2011; Williams, Martinez-Perez, 2014a, 2014b; Williams, Round, 2007, 2009), a view has emerged that enterprises operate in the informal sector due to over-regulation rather than under-regulation (Becker, 2004; De Soto, 1989, 2001; London, Hart, 2004; Nwabuzor, 2005; Small Business Council, 2004). More specifically, enterprises are viewed as operating in the informal sector enterprises as a result of high taxes, a corrupt state system and too much interference in the free market.

From this neo-liberal perspective, therefore, entrepreneurs and enterprises are making a rational economic decision to voluntarily exit the formal economy due to the costs resulting from high taxes, a corrupt public sector and state-imposed institutional constraints (e.g. Becker, 2004; De Soto, 1989, 2001; London, Hart, 2004; Nwabuzor, 2005; Perry, Maloney, 2007; Sauvy, 1984; Small Business Council, 2004). As such, those working in the informal economy are viewed by these neo-liberal scholars as heroic figures unshackling themselves from the burdensome regulations imposed by bureaucratic states (e.g. Sauvy, 1984; De Soto, 1989). Such enterprise and entrepreneurial endeavour in the informal economy is thus seen as a form of popular resistance to over-regulation, and informal workers are portrayed as a political movement that can construct a rational competitive market economy (De Soto, 1989). As Nwabuzor (2005, p. 126) asserts, "Informality is a response to burdensome controls, and an attempt to circumvent them", or as Becker (2004, p. 10) puts it, "informal work arrangements are a rational response by micro-entrepreneurs to over-regulation by government bureaucracies".

When analysing cross-national variations in the prevalence of informality, therefore, the belief is that informality will be greater in countries with higher taxes, more public sector corruption and higher levels of state interference in the workings of the free market. To evaluate critically the validity of this neo-liberal explanation, therefore, each of its tenets can be tested by evaluating the following hypotheses with regard to the proportion of enterprises starting up in the informal economy:

> *Tax rates hypothesis (H1)*: the share of informal enterprises will be greater in countries with higher tax rates;
> *State corruption hypothesis (H2)*: the share of informal enterprises will be greater in countries with higher levels of public sector corruption;
> *State interference hypothesis (H3)*: the share of informal enterprises will be greater in countries with higher levels of state interference in the workings of the free market.

Data, variables and methods

Data and variables

Here, the intention is to evaluate critically these hypotheses in relation to 116 developed and transition economies in order to investigate the validity of this neo-liberal school of thought. To do this, we employ data from the WBES, which is a data set comprising a firm-level representative sample of the economy's private sector of the participating countries. The harmonised survey questionnaire covers a broad range of business environment topics, including firm characteristics, gender participation, access to finance, annual sales, costs of inputs/labour, workforce composition, bribery, licensing, infrastructure, trade, crime, competition, capacity utilisation, land and permits, taxation, informality, business–government relations, innovation and technology, and performance measures. The normal use to which this data is put is to create several indicators that benchmark the quality of the business environment across the world.

The WBES questionnaire is completed by business owners and top managers. Typically, 1,200–1,800 interviews are conducted in larger economies, 360 interviews in medium-sized economies and 150 interviews in smaller economies. The manufacturing and service sectors are the primary sectors of interest. The number of participating countries is currently 135, and the survey data spans the period from 2002 to 2014. In this chapter, however, the sample is restricted to the 116 economies and 71,691 enterprises that provide valid information on the dependent variable: whether businesses start up their operations on an unregistered basis.

To analyse the type of businesses starting up on an unregistered basis, and based on existing research analysing cross-country differences in the informal economy using the WBES data set (Hudson *et al.*, 2012), the following firm-level explanatory variables are considered:

> *Young*: a dummy variable with value 1 indicating whether the firm was established five years ago or less, and 0 otherwise;
> *Foreign*: a dummy variable with value 1 indicating whether the share of the firm's ownership held by foreign individuals or enterprises is larger than 49 per cent;

Size: a categorical variable with value 1 for small firms with fewer than 20 employees, value 2 for medium-size firms with between 20 and 99 employees, and value 3 for large firms with more than 100 employees;

Export: a dummy variable with value 1 indicating the proportion of firm's sales which are for the export market and 0 for the share of sales for the domestic market;

Sector: a categorical variable indicating the sector in which the firm operates (i.e. textiles, leather, garments, food, metals and machinery, electronics, chemicals and pharmaceuticals, wood and furniture, non-metallic and plastic materials, auto and auto components, other manufacturing, retail and wholesale trade, hotels and restaurants, and others);

Legal status: a categorical variable indicating whether the legal form of the firm is an open shareholding, a closed shareholding, a sole proprietorship, a partnership, a limited partnership or any other form.

The firm-level vector of explanatory variables also includes a series of variables gathering the entrepreneurs' views on the business climate they face and whether various aspects of the wider business environment affected their decision on whether to register their business at the time of starting operations. These variables are:

Permits: a dummy variable with value 1 indicating that the firm regards obtaining permits and licences as a major constraint on the business and 0 otherwise;

Instability: a dummy variable with value 1 indicating that the firm regards political instability in the country as a major constraint on the business and 0 otherwise;

Transport: a dummy variable with value 1 indicating that the firm sees transportation as a major constraint on the business and 0 otherwise;

Tax: a dummy variable with value 1 indicating that the firm sees tax rates as a major constraint on the business and 0 otherwise;

Credit: a dummy variable with value 1 indicating that the firm has access to bank loans or credit lines and 0 otherwise;

Courts: a dummy variable with value 1 indicating that the firm identifies the functioning of courts as a major constraint on the business and 0 otherwise;

Bribery: a dummy variable with value 1 indicating that the firm had to pay a bribe to officials in order to "get things done" and 0 otherwise.

In order to test the neo-liberal hypotheses regarding the impact of *tax rates*, *state corruption* and *state intervention*, the multilevel models given here include a vector of country-level characteristics:

Corruption Perceptions Index (CPI): developed by Transparency International yearly since 1995 for a large number of countries. The index uses interviews with country experts and representatives of the business, media and officials from each of the participating countries; the resulting summary index ranks countries according to their level of perceived corruption, with higher scores in the index indicating lower levels of perceived corruption.

Tax revenue: tax revenue as a percentage of gross domestic product (GDP). The information comes from the IMF World Economic Outlook Database, which gathers yearly information on a wide array of economic indicators for the IMF member countries.

Social expenditure: public expenditure as a percentage of GDP in public health and education. The information comes from the World Bank Development Indicators. Unfortunately, no more comprehensive information on social expenditure is available for the years and a large number of the countries analysed comprising expenditure in social programmes likely to have a bearing on business decisions such as employment and unemployment benefits or pensions.

Total expenditure: in order to complement the analysis on social expenditure, we also use total expenditure as a percentage of GDP. The information is obtained from the IMF World Economic Outlook data set.

Finally, due to the less than comprehensive availability on a national level of the two indicators of social expenditure used to create the measure of social expenditure, the country-level analysis also reports the results for the indicators of public health and education (as a percentage of GDP) separately. As the country-level control variable for the level of development of the country, the analysis also includes the current GDP per capita of the country, expressed as the purchasing power parity in international dollars transformed into natural logs. This information was retrieved from IMF World Economic Outlook Database for the relevant years for each of the countries surveyed in the WBES. In addition, all models include survey year dummies to control for time-fixed effects.

Methods

In order to test the three neo-liberal hypotheses, we apply multilevel techniques to our data. The combination of firm- and contextual-level variables into a single analysis requires disentangling firm- and contextual-level variation for a proper estimation of standard errors. This is what a multilevel regression adds to a standard one-level regression, which only includes a single residual term (Snijders, Bosker, 2012).

Of all possible options for adding random elements to model variation between groups, we use the simplest, a logistic *random intercept model*, which only adds a single random parameter for each of the country-level contextual variables introduced at the aggregated level. In a multilevel regression, the intercept is composed of an average value for the groups, γ_{00}, and a random value which reflects the variation across groups, U_{0j}

$$\beta_{0j} = \gamma_{00} + U_{0j}$$

To this basic formulation, one can add group-level variables to explain variation in the intercept:

$$\beta_{0j} = \gamma_{00} + \gamma_{10}x_{1j} + \ldots + \gamma_q ox_{qj} + U_{0j}$$

Thus, our final model specification, including the country-level contextual variables, will be

$$log\frac{(\pi_{ij})}{(1-\pi_{ij})} = \gamma_{00} + \gamma_1 x_{1i} + \beta_1 x_{1j} + R_{ij} + U_{ij}$$

where the random effects are R_{ij} (the unexplained firm-level residual) and U_{0j} (the country-level residual). B_j and γ_i are the coefficients for the contextual- and firm-level variables, respectively. Accordingly, X_j and X_i are the vectors of contextual and firm-level variables that will be used to explain the likelihood of the enterprise starting unregistered operations.

Results

Descriptive analysis

Figure 1.1 shows the cross-national variations in the proportion of businesses that started up their operations on an unregistered basis for all countries reporting valid information for the period 2002–2014. As can be seen, there is a large variation across the 116 countries. Across all of the countries analysed, the average proportion of enterprises starting up on an unregistered basis was 12 per cent. This means, therefore, that across these 116 countries, some one in eight enterprises started up on an unregistered basis in the informal economy. In 46 of these countries, the share was above this average, and in some extreme cases, such as Egypt, Indonesia, Malaysia and Côte d'Ivoire, the share of enterprises starting up on an unregistered basis was over 40 per cent. The remaining 70 countries had a share below the average, with 63 of them witnessing fewer than 10 per cent of their enterprises starting up unregistered in the informal economy, and in 10 countries, fewer than 1 per cent started up unregistered. Indeed, in four countries (Eritrea, Hungary, Slovakia and Uzbekistan), no respondents reported starting their business unregistered. Given these significant cross-national variations in the propensity to start up on an unregistered basis in the informal economy, we here analyse whether such cross-national variations can be accounted for by the cross-national variations in tax rates, state corruption and state interference in the economy, as suggested by the neo-liberal perspective.

As a first approximation of whether this is the case, Table 1.1 reports the pairwise correlations between the propensity to start up unregistered and each of the country-level indicators used in the multilevel analysis, as well as the pairwise correlations among the explanatory country-level variables themselves. The results suggest that firms are less likely to start their operations unregistered in countries with lower levels of perceived corruption, with higher taxes and with more social (and overall

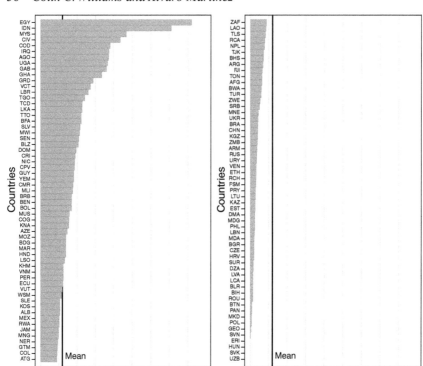

Figure 1.1 Share of firms reporting they started operations unregistered in 116 countries (average for 2002–2014).

Source: WBES (2002–2014). Own calculations (weighted).

Table 1.1 Pairwise correlations between the dependent variable and the county-level variables

	CIP	Tax revenue	Social expend.	Total expend.	Education expend.	Health expend.	GDP per capita
Unregistered	−0.06*	−0.10*	−0.14*	−0.07*	−0.06*	−0.16*	−0.13*
CIP		0.26*	0.36*	0.27*	0.15*	0.53*	0.65*
Tax revenue			0.67*	0.87*	0.52*	0.58*	0.49*
Social expend.				0.69*	0.86*	0.89*	0.54*
Total expend.					0.53*	0.62*	0.49*
Education expend.						0.53*	0.28*
Health expend.							0.62*

Source: WBES 2002–2014 data set with country-level information from various sources. Own calculations.

Note
* Significant at 1 per cent.

Table 1.2 Pairwise selected correlations between country-level and firm-level variables

	Tax	*Courts*	*Bribery*
CPI	−0.03*	−0.06*	−0.22*
Tax revenue	0.14*	0.02*	−0.06*
Total expend.	0.11*	0.03*	−0.09*
Social expend.	0.09*	0.06*	−0.17*

Source: WBES data set with country-level information from various sources. Own calculations.

Note
* Significant at 1 per cent.

public) spending. If correct, then this tentatively suggests that although the state cor-ruption hypothesis (H2) of the neo-liberal perspective is valid, the tax rates hypoth-esis (H1) and the state interference hypothesis (H3) are not. Indeed, quite the inverse appears to be the case. Countries with higher levels of taxation and greater state intervention appear to have lower levels of unregistered enterprise start-ups.

Regarding the partial correlations among the country-level explanatory vari-ables, the relationships found are as expected. There are some very high correla-tions between the different components of public expenditure and tax revenue used, which would be expected, due to how these measures were constructed. The analytical strategy followed below, therefore, will seek to minimise the potential problems caused by these high correlations.

Finally, as the multivariate analysis includes self-reported information by the inter-viewed entrepreneurs on the level of perceived corruption in the country and whether the taxes they have to pay are very high, Table 1.2 reports the pairwise correlations between this self-reported information and the country-level variables on the same topics introduced in the multilevel analysis. We do this in order to check whether there is a high correlation between the firm- and country-level information, which may have an impact on the estimation of the multilevel models, but also to investigate whether there is accordance between the business climate in the country as reported by the firms and as portrayed by the objective indicators at the country level.

The results suggest that the two corruption measures at the firm and country levels have a high correlation in the expected direction: less corrupt countries are also those where there is less likelihood of having to pay bribes. However, this correlation is not very large, which means that having the two measures at the firm and country levels is not a problem. In the same vein, countries with higher tax revenue and public expenditure are also those where entrepreneurs regard the existing tax rates as a major constraint on their business. Again, however, these correlations are not so high as to hinder the estimation of the multilevel models introducing these related firm- and country-level measures.

Multilevel analysis

Table 1.3 reports the results of the multilevel analysis to estimate the odds that firms start their business unregistered while holding other factors constant. Model 1

Table 1.3 Multilevel logistic regression for the odds of enterprises starting operations unregistered

	M1		M2	
	Coef.	*S.E.*	*Coef.*	*S.E.*
Young	−0.543***	(0.044)	−0.574***	(0.053)
Foreign	−0.783***	(0.058)	−0.764***	(0.073)
Export	−0.337***	(0.048)	−0.321***	(0.061)
Industry sector (R.C.: textile)				
Leather	−0.037	(0.157)	0.276	(0.325)
Garments	0.082	(0.072)	0.105	(0.085)
Food	−0.251***	(0.068)	−0.283***	(0.082)
Metals and machinery	−0.221***	(0.075)	−0.214**	(0.091)
Electronics	−0.411***	(0.157)	−0.629***	(0.206)
Chemicals, pharmaceuticals	−0.599***	(0.088)	−0.632***	(0.108)
Wood, furniture	−0.091	(0.117)	−0.018	(0.134)
Non-metallic, plastic materials	−0.186**	(0.076)	−0.228**	(0.093)
Auto, auto components	0.026	(0.222)	−0.143	(0.259)
Other manufacturing	−0.120*	(0.070)	−0.078	(0.082)
Retail, wholesale trade	−0.650***	(0.066)	−0.610***	(0.079)
Hotels, restaurants	−0.764***	(0.090)	−0.720***	(0.106)
Others	−0.635***	(0.076)	−0.560***	(0.089)
Legal status (R.C.: open shareholding)				
Closed shareholding	−0.346***	(0.066)	−0.335***	(0.086)
Sole proprietorship	0.371***	(0.067)	0.393***	(0.089)
Partnership	0.131*	(0.078)	0.180*	(0.104)
Limited partnership	−0.119	(0.086)	−0.164	(0.113)
Other form	−0.085	(0.109)	−0.193	(0.141)
Firm size (R.C.: small)				
Medium	−0.380***	(0.033)	−0.391***	(0.039)
Large	−0.681***	(0.047)	−0.621***	(0.058)
Business climate (firms self-reported)				
Permits			0.021	(0.048)
Instability			−0.199***	(0.062)
Transport			0.137***	(0.040)
Tax			−0.105***	(0.039)
Credit			0.008	(0.037)
Courts			−0.039	(0.047)
Bribery			0.125***	(0.041)
Year fixed effects	Yes		Yes	
Constant	−1.647***	(0.203)	−1.731***	(0.216)
Variance components (constant)	1.471***	(0.221)	1.335***	(0.211)

(continued)

Table 1.3 (Continued)

| | M1 | | M2 | |
	Coef.	S.E.	Coef.	S.E.
Observations	68,296		49,041	
Number of groups	115		112	
Wald Chi^2	1862.58		1328.98	
Prob>Chi^2	0.000		0.000	

Source: WBES 2002–2014 data set with country-level information from various sources. Own calculations.

Notes
  * Significant at p < 0.1;
 ** significant at p < 0.05; and
*** significant at p < 0.01.

shows the results controlling only for firm-level characteristics, while Model 2 adds into the model various aspects of the business climate as reported by respondents. Starting with Model 1, the results indicate that younger firms are more likely to have registered their enterprises from the outset, as are foreign-owned and export-oriented firms. Meanwhile, and examining the sectoral variations, it appears that enterprises in the textile sector (the reference category for this variable) are more likely not to have registered when starting up. With regard to the legal status of the firm, closed shareholding enterprises are less likely to have started up unregistered compared with those that now have an open shareholding legal status. Those which are now sole traders and partnerships, meanwhile, have higher odds of not having been registered when starting their operations. As for firm size, medium and large enterprises are more likely to have been registered at start-up than smaller-size enterprises. These results hold in Model 2 when one also controls for respondents' self-reported information on the business environment. Examining the features of the business environment which have an impact on the likelihood of the enterprise starting up on an unregistered basis, the finding is that political instability reduces the odds of enterprises starting up on an unregistered basis, as does the perception that tax rates are too high. However, problems with transportation and having to pay bribes to get things done increase the odds that the enterprise started without registration.

Is it the case, however, that informality (as measured here by the share of enterprises starting up unregistered) is associated with tax rates, state corruption and state interference, as suggested by the neo-liberal explanation? To test this, Table 1.4 reports the results of the multilevel analysis once country-level objective measures are introduced to analyse whether cross-national variations in state corruption, tax rates and state intervention are associated with cross-national variations in the level of informality. Given the high correlations found among some of the country-level variables used, each hypothesis is here tested in a separate model. Starting with Model 3, which introduces the CPI, evidence is found to support the neo-liberal hypothesis; countries in which public sector corruption is perceived to be lower are countries where the odds of starting up

Table 1.4 Multilevel logistic regression for the odds of enterprises starting operations unregistered

	M3		M4		M5		M6	
	Coef.	S.E.	Coef.	S.E.	Coef.	S.E.	Coef.	S.E.
Young	-0.555***	(0.054)	-0.576***	(0.053)	-0.576***	(0.075)	-0.576***	(0.053)
Foreign	-0.769***	(0.075)	-0.762***	(0.073)	-0.669***	(0.094)	-0.762***	(0.073)
Export	-0.331***	(0.063)	-0.337***	(0.061)	-0.257***	(0.079)	-0.337***	(0.061)
Industry sector (R.C.: textile)								
Leather	0.261	(0.324)	0.220	(0.322)	0.706	(0.445)	0.219	(0.322)
Garments	0.116	(0.089)	0.101	(0.085)	0.238**	(0.108)	0.101	(0.085)
Food	-0.263***	(0.086)	-0.285***	(0.082)	-0.101	(0.107)	-0.285***	(0.082)
Metals and machinery	-0.192**	(0.094)	-0.217**	(0.091)	-0.250**	(0.124)	-0.216**	(0.091)
Electronics	-0.593***	(0.208)	-0.628***	(0.206)	-0.685***	(0.313)	-0.629***	(0.206)
Chemicals, pharmaceuticals	-0.623***	(0.111)	-0.634***	(0.108)	-0.627***	(0.141)	-0.634***	(0.108)
Wood, furniture	-0.008	(0.136)	-0.023	(0.134)	0.043	(0.195)	-0.026	(0.134)
Non-metallic, plastic materials	-0.212**	(0.096)	-0.228**	(0.093)	-0.056	(0.123)	-0.228**	(0.093)
Auto, auto components	-0.089	(0.261)	-0.148	(0.259)	0.120	(0.402)	-0.148	(0.259)
Other manufacturing	-0.038	(0.089)	-0.075	(0.082)	0.009	(0.106)	-0.076	(0.082)
Retail, wholesale trade	-0.595***	(0.083)	-0.615***	(0.079)	-0.615***	(0.104)	-0.616***	(0.079)
Hotels, restaurants	-0.725***	(0.110)	-0.746***	(0.107)	-0.784***	(0.159)	-0.747***	(0.107)
Other services	-0.533***	(0.093)	-0.567***	(0.089)	-0.538***	(0.120)	-0.567***	(0.089)
Construction, transportation	-0.611***	(0.115)	-0.618***	(0.111)	-0.476***	(0.148)	-0.619***	(0.111)
Legal status (R.C.: open shareholding)								
Closed shareholding	-0.361***	(0.087)	-0.332***	(0.086)	-0.338***	(0.109)	-0.332***	(0.086)
Sole proprietorship	0.384***	(0.090)	0.400***	(0.089)	0.477***	(0.112)	0.400***	(0.089)
Partnership	0.188*	(0.106)	0.192*	(0.104)	0.264*	(0.136)	0.192*	(0.104)
Limited partnership	-0.195*	(0.117)	-0.158	(0.113)	-0.110	(0.157)	-0.157	(0.113)
Other form	-0.220	(0.142)	-0.186	(0.141)	-0.218	(0.175)	-0.186	(0.141)

	(1)	(2)	(3)	(4)
Firm size (R.C.: small)				
Medium	−0.409*** (0.040)	−0.392*** (0.039)	−0.348*** (0.052)	−0.393*** (0.039)
Large	−0.639*** (0.059)	−0.616*** (0.058)	−0.761*** (0.078)	−0.616*** (0.058)
Business climate (firms self-reported)				
Permits	0.026 (0.049)	0.019 (0.048)	0.069 (0.063)	0.019 (0.048)
Instability	−0.199*** (0.063)	−0.197*** (0.062)	−0.085 (0.085)	−0.197*** (0.062)
Transport	0.129*** (0.041)	0.132*** (0.040)	0.067 (0.054)	0.132*** (0.040)
Tax	−0.090** (0.040)	−0.108*** (0.039)	−0.070 (0.053)	−0.107*** (0.039)
Credit	0.009 (0.038)	0.012 (0.037)	−0.003 (0.049)	0.012 (0.037)
Courts	−0.050 (0.048)	−0.050 (0.047)	−0.061 (0.061)	−0.051 (0.047)
Bribery	0.124*** (0.041)	0.120*** (0.041)	0.141** (0.056)	0.120*** (0.041)
Year fixed effects	Yes	Yes	Yes	Yes
Country-level variables				
Perceived corruption	−0.269*** (0.092)			
Tax revenue (% GDP)		−0.018* (0.010)		
Social expend. (% GDP)			−0.064 (0.051)	
Total expend (% GDP)				
GDP per capita (log)	−0.270** (0.126)	−0.374*** (0.120)	−0.481*** (0.159)	−0.409*** (0.010)
Constant	1.714* (1.005)	2.002** (0.992)	2.715** (1.302)	2.196** (0.116)
Variance (constant)	1.142*** (0.192)	1.124*** (0.179)	1.135*** (0.235)	0.972
Observations	47,155	48,825	27,267	48,825
Number of groups	100	111	68	111
Wald Chi²	1,336.55	1,361.85	958.37	1,361.18
Prob>Chi²	0.000	0.000	0.000	0.000

Source: WBES 2002–2014 data set with country-level information from various sources. Own calculations.

Notes
* Significant at p < 0.1;
** significant at p < 0.05; and
*** significant at p < 0.01.

on an unregistered basis are lower. Interestingly, this result holds even when one controls for the perceptions of the respondents regarding whether corruption has been a major constraint on the development of their business.

Is it also the case, therefore, that the neo-liberal tax rates hypothesis holds: that the share of enterprises starting up unregistered will be greater in countries with higher tax rates? Model 4 introduces the cross-national variations in the level of tax revenue as a percentage of GDP from the IMF Economic Outlook Database. The results display an association, but not in the direction proposed by the neo-liberal approach. Countries with higher tax rates are those where enterprises are less likely to start up unregistered. To test the state interference hypothesis, meanwhile, Models 5 and 6 introduce two measures of the intensity of state intervention in the economy. Model 5 uses the share of social spending as a percentage of GDP, which combines the total public spending on education and on health, although, as suggested earlier, this is an imperfect indicator of social spending, not least because it does not include any labour market-related spending. The problem, moreover, is that the data on public spending on education provided by the World Bank does not cover all the countries and years covered by the WBES. As a complement, therefore, and to overcome the drawbacks of the social spending indicator, Model 6 uses an alternative indicator of state interference in the economy for which more complete information was found. Specifically, Model 6 repeats the analysis with a measure of total government expenditure as a percentage of GDP. Nevertheless, the results of Models 5 and 6 suggest that cross-national variations in the level of state interference are not associated with cross-national variations in the likelihood of starting up on an unregistered basis. As such, the neo-liberal state interference hypothesis is not validated.

To further investigate this state interference hypothesis, Table 1.5 investigates state expenditure on education and health separately. Again, the quality of the data available varies considerably (although it is better for the latter than for the former). However, and as Models 7 and 8 demonstrate, although there is no association between cross-national variations in education expenditure and cross-national variations in informality, there is a significant association between cross-national variations in public spending on health and the odds of an enterprise starting up unregistered. This suggests that if more targeted social spending programmes are considered, this may well influence the decisions of entrepreneurs regarding whether they start up unregistered. Finally, all models in Tables 4 and 5 control for the natural log of GDP per capita. As expected, this indicates that in more affluent countries (also those where the rule of law is stronger), entrepreneurs are less likely to start up unregistered.

These results from 116 countries thus provide some support for the neo-liberal state corruption hypothesis, but find no support for either the neo-liberal tax rates hypothesis or the neo-liberal state interference hypothesis. Indeed, if anything, they find that the association is in the opposite direction, with increased tax rates and social spending (in the form of health spending) leading to a reduction (rather than an increase) in the extent of informality (measured by the proportion of enterprises starting up on an unregistered basis). However, the regression coefficients

Table 1.5 Multilevel logistic regression for the odds of enterprises starting operations unregistered

	M7		M8	
	Coef.	*S.E.*	*Coef.*	*S.E.*
Young	−0.577***	(0.075)	−0.588***	(0.055)
Foreign	−0.668***	(0.094)	−0.750***	(0.075)
Export	−0.257***	(0.079)	−0.318***	(0.063)
Industry sector (R.C.: textile)				
Leather	0.687	(0.443)	0.527	(0.353)
Garments	0.240**	(0.108)	0.171*	(0.090)
Food	−0.099	(0.107)	−0.222**	(0.088)
Metals and machinery	−0.250**	(0.124)	−0.162*	(0.097)
Electronics	−0.685**	(0.313)	−0.573***	(0.217)
Chemicals, pharmaceuticals	−0.626***	(0.141)	−0.569***	(0.114)
Wood, furniture	0.042	(0.195)	0.047	(0.153)
Non-metallic, plastic materials	−0.055	(0.123)	−0.141	(0.098)
Auto, auto components	0.120	(0.402)	−0.311	(0.329)
Other manufacturing	0.010	(0.106)	−0.040	(0.086)
Retail, wholesale trade	−0.613***	(0.104)	−0.586***	(0.084)
Hotels, restaurants	−0.782***	(0.159)	−0.678***	(0.117)
Others	−0.537***	(0.120)	−0.564***	(0.096)
Construction, transportation	−0.476***	(0.148)	−0.579***	(0.116)
Legal status (R.C.: open shareholding)				
Closed shareholding	−0.336***	(0.109)	−0.326***	(0.089)
Sole proprietorship	0.477***	(0.112)	0.416***	(0.092)
Partnership	0.264*	(0.136)	0.267**	(0.109)
Limited partnership	−0.109	(0.157)	−0.070	(0.118)
Other form	−0.221	(0.175)	−0.146	(0.143)
Firm size (R.C.: small)				
Medium	−0.348***	(0.052)	−0.398***	(0.041)
Large	−0.761***	(0.078)	−0.598***	(0.060)
Business climate (Firms self-reported)				
Permits	0.069	(0.063)	0.026	(0.050)
Instability	−0.085	(0.085)	−0.125*	(0.067)
Transport	0.066	(0.054)	0.121***	(0.042)
Tax	−0.071	(0.053)	−0.083**	(0.040)
Credit	−0.004	(0.049)	0.024	(0.039)
Courts	−0.060	(0.061)	−0.055	(0.049)
Bribery	0.141**	(0.056)	0.107**	(0.043)
Year fixed effects	Yes		Yes	
Country-level variables				
Education expend. (% GDP)	−0.021	(0.082)		
Health expend. (% GDP)			−0.146**	(0.064)
GDP per capita (log)	−0.555***	(0.154)	−0.358***	(0.112)
Constant	2.991**	(1.311)	1.781*	(0.959)
Variance components (constant)	1.191***	0.245	1.034***	0.168

(continued)

Table 1.5 (Continued)

	M7		M8	
	Coef.	*S.E.*	*Coef.*	*S.E.*
Observations	27,267		45,493	
Number of groups	68		108	
Wald Chi^2	955.67		1272.53	
Prob>Chi^2	0.000		0.000	

Source: WBES 2002–2014 data set with country-level information from various sources. Own calculations.

Notes
 * Significant at $p < 0.1$;
 ** significant at $p < 0.05$; and
 *** significant at $p < 0.01$.

make it difficult to quickly understand the actual impact of state corruption, tax rates and state intervention, given the large variation in these three state-level characteristics across the countries analysed. In order to provide a better portrait of their impact, therefore, we have here performed a post-estimation exercise allowing the predicted odds of starting the business unregistered to vary as the three country-level indicators we have found to be significant also vary.

This post-estimation exercise is undertaken for a representative enterprise using the mean and modal values of the explanatory variables across the countries and years surveyed and the sample used in the estimation of Model 2. In other words, the representative firm is one established more than five years ago, a domestic enterprise, oriented to the internal market, working in the retail and wholesale sector, a closed shareholding company of small size whose owner does not see permits and licences as a major constraint and does not regard political instability, transportation, courts or tax rates as constraints on the business. This enterprise has no access to credit or bank loans and does not need to resort to bribes to get things done. GDP per capita and the year dummies are set in their mean values.

Figure 1.2 shows the predicted odds of this representative enterprise starting up unregistered as the index of perceived public sector corruption decreases (higher scores in the index mean less perceived corruption). The range of the index uses the minimum and maximum values of the sample used in the estimation as lower and upper bounds. The finding is that while this representative firm has 10 per cent odds of starting up on an unregistered basis in more corrupt countries, this likelihood is only 2 per cent in less corrupt countries. This is an 80 per cent reduction in the odds of starting up unregistered from the minimum to the maximum value of the CPI.

Figure 1.3 similarly reports the predicted odds of the representative firm not being registered when starting operations as tax revenue increases. The impact is considerable. The odds of starting up unregistered reduce from 8.5 per cent in the countries with the lowest tax rate to 3 per cent in those with the highest tax burden

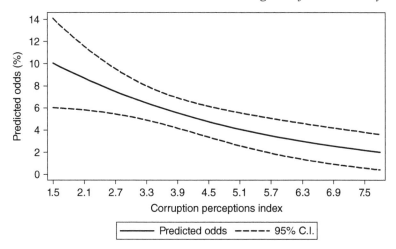

Figure 1.2 Predicted odds of starting business without registration as perceived corruption changes.

Source: WBES (2002–2014). Own calculations.

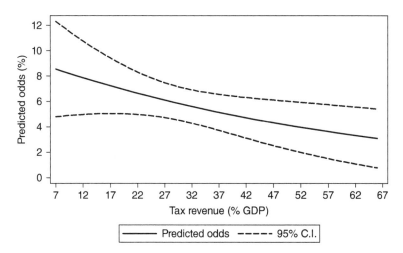

Figure 1.3 Predicted odds of starting business without registration as tax revenue changes.

Source: WBES (2002–2014). Own calculations.

as a percentage of GDP. It is, thus, the case, as suggested by the neo-liberals, that tax rates do have a major impact on the propensity to start up unregistered, but not in the direction they suggest. Instead, it is the case that countries with higher taxes are also those with a lower propensity to informality. Indeed, comparing this result with the above result regarding perceptions of public sector corruption,

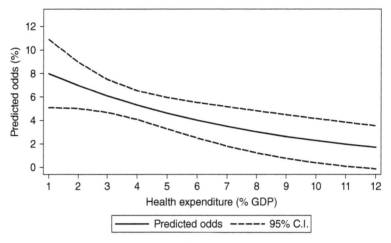

Figure 1.4 Predicted odds of starting business without registration as public spending in health changes.

Source: WBES (2002–2014). Own calculations.

it becomes apparent that the latter has a stronger effect on the odds of starting up unregistered.

Finally, Figure 1.4 reports the predicted odds of a representative firm starting up unregistered with regard to variations in the level of public spending on health (the only significant measure for the state intervention hypothesis). Again, the results suggest that countries with higher spending in health services are also those where firms are less likely to start up unregistered. The odds vary between 8 per cent for countries with lower spending to nearly 2 per cent for those with higher spending. This result resembles that found for the share of tax revenue. Hence, it seems that among the three country-level drivers of informality, corruption plays a leading role, with tax rates and state intervention in the economy having a very similar impact on entrepreneurs' decisions on whether to operate unregistered.

Conclusions

Across the world in the current neo-liberal era, and encouraged by supranational institutions such as the World Bank and the IMF, governments seeking to tackle the informal economy are pursuing a policy approach which seeks to reduce tax rates, diminish public sector corruption and decrease state interference in the working of the free market. Until now, however, there has been little, if any, evaluation of the validity of pursuing such an approach. To fill this lacuna, the aim of this chapter has been to evaluate critically whether cross-national variations in informality are associated with cross-national variations in tax rates, public sector corruption and state intervention. According to neo-liberal theory, countries with higher tax rates, more public sector corruption and greater levels of public spending should display greater levels of informality.

To evaluate critically this neo-liberal theorisation of informality, this chapter has taken as a measure of informality the proportion of enterprises starting up unregistered. It has then used data from 116 countries in the WBES, which reports the extent to which enterprises start up on an unregistered basis, and compared the findings regarding their degree of informality with cross-national variations in tax rates, corruption perceptions and public spending levels. The finding is that although public sector corruption is associated with informality in the direction assumed by neo-liberal theory, this is not the case with either tax rates or public spending. No evidence is found that higher rates of taxation or higher levels of public spending across countries are associated with increasing levels of informality. Instead, if anything, the direction of association is that higher tax rates are associated with lower levels of informality, and there is also evidence that some forms of public spending (e.g. on health) reduce, rather than increase, the level of informality. The result is that caution is urged regarding the continuing implementation of a neo-liberal agenda of cutting taxes and reducing state expenditure as the way to tackle informality.

In sum, if this chapter stimulates further research on the validity of the neo-liberal explanation of informality, then one of its intentions will have been fulfilled. If this then leads to questions being raised about the validity of the current neo-liberal policy approach and the investigation of alternative ways forward when tackling informality, then this chapter will have achieved its fuller intention. What is certain, however, and whether or not new policy approaches are developed, is that the current neo-liberal explanation has little or no evidence base for its promulgation of lower taxes and reduced public spending as a remedy for tackling informality.

References

Ahmad, A.N. (2008). Dead Men Working: Time and Space in London's ("Illegal") Migrant Economy. *Work, employment and society*, 22(2), pp. 301–308.

Becker, K.F. (2004). *The Informal Economy*. Stockholm: Swedish International Development Agency.

Boeke, J.H. (1942). *Economies and Economic Policy in Dual Societies*. Harlem: Tjeenk Willnik.

Buehn, A., Schneider, F. (2012). Shadow Economies around the World: Novel Insights, Accepted Knowledge and New Estimates. *International tax and public finance*, 19(1), pp. 139–171.

Castells, M., Portes, A. (1989). World Underneath: The Origins, Dynamics and Effects of the Informal Economy. In A. Portes, M. Castells, L. Benton (Eds), *The Informal Economy: Studies in Advanced and Less Developing Countries* (pp. 19–41). Baltimore: John Hopkins University Press.

Cross, J., Morales, A. (2007). Introduction: Locating Street Markets in the Modern/Postmodern World. In J. Cross, A. Morales (Eds), *Street Entrepreneurs: People, Place and Politics in Local and Global Perspective* (pp. 1–20). London: Routledge.

Cross, J.C. (2000). Street Vendors, Modernity and Postmodernity: Conflict and Compromise in the Global Economy. *International journal of sociology and social policy*, 20(1), pp. 29–51.

Davis, M. (2006). *Planet of Slums*. London: Verso.

De Soto, H. (1989). *The Other Path*. London: Harper and Row.

De Soto, H. (2001). *The Mystery of Capital: Why Capitalism Triumphs in the West and Fails Everywhere Else*. London: Black Swan.

Feld, L., Schneider, F. (2010). Survey on the Shadow Economy and Undeclared Earnings in OECD Countries. *German economic review*, 11, pp. 109–149.

Gallin, D. (2001). Propositions on Trade Unions and Informal Employment in Time of Globalisation. *Antipode*, 19(4), pp. 531–549.

Geertz, C. (1963). *Old Societies and New States: The Quest for Modernity in Asia and Africa*. Glencoe, IL: Free Press.

Geetz, S., O'Grady, B. (2002). Making Money: Exploring the Economy of Young Homeless Workers. *Work, employment and society*, 16(3), pp. 433–456.

Ghezzi, S. (2010). The Fallacy of the Formal and Informal Divide: Lessons from a Post-Fordist Regional Economy. In E. Marcelli, C.C. Williams, P. Joassart (Eds), *Informal Work in Developed Nations* (pp. 141–160). London: Routledge.

Hudson, J., Williams, C.C., Orviska, M., Nadin, S. (2012). Evaluating the Impact of the Informal Economy on Business in South East Europe: Some Lessons from the 2009 World Bank Enterprise Survey. *South East European journal of economics and business*, 7 (1), pp. 99–110.

Hussmanns, R. (2005). *Measuring the Informal Economy: From Employment in the Informal Sector to Informal Employment*. Geneva: Working Paper no. 53, ILO Bureau of Statistics.

ILO (2002). *Decent Work and the Informal Economy*. Geneva: International Labour Office.

ILO (2011). *Statistical Update on Employment in the Informal Economy*. Geneva: ILO Department of Statistics.

ILO (2012). *Statistical Update on Employment in the Informal Economy*. Geneva: ILO Department of Statistics.

ILO (2013). *Measuring Informality: A Statistical Manual on the Informal Sector and Informal Employment*. Geneva: ILO Department of Statistics.

International Monetary Fund (2014). World Economic Outlook Database: http://www.imf.org/external/pubs/ft/weo/2014/01/weodata/index.aspx (Accessed 17 August 2014).

Jütting, J.P., Laiglesia, J.R. (2009). Employment, Poverty Reduction and Development: What's New? In J.P. Jütting, J.R. Laiglesia (Eds), *Is Informal Normal? Towards More and Better Jobs in Developing Countries* (pp. 1–20). Paris: OECD.

Lewis, A. (1959). *The Theory of Economic Growth*. London: Allen and Unwin.

London, T., Hart, S.L. (2004). Reinventing Strategies for Emerging Markets: Beyond the Transnational Model. *Journal of international business studies*, 35(5), pp. 350–370.

Neuwirth, R. (2011). *Stealth of Nations: The Global Rise of the Informal Economy*. New York: Pantheon Books.

Nwabuzor, A. (2005). Corruption and Development: New Initiatives in Economic Openness and Strengthened Rule of Law. *Journal of business ethics*, 59(1/2), pp. 121–138.

OECD (2012). *Reducing Opportunities for Tax Non-Compliance in the Underground Economy*. Paris: OECD.

Perry, G.E., Maloney, W.F. (2007). Overview: Informality – Exit and Exclusion. In G. E. Perry, W.F. Maloney, O.S. Arias, P. Fajnzylber, A.D. Mason, J. Saavedra-Chanduvi (Eds), *Informality: Exit and Exclusion* (pp. 1–20). Washington, DC: World Bank.

Rodgers, P., Williams, C.C. (2009). The Informal Economy in the Former Soviet Union and in Central and Eastern Europe. *International journal of sociology*, 39(1), pp. 3–11.

Sassen, S. (1996). Service Employment Regimes and the New Inequality. In E. Mingione (Ed.), *Urban Poverty and the Underclass* (pp. 142–159). Oxford: Basil Blackwell.

Sauvy, A. (1984). *Le Travail Noir et l'Economie de Demain*. Paris: Calmann-Levy.

Schneider, F., Williams, C.C. (2013). *The Shadow Economy*. London: Institute of Economic Affairs.

Slavnic, Z. (2010). Political Economy of Informalization. *European societies*, 12(1), pp. 3–23.

Small Business Council (2004). *Small Business in the Informal Economy: Making the Transition to the Formal Economy*. London: Small Business Council.

Snijders, T.A.B., Bosker, R.J. (2012). *Multilevel Analysis: An Introduction to Basic and Advanced Multilevel Modeling*. Los Angeles; London: SAGE.

Snyder, K.A. (2004). Routes to the Informal Economy in New York's East Village: Crisis, Economics and Identity. *Sociological perspectives*, 47(2), pp. 215–240.

Taiwo, O. (2013). Employment Choice and Mobility in Multi-Sector Labour Markets: Theoretical Model and Evidence from Ghana. *International labour review*, 152(3–4), pp. 469–492.

Transparency International (2013). Corruption Perceptions Index (CPI): http://www.transparency.org/research/cpi/ (Accessed 12 January 2014).

Venkatesh, S.A. (2006). *Off the Books: The Underground Economy of the Urban Poor*. Cambridge, MA: Harvard University Press.

Williams, C.C. (2007a). The Nature of Entrepreneurship in the Informal Sector: Evidence from England. *Journal of developmental entrepreneurship*, 12(2), pp. 239–254.

Williams, C.C. (2007b). Entrepreneurs Operating in the Informal Economy: Necessity or Opportunity Driven? *Journal of small business and entrepreneurship*, 20(3), pp. 309–320.

Williams, C.C. (2009a). Beyond Legitimate Entrepreneurship: The Prevalence of Off-the-Books Entrepreneurs in Ukraine. *Journal of small business and entrepreneurship*, 22(1), pp. 55–68.

Williams, C.C. (2009b). The Motives of Off-the-Books Entrepreneurs: Necessity- or Opportunity-Driven? *International entrepreneurship and management journal*, 5(2), pp. 203–217.

Williams, C.C. (2010). Spatial Variations in the Hidden Enterprise Culture: Some Lessons from England. *Entrepreneurship and regional development*, 22(5), pp. 403–423.

Williams, C.C. (2013). Beyond the Formal Economy: Evaluating the Level of Employment in Informal Sector Enterprises in Global Perspective. *Journal of developmental entrepreneurship*, 18(4), pp. 1–18.

Williams, C.C. (2014). Out of the Shadows: A Classification of Economies by the Size and Character of their Informal Sector. *Work, employment and society*, 28(5), pp. 735–753.

Williams, C.C., Gurtoo, A. (2011). Evaluating Competing Explanations for Street Entrepreneurship: Some Evidence from India. *Journal of global entrepreneurship research*, 1(2), pp. 3–19.

Williams, C.C., Martinez-Perez, A. (2014a). Is the Informal Economy an Incubator for New Enterprise Creation? A Gender Perspective. *International journal of entrepreneurial behaviour and research*, 20(1), pp. 4–19.

Williams, C.C., Martinez-Perez, A. (2014b). Do Small Business Start-Ups Test-Trade in the Informal Economy? Evidence from a UK Small Business Survey. *International journal of entrepreneurship and small business*, 22(1), pp. 1–16.

Williams, C.C., Round, J. (2007). Entrepreneurship and the Informal Economy: A Study of Ukraine's Hidden Enterprise Culture. *Journal of developmental entrepreneurship*, 12(1), pp. 119–136.

Williams, C.C., Round, J. (2009). Evaluating Informal Entrepreneurs' Motives: Some Lessons from Moscow. *International journal of entrepreneurial behaviour and research*, 15(1), pp. 94–107.

World Bank (2013). World Development Indicators. Washington DC: World Bank. http://data.worldbank.org/data-catalog/world-development-indicators (Accessed 18 February 2014).

2 The informal economy and the state

Zoran Slavnic

Introduction

Since the late 1980s, the concept of the informal economy has increasingly occupied the attention not only of social scientists, but also of politicians, policy-makers and, not the least, journalists. Despite this focus on the phenomenon, or perhaps just because of it, the general concept of what it is still remains vague and uncertain. This chapter is going to discuss some of these ambivalences, relevant not only to the conceptualisation of the phenomenon, but also to the related policy praxis.

I am going to open this discussion by presenting controversies about the definition of the informal economy, the tendency to disregard the unity of the economic system by dividing it into several separate economies, and preconceived ideas about who operates in the informal economy and who does not. Then, I am going to present an alternative view of these issues, which will include informal economic actors that conventional research in this field has had trouble comprehending as participants. These are big businesses and the state. Finally, I shall present an empirical case of informalisation of the Swedish taxi industry, which illustrates not only how the state can be involved in the informal economy, but also how complex is the political/policy engagement with the problem.

The informal economy: the problem of definition

Originally, the concept was developed within the International Labour Organization's (ILO) Research Program on Urban Unemployment at the beginning of the 1970s (Bangasser, 2000), and was associated exclusively with the analyses of economic and social processes in the so-called Third World countries. Even at that initial stage, the question of how to conceptualise the phenomenon was controversial.

Keith Hart, an economic anthropologist who led the research programme and who coined the term, was impressed by the creativity with which ordinary people generated incomes, considering the circumstances of their everyday life (Hart, 2005). At that time, development in most African countries was characterised by explosive population growth. Most of the people lived in the countryside, but since the agricultural sector remained undeveloped, thanks to the cheap food imported from subsidised food producers in the so-called First World countries, most of the inhabitants were pushed to migrate to rapidly growing cities. At the same time, the capacity of cities to welcome these people was limited, because of weak industrial development. There was a lack of housing, infrastructure and jobs. People were forced to find their own ways of generating incomes.

Hart described this popular entrepreneurial dynamism as the *informal economy*. For him, it was not only about self-help; it was also about "people taking back in their own hands some of the economic power that centralized agents sought to deny them" (Hart, 1990, cf. Portes, 1994). But even before he published his academic article on this (Hart, 1973), the ILO had already institutionalised the notion of the informal economy, reducing its meaning to become synonymous with poverty. The informal economy in developing countries was viewed as a result of a political inability to modernise the society, to provide prerequisites for ordered urbanisation, to provide universal education for all citizens and to provide employment opportunities within the formal economy (Sassen, 1998).

During the 1980s, the concept of the informal economy was brought into play as a useful way to explain social and economic processes in the First World countries as well. However, it immediately came to be associated with increased immigration from the Third World countries. According to Williams and Windebank (1998), this is due to the widespread opinion that the informal economy is related more to the traditional way of generating income, which characterises developing economies, as opposed to the modern way of organising economic and social life in so-called advanced economies, which is increasingly rational and formal. According to this view, informalisation in the advanced economies grew as the number of immigrants from developing countries increased, bringing with them the customs of their homelands.

This interpretation, characterised by direct causal association between immigration and informalisation, was criticised both in the American (Portes *et al.*, 1989; Sassen, 1997, 1998) and European literature (Reyneri, 1998; Wilpert, 1998; Williams, Windebank, 1998; Kloosterman *et al.*, 1999; Samers, 2003, 2004, 2005; Jones, Ram, 2006; Slavnic, 2010); the argument was that the informalisation of First World economies is not generated by immigrants and their culture but, rather, by the structural changes taking place in these economies. Either way, the notion of an informal economy has become a sort of an umbrella concept describing economic activities outside the so-called formal economy (Leonard, 1998). Its ambivalence has been manifested in several ways. One of them is the confusion relating to the terminology of this phenomenon. Henry (1981) found that within the English-speaking academic community alone, there were at least 15 different designations for it. Williams and Windebank (1998) listed as many as 22 adjectives that are used as synonyms for "informal"[1] and at least four nouns that are used as synonyms for "economy."[2] In such a situation, not only is it difficult to determine the content and scope of the notion of an informal economy, but also it is more than difficult for researchers to disentangle the confusion in the relevant literature.

Too many names in circulation are not the only problem here. Scholars have also developed many classifications for the different kinds of economy in this context.[3] Thus, Edgell and Hart (1988) talk about "formal, informal and domestic economy"; Ferman and Berndt (1981) write about "regular, irregular and social economic activities"; Rose (1985) classified economy as "official, unofficial and domestic"; Henry (1981) as "legal, extra-legal and illegal"; while Davies (1985) talks about "black and blue economies" and Handy (1984) about "white, black, mauve and gray economies".

A related conceptual problem is, then, how to define the informal economy. There are at least two demarcations that trouble scholars. The first is the distinction between the informal and the criminal economies. Some scholars include the criminal economy in their definition of the informal economy; some do not. There is even a third approach. Hernando De Soto (1989), promoting the neo-liberal explanation, clearly states that the informal economy is in fact an illegal but still legitimate economic strategy ("... Illegal pursuit of legal economic ends ..."). People are, in his view, obliged to deploy informal economic strategies because of the over-regulation of the free market that is imposed by the state. Deregulation and decreased state interference in the free market would make economic agents less prone to use informal economic strategies (ibid.).

Those scholars who do not explicitly equate the informal and the criminal economy still define the informal economy as criminal (illegal) activities, although in a somewhat milder, euphemistic manner. Examples are: "... fail to adhere to the established institutional rules ..." (Feige, 1990, p. 990); "... terms of legislation and regulation ... are not being met ..." (Renooy, 1990, p. 24); "... bypass existing laws ..." (Portes, 1994, p. 431); "... activities that take place outside of the formal regulatory framework ..." (Sassen, 1997); "... activities ... that circumvent government regulation ..." (Feige, 1989, p. 1). See also Del'Anno, 2003 and Del'Anno, Schneider, 2004: "... production and services that are deliberately concealed from public authorities ..." (Schneider, 2014). Economic activities that fail to adhere to, or bypass, existing laws are nothing other than illegal or criminal, even if most of the definitions listed above obviously avoid labelling them as such. Paradoxically, economic activities taking place outside the formal regulatory framework (Sassen's definition) do not necessarily need to be either illegal/criminal or informal.[4]

The reason why these activities are regarded as informal might be related to the fact that the state tolerates them. The state does not employ instruments of legal coercion in order to stop them. Before I return to this quite important issue, I need to round off the story of how scholars deal with this informal/criminal ambivalence.

Most of the definitions that have been offered by relevant national and international institutions try even harder to tone down the possible connection between the informal and the criminal economies. The ILO's definition (2002) ("sale of goods and services that are licit in every sense other than that they are unregistered"), and the European Commission's definition (2007) ("activities that are lawful as regards their nature but not declared"), where the accent is on what is formal, rather then what is informal, about the informal economy, are examples. The ILO's more recent definition (2012, p.1) ("private unincorporated enterprises that are unregistered or small in terms of the number of employed persons"), where actors within the informal economy are passive, excluded subjects who are unincorporated and unregistered by somebody else, is another example.

Some scholars have tried to make the conceptual distinction between the illegal and the informal economy clearer. Thus, Castells and Portes (1989, see also Portes, 1994) define illegal economic activities as being involved in the illegal production and distribution of goods and services that are by law defined as illicit, while informal enterprises in the first place deal with licit goods and services, and the way of operating the business may to varying extents be illicit. Others (Kloosterman *et al.*, 1998) see the informal economy as an income-generating process, rather than the individual characteristics of those involved in these activities. This brings us back to the role of the state. According to Kloosterman *et al.* (1998, pp. 252–253),

> law enforcement is not self-evident nor does it follow a fixed course ... The government may assign many or only a few powers to enforcement agencies, and/or may give them the power to establish their own priorities. These priorities are affected by political decisions as well as the caseload, the interpretation of the job, the motivation and the efforts of the law enforcers themselves.

The second important conceptual distinction that concerns scholars in the field is the distinction between the informal and the formal economy.[5] If we take a closer look at these definitions, we can see that the notion of the informal economy includes any economic activity that circumvents actual legal standards. In other words, we have, on the one hand, institutional norms that regulate the activities of economic operators. On the other hand, there are the economic operators themselves, whose activities are expected to comply with these standards. Those who fail to do so end up in the domain of the informal (or illegal) economy. The problem is, however, that scholars within this field show a clear tendency to categorise some economic agents into the informal economy more often than others. Thus, members of marginal social groups, such as immigrants, the unemployed, those with little education, and/or small economic agents such as small business owners, are more prone to be counted as part of the informal economy, while, at the same time, big businesses as well as the state, which, together with its institutions, partly creates the rules and regulations, and partly appears as an economic actor itself, tend to be perceived a priori as part of the formal economy, always operating in harmony with existing regulations.

The informal economy: definition of the problem

In the preceding sections of this chapter, I have illustrated the problems related to defining the informal economy, to determining the differences between the formal, informal and criminal economies, and to naming the most important participants in the informal economy. I have also tried to point out the tendencies to simplify which still dominate the conceptualisation of the phenomenon. In what follows, I am going to present a growing body of literature that criticises the trend towards simplification,[6] and then present a different perspective on the informal economy.

The criticism of the simplified causal association between immigration and informalisation has already been introduced. However, associating immigrants with the process of informalisation has continued to dominate the field in two slightly different ways. The first is the so-called "marginality thesis", which describes the informal economy as predominantly employing marginal social groups: poor, unemployed and immigrants. This thesis is quite influential, even if it has been revealed as a sheer myth (Williams, Windebank, 1998, 2005; Williams, 2014a; Slavnic, 2011; Likic-Brboric *et al.*, 2013). Studying the 2007 Eurobarometer survey, Williams (2014a, p. 3) has shown, for instance, that British unemployed people earn only about 1 per cent of the total national earnings from informal work, compared with the 97 per cent of total informal earnings taken by those having formal jobs. Unemployed, the poor and immigrants are presumably most severely affected by informalisation, but they are definitely not the most important actors in the informal economy.

Another way in which scholars continue systematically to relate immigrants and the informal economy is within the field of ethnic minority concerns. The argument behind this is that "cultural distance" (differences in norms, business methods and/or expectations of what is and what is not acceptable in business activities) between immigrant communities and the host society often generate informal economic activities among immigrant entrepreneurs (see, for instance, Freeman, Ögelman, 2000). This academic discourse persists, despite the growing literature showing that immigrants' culture does not generate informalisation. Rather, the host countries' social and economic structure, characterised by unemployment and discrimination in the labour market, forces immigrants not only to start up small businesses more often than other segments of the population, but also to deploy informal economic strategies in order to survive in the market (Slavnic, Urban, 2008; Slavnic, 2012, 2013; Schierup *et al.*, 2014).

The second general trend towards simplification is related to what Harding and Jenkins (1989) call systematic representation of the informal economy as a negation of the formal economy. This way of conceptualising in terms of binary oppositions is problematic, not only because it tends to divide the economic system in at least two different ways (Leonard, 1998; Williams, 2014b), but also by preventing us from including so-called formal economic actors in our analysis of the phenomenon of the informal economy (Slavnic, 2010). We tend to *reify* or to over-emphasise the formal nature of our societies (Harding, Jenkins, 1989). Why is this so?

To be able to find an answer to this question, we need to refer to Max Weber (1978, pp. 311–312), who makes a clear methodological distinction between the sociological and legal concepts of social order. As a juridical concept, social order can be perceived only as a legal order, i.e. as a collection of mutually coherent propositions, free from internal contradictions, which therefore

56   *Zoran Slavnic*

constitute a regime that mandates social actors' behaviour. Sociology (or social economy – *Sozialökonomie*, as Weber calls it) is more interested in the actors' actual behaviour to the extent that it is determined by concrete economic and social factors. These two realms – the realm of the ideal "legal order" (the realm of the "ought"), on the one hand, and the realm of the real economic activity (the realm of the "is"), on the other hand – are, as stated by Weber, two completely separated spheres, which have nothing to do with one another. In everyday life, there is no activity that is fully congruent with the legal norms that regulate this type of activity. Each concrete, individual or collective human action (financial or other) deviates somewhat from this ideal.

If Weber is right, then our aforementioned tendency towards reification, or an over-emphasis on the formal nature of our societies, results in yet another method-ological problem. If we treat some part of reality (in this case big businesses and the state) as completely congruent with the ideal concept of the formal economy, than these institutions cease to be part of reality, and in this way also cease to be a suitable subject for a sociological study. There is obviously something wrong – either with these activities and these actors, or with the way that a large part of the research community engages in this field.

At the same time, activities of those economic agents that are perceived as oper-ating in the so-called informal economy are certainly suitable as research subjects, although even here there is a problem. Their (informal) economic activities/strat-egies are usually studied in relation to rules and regulations (which they do not respect), rather than in relation to other economic agents. Even here, we may refer to Weber (ibid., p. 312), who writes that a primary end of social actors' action is not to obey rules and legal norms, but to achieve their personal goals or to satisfy their needs. The way they act is further defined by their routines, habits and customs, as well as by the environment in which they operate. This is affected by how other social actors react to their actions, and also by how far the state is willing and pre-pared to use its apparatus of coercion in order to force these actors to obey the rules.

Having this in mind, I have elsewhere (Slavnic, 2010) tried to define the infor-mal economy as a consequence of broader structural processes that characterise contemporary capitalism. It is the result of structural conflict between old, welfare modes of regulation and new, neo-liberal regimes of accumulation. What happens is that traditional welfare regulatory frameworks become increasingly constrain-ing and thereby disrupt neo-liberal capital accumulation. This, in turn, results in an increasing number of economic actors choosing to bypass existing regulatory frameworks, i.e. to deploy informal economic strategies, in order to accomplish their economic aims.

The informal economic strategies of powerful economic actors, such as big businesses and state institutions, have been identified as "informalisation from above". Those developed by small and usually marginalised economic actors, partly as survival strategies and partly to resist the pressures from above, have been identified as "informalisation from below" (ibid.).

The state, together with its institutions, partly creates the legal order, and partly plays the role of an economic actor[7] because it is also "capable" of bypassing the regulatory frameworks. As such, it is a legitimate research subject within the field of the informal economy. Several ways in which states can be involved in the informal economy have been identified (Slavnic, 2007). The first relevant strategy deployed by the state is that, at the same time as it increasingly introduces neo-liberal policies of deregulation, privatisation and marketisation, it continues to use its usual political welfare rhetoric, and maintain its traditional welfare ideology. The point here is that the state, even while it increasingly exposes its citizens to "pure market forces" (i.e. to commodification), continues to assure them that they can count on the state for protection from these same market forces (decommodi-fication) in the future.

The second relevant informal strategy developed by the state is selective politi-cal and economic practice in relation to different social and economic actors. The fact is that the re-commodification process described above affects neither all economic actors nor all population categories in the same way or to the same extent. On the contrary, these processes result in an increasingly polarised society divided between winners and losers. The state is not outside these processes, but contributes to them, both as an active participant and as an external coordinator.

Finally, the third relevant informal strategy occurs when states tend, more or less directly, to involve the informal economy. Castells and Portes (1989) describe how the Mexican state, in its attempt during the 1980s to create attrac-tive conditions for American companies to establish their businesses on Mexican territory near the border with the United States, adopted economic and political measures that were in direct conflict with politically agreed national standards and regulations developed earlier. Another example may be the role of the states in the so-called *offshore economy* during the past three decades or so. The off-shore economy is related to third spaces, which include highly integrated capital markets, export processing zones and tax havens. Within these protected zones, a certain number of, but not all, economic actors have the opportunity of evading the established regulations which apply to all other actors.

In contrast to most proponents of globalisation theory, who use the offshore economy as a key argument for their thesis about diminishing state sovereignty, at least as regards economic policy, Cameron and Palan (2003; Palan, 1998; Palan, Nesvetailova, 2013) argue not only that the offshore economy is intimately related to states, but that most of the leading national states of the "First World" play an important role in the emergence as well as the expansion of the offshore econ-omy. In the following section of the chapter, I first discuss the role of the state in a more concrete situation, where it chooses policy strategies in order to tackle the complex phenomenon of the informal economy. Then I present an empirical case illustrating these practices – namely, the informalisation of the Swedish taxi industry and the role of the state in these processes.

Possible policy options

For politicians, dealing with the informal economy may be quite a frustrating occupation. Their priority is to support and protect the "legal order", since it is the foundation for the functioning of the rule of law, on which rests the basic premise of democratic political systems and within which these politicians exist and work. At the same time, they act in a particular (political) reality. They have their own lists of objectives, which were promised to the voters, but the (usually) constrained budget necessitates a constant definition and redefinition of political and policy priorities. At the same time, politicians have to strike a balance between the different political, economic, cultural and social actors, who have different amounts of power to influence actual policies. All this, then, results in at least three kinds of consequences, which in one way or another may make the state and different state institutions operate outside "the legal concept of the legal order".

The first is most directly tied to using coercion in order to eliminate economic activities that are informal or illegal. Kloosterman *et al.* (1998) have already indicated that the enforcement of law in this context depends on resources; the efficiency of enforcement agencies; their capacity and workload; motivation of politicians, policy-makers and officials in enforcement agencies to enforce the law; and so on. All these factors vary locally, regionally, nationally and, of course, internationally, but generally speaking, policy-makers have, according to Williams (2014a, 2014b), four options at their disposal: to do nothing, to try to eradicate the informal economy, to deregulate the formal economy, or to formalise the informal economy. Each of these has its benefits but also its costs.

For instance, doing nothing to amend the informal economy is unfair to businesses operating within the formal economy; but for businesses operating within the informal economy, there are also costs. They have no access to "formal" capital and "formal" business support; their workers lack labour rights; their customers lack legal protection, insurance and/or guarantees; and governments suffer loss of tax revenues and loss of political legitimacy (Williams, 2014b, p. 10). At the same time, eradicating the informal economy is in many cases very difficult to achieve, and where it is possible it is usually rather costly, in both financial and political terms. As a consequence, it may result in the disappearance of income opportunities for a great number of individuals and groups, who would then become dependent on the government's social support programmes.

Furthermore, many formal businesses start their operations within the informal economy before they move into the formal economy. By eradicating the informal economy, this "test-trading" opportunity disappears (ibid., p. 10). Besides, people do not engage in the informal economy exclusively to achieve financial gain. Sometimes they do it for moral reasons, such as to help their neighbours, relatives or friends; this can lead to "active citizenship" and/or "community building" (Williams, 2005; Williams, Windebank, 2005). By reducing the informal economy, governments reduce the opportunities for such active citizenship, which they would normally encourage (Williams, 2014b).

The same benefit–costs ratio may be related to any of the above policy strategies. The most appropriate one, according to Williams (2014a, 2014b), is helping informal economic activities become formal. This strategy, however, is most efficient if it is deployed in combination with the others.

It should be noted, however, that from the perspective of Weber's concept of "legal order", the only legitimate policy strategy would be the eradication of the informal economy. All others are, in one way or another, contrary to the legal order. Thus, the state, by the judicious use of coercion, ensures law enforcement. "To do nothing" cannot in any way be legitimate, because by doing nothing, the state itself acts illegally. The strategy of deregulation or removal of the informal/ illegal economy by abolishing the laws that had made it illegal is not legitimate, because all illegal acts committed prior to the abolition of the law remain illegal and should be punished according to the law.

The same legal principle applies equally to the strategy of moving the informal economy into the formal one. Informal economic activities carried out before the formalisation must continue to be subject to the enforcement of the rule of law and punished as such. If, however, we try to view this phenomenon sociologically, we see how complex is the implementation task for state and policy-makers. The Swedish taxi sector is a good example, because after deregulation, informalisation was rife, and the state had to face up to that.

Exposition of the problem: informalisation of the Swedish taxi industry and the role of the state

In Sweden during the 1990s, there was widespread deregulation, and in July 1990, the taxi industry was included in this process. It was expected that this would improve efficiency and result in better service and lower prices. Few of these goals have, however, been achieved (Laitila *et al.*, 1995). Efficiency remained low, profitability decreased, prices decreased slightly for some customers, but increased for others, while working conditions for those employed within the industry worsened significantly. At the same time, the increasing number of actors within the sector had to employ different kinds of irregular/informal business strategies in order to survive in the market (Slavnic, 2011, 2015).

Research into this empirical case showed that the deregulation strategy did nothing to combat the informal economy (Williams, Renooy, 2014; Williams, 2014b). In any case, irregularities in the Swedish taxi industry have continued to worry policy-makers ever since deregulation started. During the past two decades or so, several commissions have been appointed by the government[8] or different state agencies/departments,[9] which have been charged with investigating irregularities in the taxi sector. But despite these investigations, which clearly pointed out the problems, as well as making proposals for how to deal with them, the government has actually done nothing concrete.

The example, which is quite illustrative in this context, is the history of the proposal for special de-tanking centres (or *reporting centres for taxis*, as they are called in most recent documents), where the data from all taximeters were to be registered and saved. This proposal was first presented in 1997, but in SOU 1999:60, it was officially offered as a strategy for dealing with tax evasion by the taxi companies.

This particular story has been going on for the past 17 years, covering two mandates of social democratic government and additionally two mandates of conservative government. During this period, the state has lost tens of billions of kronor as a result of tax evasion. Besides, throughout this period, basically all relevant actors – media, various state agencies (among others the Competition Board and the National Tax Agency), trade unions and branch associations – have repeatedly pressed the state to implement effective legislation in order to do something about the problems. Politicians have, nevertheless, ignored all these requests. The following clip from a Malmö-based newspaper, *Sydsvenskan*, illustrates how these issues were dealt with by the social democratic government in the early 2000s:

The third official investigation in ten years

Much to the disappointment of the unions, there is still no single bill against cheating in the taxi business. Under the current legislation the authorities have no chance against the cheaters. Both the Economic Crimes Bureau and the Swedish Tax Agency have requested tougher measures, but from Stockholm comes only a series of investigations.

And the provincial government is criticised for being too generous with taxi permits. Meanwhile cheating continues in Scania's taxi market, which is the worst in the country.

A mandatory taximeter de-tanking for all taxis would help authorities keep better track of how much taxi companies actually earn. This is something that the Tax Office, Economic Crimes Bureau, Taxi Association and the Transport Workers' Union have agreed on for several years. Two state public inquiries have been made into the issue, and a third is on the way, but no bill has come yet, despite positive responses.

– The government has not wanted to propose new bills. The investigations are just a way to hide the issue and avoid taking a position, says Karin Svensson-Smith (V), who sits on the Parliamentary Traffic Committee. She has for some years been working on taxi issues, usually against the dominant trends. (Source: Sydsvenskan, 1 February 2004, author's translation)

During the summer of 2006, in the glare of significant media coverage, new, more stringent legislation against black (illegal) taxis was introduced.[10] According to the previous regulations, it was possible to take these taxi operators to court only if they had been caught several times in the act of operating without a licence. According to the new regulation, which came into force after a long political debate in July 2006, one single illegal journey for illegal taxi drivers was enough to warrant prosecution; continuous illegal activity would result in a prison sentence. The new rule was presented as an important contribution to the struggle against irregularities, even if it was actually of marginal importance and only cosmetic in character.

The new conservative government, which came into power at the end of 2006, has continued with the same ambivalent approach to the problems. During the first mandate period, the most important argument presented by the government was that any additional regulation directed against infringements in the taxi sector would necessarily challenge one important policy ambition, namely, reducing regulations on small business by 25 per cent (Taxiförbundet, 2008). During the second mandate period, several other arguments were presented: for instance, that to record the data from all taximeters would be a slur on the personal integrity of taxi drivers. The other argument was that linking reporting centres and special de-tanking centres would be relatively costly for taxi business owners. According to government estimates, the entry costs alone would lie somewhere between 80,000 and 150,000 kronor, and an additional monthly fee of 10,000 to 20,000 might be added to this sum (Taxiförbundet, 2011). In opposition to these estimates, the Swedish taxi association's figures included costs for a GPRS subscription (40 kronor per month) and a modem with SIM card to the taximeter. The total connection would cost about 1,000 kronor. In addition, a monthly subscription of 250–400 kronor would be required.

Eventually, after continuous political demand underpinned by a number of reports issued by various organisations, agencies and institutions, the government appointed another commission on 25 July 2012 to investigate the possibility of establishing reporting centres for taxis. The report was presented in February 2013 and led to a new law. The parliamentary decision was made on 10 July 2014, and the law was scheduled to come into force on 1 January 2016.

This looks like the end of this story. It was suggested that the state would expect to collect at least one billion kronor more in income tax and that taxi customers could expect better and safer services. But there are rumours within the taxi sector about the newest technical solutions, making it possible both to order the nearest taxi cab and to pay for the service via a smartphone app (Taxiförbundet, 2014). Certain groups within the sector are said to believe that this new technology makes taximeters useless and unnecessary.

I do not want to speculate about the possible effects of the new technology. My intention has been primarily to point to the obvious lack of political will and the need for something to be done about the problems within the taxi sector. If we look back at this story, we see that the Swedish government has tried several strategies. The first one was inspired by the neo-liberal idea that all problems could be solved simply by deregulation. As we have seen, this strategy not only failed to resolve old problems but has brought a number of new ones. It was followed by the *laissez-faire* strategy, which was, in a sense, also influenced by neo-liberal ideology. That is, the re-regulation (regardless of whether it is a partial or complete re-regulation) was (and obviously still is) contrary to the now official "deregulatory" ideology. At the same time, the taxi industry has offered the opportunity of employment to a great number of people who would otherwise be unemployed. Any effective elimination of irregularities within the sector would have left these people without jobs and made them dependent on public welfare programmes.

Simultaneously, during this entire period, there has been growing pressure on the state to do something in this regard. Interestingly, the key proponent of these demands for "change" has been the Swedish taxi association. Currently, there are no concrete research results that can lead to decisive conclusions, but clues from earlier studies (Slavnic, 2011; Slavnic, Urban, 2008) indicate that the Swedish taxi association is under the control of large taxi companies that were oligopolistic even before deregulation. Debates about these issues indicate that these big actors within the industry, by insisting on eliminating the so-called *black taxis* and *freewheelers*, are trying to achieve again their former monopolistic/oligopolistic positions.

To confirm or disprove these indications, we need more research, but if they are at least partly true, then the reluctance of the state to implement radical measures against irregularities within the sector may have dual causes. On the one hand, it may be understood as a necessary anti-monopolistic policy, and on the other hand, these measures may be seen as a desirable endeavour to prevent further erosion of social cohesion, which would deepen the gap between the haves and have-nots in society. Paradoxically, by using basically informal strategies, the state seems to be trying to achieve formal and legitimate policy goals.

Concluding remarks

In this chapter, I have endeavoured to go beyond a simplified conceptualisation of the relationship between the formal, the informal and the criminal economy, as well as beyond preconceived ideas about the participants in the informal economy. According to these ideas, which in fact dominate the research field, the principal participants in the informal economy are marginal, weak and/or small economic actors. At the same time, proponents of the ideas are more or less incapable of conceiving big economic actors, namely, states, together with their institutions and big businesses, as parts of the informal economy. This chapter has shown, however, that the state may be deeply involved in the process of informalisation. In a constant striving to create and re-create social, economic and legal order, states often employ strategies that go beyond their own regulatory frameworks. What they say about an unfair distribution of resources and opportunities among different individuals and groups, or in terms of direct involvement in the informal economy, does not accord with what they do. At the same time, my empirical case has shown that the state may employ strategies that, even if they do not adhere to existing rules and regulation, may serve as a means of achieving absolutely legitimate and just policy goals.

Notes

1 Black, cash-in-hand, clandestine, ghetto, hidden, invisible, irregular, non-official, off-the-books, other, parallel, precarious, second, shadow, subterranean, twilight, underground, unobserved, unofficial, unorganised, unrecorded, unregulated.
2 Economy, sector, activity, work.
3 The summary of the classifications that follows relies on Leonard (1998).
4 Crime is, by definition, "an act or the commission of an act that is forbidden or the omission of a duty that is commanded by a public law and that makes the offender liable to punishment by that law" (Merriam-Webster online dictionary, http://www.merriam-webster.com/dictionary/crime (Accessed 17 January 2015)). Consequently, what is not

against a law, or the commission of an act that is outside the framework of the law, meaning that it is not by law defined as illegal, is not illegal/criminal.

5 For further discussion on this issue, see Routh and Borghi's introduction to this edited volume.

6 See also the editors' introduction to this volume.

7 Not only direct engagement in market transactions counts, but also what Weber (1978) calls *economically oriented activities*, i.e. creating policies which may open or close market opportunities for different economic actors.

8 SOU 1997:111, *Branschsanneringsutredningen*; SOU 1999:60, *Taxiutredning "Kundvänligare taxi"*; SOU 2004:102, *Ekonomisk brottslighet inom taxibranschen*; SOU 2010:76 *Transportstyrelsens databaser på vägtrafikområdet - integritet och effektivitet*.

9 Näringsdepartementet (2013). *Redovisningscentraler för taxi* - Ds 2013:66, Departementsserien (Ds) 5 november 2013; Skatteverket (2008) *Skattefelskarta för Sverige* (2008:1); Skatteverket (2014) *Skattefelets utveckling i Sverige 2007–2012* – note that these two reports by the Swedish tax agency deal with tax evasion in all economic sectors, including the taxi sector.

10 Transport Committee's proposal 2005/06: TU14: Measures against unregistered taxis; Parliamentary decision 15 May 2006; Basic Legislative 1998: 490; amendment 2006: 512 – came into force 1 July 2006.

References

Bangasser, P.E. (2000). *The ILO and the Informal Sector: An Institutional History*. ILO Employment paper, 9, Geneva.

Cameron, A., Palan, R. (2003). The Imagined Economy: Mapping Transformations in the Contemporary State. In N. Brenner, B. Jessop, M. Jones, G. MacLeod (Eds), *State/Space, A Reader*. Malden, UK: Blackwell Publishing.

Castells, M., Portes, A. (1989). World Underneath: The Origins, Dynamics, and Effects of the Informal Economy. In A. Portes, M. Castells, L.A. Benton (Eds), *The Informal Economy. Studies in Advanced and Less Developed Countries*. Baltimore & London: The Johns Hopkins University Press.

Davies, J. (1985). Rules not Laws: Outline of an Ethnographic Approach to Economies. In B. Roberts, R. Finnegan, D. Gallie (Eds), *New Approaches to Economic Life: Economic Restructuring, Unemployment and the Social Division of Labour*, Manchester: Manchester University Press.

De Soto, H. (1989). *The Other Path*. New York, NY: Harper & Row.

Dell'Anno, R. (2003). *Estimating the Shadow Economy in Italy: A Structural Equation Approach*. Working Paper 7, Department of Economics, University of Aarhus, Aarhus, Denmark.

Del'Anno, R., Schneider, F. (2004). *The Shadow Economy of Italy and other OECD Countries: What Do We Know?* Discussion Paper, Department of Economics, University of Linz, Linz, Austria.

Edgell, S., Hart, G. (1988). *Informal Work: A Case Study of Moonlighting Fireman*, Salford: Salford Papers in Sociology and Anthropology.

European Commission (2007). *Communication from the Commission to the Council, the European Parliament, the European Economic and Social Committee and the Committee of the Regions, Stepping up the fight against undeclared work*, COM (2007) 628. http://eur-lex.europa.eu/legal-content/EN/TXT/PDF/?uri=CELEX:52007DC0628 &from=EN (Accessed 29 January 2015).

Feige, E.L. (1989). Introduction. In Feige E.L. (Ed.), *The Underground Economies: Tax Evasion and Information Distortion*. Cambridge: Cambridge University Press.

Feige, E.L. (1990). Defining and Estimating Underground and Informal Economies: The New Institutional Economics Approach. *World development*, 18(7), pp. 989–1002.

Ferman, L., Berndt, L. (1981). The Irregular Economy. In Henry, S. (Ed.) *Can I Have It in Cash*. London: Astragal Books.

Freeman, N., Ögelman, G.P. (2000). State Regulatory Regimes and Immigrants' Informal Economic Activity. In Rath, J. (Ed.), *Immigrant Businesses. The Economic, Political and Social Environments*. Warwick: Macmillan Press Ltd & CRER.

Handy, C. (1984). *The Future of Work: A Guide to a Changing Society*. Oxford: Blackwell.

Harding, P., Jenkins, R. (1989). *The Myth of the Hidden Economy*. Milton Keynes and Philadelphia: Open University Press.

Hart, K. (1973). Informal Income Opportunities and Urban Employment in Ghana. *Journal of modern African studies*, 11(1), pp. 61–89.

Hart, K. (1990). The Idea of Economy: Six Modern Dissenters. In Friedland R. and Robertson A. F. (Eds.), *Beyond the Marketplace: Rethinking Economy and Society*. New York: Walter de Gruyter, pp. 137–160.

Hart, K. (2005). *Formal Bureaucracy and the Emergent Forms of the Informal Economy*. Research Paper No. 11, Expert Group on Development Issues (EGDI) of the Swedish Ministry of Foreign Affairs and UNU-WIDER, Stockholm, available at: www.rrojasdatabank.info/unurp05/rp2005-11_1.pdf (Accessed 1 October 2012).

Henry, S. (1981). *Can I Have It in Cash*. London: Astragal Books.

ILO (2002). *Decent Work and the Informal Economy*. Geneva: International Labour Organization.

ILO (2012). *Statistical Update on Employment in the Informal Economy*. Geneva: ILO Department of Statistics.

Jones, T., Ram, M. (2006). Shades of Grey in the Informal Economy. *International journal of sociology and social policy*, 26(9/10), pp. 357–373.

Kloosterman, R., Leun, J. v. d., Rath, J. (1998). Across the Border: Immigrants' Economic Opportunities, Social Capital and Informal Business Activities. *Journal of ethnic and migration studies*, 4(2), pp. 249–268.

Kloosterman, R., Leun, J. v. d., Rath, J. (1999). Mixed Embeddedness: (In)formal Economic Activities and Immigrant Business in the Netherlands. *International journal of urban and regional research*, 23, pp. 252–266.

Laitila, T., Marell, A., Westin, K. (1995). *Taxitrafikens egenskaper och taxikundernas uppfattning fyra år efter avreglering*. Stockholm: KFB – Kommunikations Forsknings Beredningen.

Leonard, M. (1998). *Invisible Work, Invisible Workers – The Informal Economy in Europe and the US*. London: Macmillan Press Ltd.

Likic-Brboric, B., Slavnic, Z., Woolfson, C. (2013). Labour Migration and Informalisation: East Meets West. *International journal of sociology and social policy*, 33(11/12), pp. 677–692.

Näringsdepartement (2013). *Redovisningscentraler för taxi*. Stockholm: Ds 2013:66, Departementsserien (Ds), 5 November.

Palan, R. (1998). Trying to Have Your Cake and Eating It: How and Why the State System Has Created Offshore. *International studies quarterly*, 42, pp. 625–644.

Palan, R., Nesvetailova, A. (2013). *The Governance of the Black Holes of the World Economy: Shadow Banking and Offshore Finance*. London: CITYPERC Working Paper Series, No. 2013/03, City Political Economy Research Centre, Department of International Politics, City University.

Portes, A. (1994). The Informal Economy and Its Paradoxes. In N.J. Smelser, R. Swedberg (Eds), *The Handbook of Economic Sociology*. Princeton & NY: Princeton University Press.

Portes, A., Castells, M., Benton, L.A. (1989). *The Informal Economy. Studies in Advanced and Less Developed Countries*. Baltimore and London: The Johns Hopkins University Press.

Renooy, P. (1990). The Informal Economy: Meaning, Measurement and Social Significance, *Netherlands Geographical Studies*, no. 115, Utrecht: Royal Dutch Geographical Society.

Reyneri, E. (1998). The Underground Economy and Irregular Migration in Italy. *Journal of ethnic and migration studies*, 24(2), pp. 313–332.

Rose, R. (1985). Getting By in the Three Economies: The Resources of Official, Unofficial and Domestic Economies. In J. Lane (Ed.) *State and Market: the Politics of the Public and the Private*. London: Sage Publications.

Samers, M. (2003). Invisible Capitalism: Political Economy and the Regulation of Undocumented Immigration in France. *Economy and society*, 32(4), pp. 555–583.

Samers, M. (2004). The "Underground Economy", Immigration and Economic Development in the European Union: An Agnostic-Sceptic Perspective. *International journal of economic development*, 6(2), pp. 199–272.

Samers, M. (2005). The myopia of "diverse economies", or a critique of the "informal economy". *Antipode*, 37(5), pp. 875–886.

Sassen, S. (1997). *Informalisation in Advanced Market Economies*. Issues in Development Discussion, paper 20, Geneva: Development Policies Department, International Labour Office.

Sassen, S. (1998). *Globalization and Its Discontents. Essays on the New Mobility of People and Money*. New York: The New Press.

Schierup, C.-U., Ålund, A., Likić-Brborić, B. (2014). Migration, Precarization and the Democratic Deficit in Global Governance. *International migration*, 53(3), pp. 50–63.

Schneider, F. (2014). *The Shadow Economy and Shadow Labor Force: A Survey of Recent Developments*, IZA Discussion Papers, No. 8278.

Skatteverket (2008). *Skattefelskarta för Sverige*.1, Stockholm.

Skatteverket (2014). *Skattefelets utveckling i Sverige 2007–2012*, Stockholm.

Slavnic, Z. (2007). Informalisation of the Economy and the Recommodification of Labour. In E. Berggren, B. Likic-Brboric, G. Toksoz, N. Trimikliniotis (Eds), *Irregular Migration, Informal Labour and Community in Europe*. Maastricht: Shaker Publishing.

Slavnic, Z. (2010). Political Economy of Informalisation. *European societies*, 12(1), pp. 3–23.

Slavnic, Z. (2011). Struggle for Survival in the Deregulated Market: Re-Commodification and Informalisation of the Taxi Sector in Stockholm. *Forum for social economics*, 40(2), pp. 233–251.

Slavnic, Z. (2012). Breaking out – Barriers against Effort, Biographical Work against Opportunity Structures, *Journal of business administration research*, 1(2), pp. 1–17.

Slavnic, Z. (2013). Immigrant Small Business in Sweden: A Critical Review of the Development of a Research Field. *Journal of business administration research*, 2(1), pp. 29–42.

Slavnic, Z. (2015). Taxi Drivers: Ethnic Segmentation, Precarious Work, and Informal Economic Strategies in the Swedish Taxi Industry. *Journal of business anthropology*, 4(2), pp. 298–319.

Slavnic, Z., Urban, S. (2008). Socio-Economic Trends in the Swedish Taxi Sector: Deregulation, Recommodification, Ethnification. *International journal on multicultural societies (IJMS)*, 10(1), pp. 76–94.

SOU 1997:111. *Branschsanneringsutredningen*.

SOU 1999:60. *Taxiutredning "Kundvänligare taxi"*

SOU 2004:102. *Ekonomisk brottslighet inom taxibranschen.*

SOU 2010:76. *Transportstyrelsens databaser på vägtrafikområdet - integritet och effektivitet.*

Taxiförbundet (2008). *Branschläget 2008*, Stockholm.

Taxiförbundet (2011). *Branschläget 2011*, Stockholm.

Taxiförbundet (2014). *Branschläget 2014*, Stockholm.

Weber, M. (1978). *Economy and Society. An Outline of Interpretive Sociology.* Berkeley: University of California Press.

Williams, C.C. (2005). Unravelling the Meanings of Underground Work. *Review of social economy*, 63(1), pp. 1–18.

Williams, C.C. (2014a). Tackling Enterprises Operating in the Informal Sector in Developing and Transition Economies: A Critical Evaluation of the Neo-Liberal Policy Approach. *Journal of global entrepreneurship research*, 2, 1, 9. http://www.journal-jger.com/content/2/1/9/.

Williams, C.C. (2014b). *Policy Approaches towards Undeclared Work: A Conceptual Framework*, GREY Working Paper No. 4, Sheffield: University Management School, University of Sheffield.

Williams, C.C., Windebank, J. (1998). *Informal Employment in the Advanced Economies. Implications for Work and Welfare.* London & New York: Routledge.

Williams, C.C., Windebank, J. (2005). Refiguring the Nature of Undeclared Work. *European societies*, 7(1), pp. 81–102.

Williams, C.C., Renooy, P. (2014). *Bringing the Undeclared Economy out of the Shadows: the Role of Temporary Work Agencies.* Yearly report on flexible labor and employment, Amsterdam, April, commissioned by Randstad.

Wilpert, C. (1998). Migration and Informal Work in the New Berlin: New Forms of Work or New Sources of Labour? *Journal of ethnic and migration studies*, 24(2), pp. 269–294.

3 Reforms, individualisation and informal employment in urban China

Sandra V. Constantin

Introduction

In post-Maoist China, the economic and labour market neo-liberal deregulation that has been taking place over the last three decades has induced rapid economic growth at the national level, and it has increased per capita income at the level of the individual. This economic development is still strongly uneven, and characterised by salient socio-economic disparities in terms of region, locality, citizenship and gender (Angeloff, Lieber, 2012; Perry, Selden, 2010 [2000]; Whyte, 2010). One of the consequences of these inequalities is the continuous flow of migrations from rural to urban areas allowed by the relaxation of the *hukou* system. This residence booklet – *jumin hukou bu* – was introduced in China in the 1950s, and since then it has created an institutionalised division among the population according to place of residence (city or countryside)[1] (Wang, 2005; Liu, 2005; Peter, Chan, 2004). If the reforms have induced a sharp increase of the urban workforce over the period through internal migration, at the same time they have produced drastic changes in the urban employment structure. According to official statistics published in China, in 1995, 76 per cent of all urban employment was located in the state and collective sectors. This figure shrank to 41 per cent in 2000, and to 27 per cent in 2005, because the economic and labour market reforms gave rise to new forms of enterprise ownership, such as private ownership, joint venture and liability corporations, that still constitute a substantial part of urban employment (Park, Cai 2011, pp. 17–18; Naughton, 2007, p. 184). However, based on the China National Bureau of Statistics (NBS) data, Park and Cai estimate that at least 36 per cent of all urban employment was informal in 2005 (2011, pp. 17–19), adding that their "estimates of informal employment are likely to be underestimates of actual informal employment" because of the difficulty of counting migrants working in cities without a resident permit for the location in which they actually reside (Park, Cai, 2011, p. 20).

This chapter analyses, in the light of Beck's theory of individualisation and based on the case study of Beijing, the changes in employment security in post-Maoist China and the current trend towards the informalisation of employment. In this chapter, informal employment is understood as "employment that is not stable or secure, that lacks a written agreement or contract, and that does not provide social insurance or benefits" (Gallagher *et al.*, 2011, p. 2).

To begin with, this chapter provides an overview of the evolution of the employment structure in urban China over six decades. Then, the theoretical background and the research design of the present study are introduced. And in the last section, this chapter examines, through the case study of Beijing, why, despite the efforts made by the party-state since 1994 to protect workers through legal reforms, informal employment (*fei zhenggui jiuye*) has grown to reach more than one-third of urban employment in 2005 (Peng, 2009). If self-employed workers are also counted, since they do not have a labour contract and most of them do not have social insurance, the share of the urban workforce employed informally in 2005 reaches 46 per cent (Park, Cai, 2011, p. 20).

The neo-liberal deregulation of the economy and labour market in China

The urban employment structure in Maoist China

Under Mao (1949–1976), the free market system was replaced by a planned economic system controlled by the party-state. In this socialist system, private companies were gradually removed. In urban areas, the state took the responsibility for allocating a job to everyone in a work unit (*danwei*). The *danwei* used to regulate all aspects of people's lives: it provided a job for life, housing, medical care and retirement allowance. It also bore the financial costs of education for the children of its employees, and was used by the party-state as a means to monitor and control the population through a system of political files (Bray, 2005; Lü, Perry, 1997). Individuals were educated to collectivism. The central government used propaganda and created new social norms and values "to subdue individual preference in seeking a career, even choosing a residence, subjecting people to the economic needs of the party and the government" (Bray, 2005, pp. 74–75).

In Maoist China, the party-state created an "organized dependency" of the individual on the collective. New roles, norms, status and identities were imposed on the individual through the Maoist institutions. The individuals were socio-economically dependent on their work units, politically dependent on the political organisation, and personally dependent on cadres (Walder, 1986). The work units in particular replaced traditional and interpersonal solidarities. However, Maoist institutions induced, paradoxically, a first step towards individualisation. As stated by Yan, on the surface, the society "was a highly developed collectivist society where the individual almost entirely had lost her/his freedom and autonomy as she/he could not even choose where to work or to reside [...]. At a deeper level, however, the Chinese individual was dis-embedded, in many cases forcefully, from the traditional networks of family, kinship, and community and the constraints of the traditional, mostly Confucian and patriarchal, values and behavioural norms" (Yan, 2010, pp. 492–493). These major shifts in the social organisation reflect a partial process of individualisation. That is to say a process of societisation that does not result from the free choice of individuals (Beck, Beck-Gernsheim, 2011 [2002]; Bauman, 2001; Giddens, 2015 [1991]). This individualisation is partial because the individuals were freed from "traditional" social categories (such as community and kinship) that prescribed their conducts and their forms of social engagement, but meanwhile they were re-embedded in new collectivist solidarities that emerged from the Maoist organisation of the society. Afterwards, in post-Maoist China, institutional and socio-economic changes induced again a new relationship between individual, society, and the state (Yan, 2010).

The reforms and the emergence of informal employment in urban China

China's transition towards a market economy has not only liberalised the Chinese market; it has also gradually dissolved and transformed the social constraints that bound the individual to the workplace (Lü, Perry, 1997; Cheng, 2009). By the late 1970s, Deng returned to power with the aim of boosting the socio-economic development of the country (Fairbank, Goldman, 2010 [1992], p. 577). To this end, the party-state began to shape a "new Chinese citizen", who would still be subject to the party-state politically, but emancipated at the economic and social levels. It had two great assets to realise its ambitions and undertake socioeconomic reforms: a male and a female population that were both literate and healthy, thanks to the previous policies in these fields conducted under Mao.

This state project has resulted in a process of individualisation, which is characterised by a radical change in the relationship between individual and society (Beck, 2008 [1986], p. 127). During this process, according to the individualisation theory, it should be observed that the individual is first disembedded from traditional social categories that used to prescribe his conduct and social commitments. Second, the individual should lose the "traditional" forms of security played by the family group and the community, because the welfare state is substituted for them. Third, because of the role played by the new institutions, the individual is expected to re-embed in a new type of social commitment (Beck, 2008 [1986], p. 128; Beck, Beck-Gernsheim, 2011 [2002], p. 158). However, in China, individuals have been called upon to become responsible for their own destinies before the institutionalisation of a post-Maoist nationwide welfare system. Therefore, in the case of accidents during the life-course, most Chinese people cannot exclusively rely on social institutions. They have to be reflexive and find biographical answers to social and economic uncertainties: informal employment is one of them. "Reflexive" means individuals have to make choices over their life-course, where previous generations had no such choices. According to Beck, contemporary individuals are characterised by choices and as a consequence they are reflexive (Beck, Beck-Gernsheim, 2011 [2002]).

Initially, the central government turned a blind eye to the emerging informal economy in Chinese cities. These informal activities were primarily the result of the rural population living in the urban periphery, who tried to sell part of their harvest informally in the cities, and young urbanites not wanting to return to the countryside, where they were sent to be re-educated by the peasants (Bonnin, 2004; Peng, 2009). The party-state had an ambivalent attitude regarding the re-emergence of informal activities, such as street vendors, as "on the one hand, they represented a real threat to the socialist planned economy, but on the other hand, they also helped the party-state to solve the problem of mounting unemployment and declining economic growth" (Yan, 2010, p. 496). After a decade of Cultural Revolution (1966–1976),[2] the country was paralysed both economically and politically. In cities, the rise of strikes, absenteeism, and the gathering of youths into gangs illuminated the discontent of the urban population (De Beer, Rocca, 1995, p. 47). In this context, the central government, fearing a strong opposition from the population, decided to wait until 1984 to start the reforms and opening-up policies in urban areas. In order to maintain as much social stability as possible, the party-state started to open pockets of market economy in the planned economy system. People started to slip into these pockets and to use this opportunity to increase their incomes.

In such a dual system (*shuangguizhi*), in which a planned economy and a "free" market coexisted, public enterprises started to produce a part of their output "outside the plan". Meanwhile, "individual industrial and commercial households" (*geti gongshang hu* or *getihu*) began to emerge. The party-state recognised, during the third plenum of the XIIth congress of the Chinese Communist Party in 1984, the irreplaceable value of these informal activities to improve the living conditions of the people (Monteil, 2010, p. 104). This gave private companies the impulse to gradually mushroom.[3] In the streets of the country, little shops, street vendors and small crafts also re-emerged. In 1991, informal employment was still relatively marginal, amounting to 6.99 per cent of the active population (Tong, 2009, p. 306).

Informality and social protection

The opening up to market economy and the reintroduction of a partial labour market in China were still far from a linear process. If already in the 1980s the individual was called upon to become reflexive and not rely only on the Maoist system of dependency, it was only after 1992 that the reforms and opening-up policies were extended. This second phase of reforms (1992–2013) was marked by the sharp decline of the welfare state and an increased exposure of the population to socio-economic risks.

With the dismantling of state-owned enterprises (SOEs) and collectively owned enterprises, by the mid-1990s, 40 per cent of workers had been laid off. This meant that almost 50 million people were unemployed in Chinese cities (Naughton, 2007, p. 184). The transition was overwhelming. Within a generation, the urban population had to adapt from a highly protected system (*tiefanwan* or the iron rice bowl), which guaranteed permanent employment, lifelong benefits and a relatively high degree of equality, to a new system which makes them responsible for risks during their life-course. Individuals had no choice but to move, to seek employment on their own and to change job if necessary. Research shows that self-employment became "the main avenue of re-employment" for urban workers (Hurst, 2009; Yan, 2010, p. 499). The market-determined employment system is also "characterized by considerable variation in wages, labour law enforcement, and job security" (Gallagher *et al.*, 2011, pp. 3–4).

This institutionalised disembedding of individuals from the work-unit system had a unique impact on the individualisation process in contemporary China.

The reforms, by emancipating the individuals from the tutelage of the party-state, have created, on the one hand, new opportunities and a rise in their incomes for some people; on the other hand, they have induced degradation in their living conditions for others. Along with the dismantling of the *danwei* system, the welfare state inherited from the Maoist period was demolished. As a result, individuals have to internalise the negative externalities of economic liberalisation of the labour market and of cost in the health, education, housing and food sectors, which were previously supported by the collective (Naughton, 2007). In three decades, access to these resources has become highly competitive and the responsibility of the individual.

The process of individualisation in China is therefore limited and controlled by the party-state, which encourages it in social, economic and private (to some extent) spheres, promoting individual actions and "do it yourself biographies", but still restricts it at the political level (Beck, Beck-Gernsheim, 2010; Yan, 2010). Since the opening up of China to the market economy, Chinese workers have to adapt to the competitive pressure of global capitalism and the continuing demand for labour flexibility, detrimental to labour security and stability. SOEs and private companies have continuously and increasingly used informal employment as a means to adapt to the changing environment and to benefit from their comparative advantage: a cheap labour force (Swider, 2011; Zhang, 2011; Lin, 2011; Peng, 2009). In 2005, between 27 per cent and 36 per cent of the employment in China was informal (Tong, 2009; Park, Cai, 2011; Peng, 2009). This variation in the figures among studies can be explained by their different definitions of informal work, but it is beyond the scope of this chapter to discuss this.

Theoretical background and research design

Research question and research design

China is not unique in its process of transformation of the employment structure and the precariousness of labour conditions under the pressure of the global economy and the neo-liberal ideology. Nevertheless, the transformation of the labour market and the rise of informal employment in urban China represent a number of major challenges, as they took place before the institutionalisation of a post-Maoist welfare state and the adoption of formal legislation to protect workers. The first labour and employment legislation, the National Labour Law, was adopted in 1994, 15 years after the beginning of the opening-up policy.[4] First, the law unified in a single legislation the multiplicity of laws, regulations and directives that had been used to govern labour relations across ownership sectors since the mid-1980s. The National Labour Law (1994) took precedence over earlier legislations and regulations, and it encompassed a wide range of aspects of employment practices (minimum wage, social insurance, conflict resolution mechanisms, working-time limitations, etc.). Second, the law introduced written labour contracts "as the basic mode of employment relations" (Gallagher, Dong, 2011, p. 39). However, after the National Labour Law was passed, it took another

14 years to implement the Labour Contract Law (2008). The major objective of this law was to reduce employment precariousness by mandating employers to sign contracts with workers. The law even requires employers to sign open-term labour contracts with their employees after two consecutive fixed-term contracts and to show termination causes when they want to end contracts (LDF, 2008). But despite their late adoption, have these legal regulations helped contain the rise of informal employment in Beijing? If not, why has the level of informal employment been continuously growing?

To answer these questions, this chapter relies on retrospective longitudinal data collected in Beijing between September 2012 and August 2013. With a team of 20 students hired in three different universities in Beijing, I reconstructed the life-course of 916 respondents. These data were collected using a computer-administered life-course matrix. The life-course is defined as a sequence of events and socially defined roles that the individual assumes over time. Thus, this matrix is well adapted to collect retrospective data on the timing and the sequencing of events that occurred during the lives of the interviewed individuals. It captures the relationship between history, cohort and age (Giele, Elder, 1998, pp. 22–25). And it allows these dimensions to be linked to each other with, as common denominator, the dimension of temporality (date of occurrence of the events, their duration and chronology). The data collected do not only include demographic and socio-economic information but also reconstruct the family, school, professional and migratory trajectories of the respondents from their year of birth until 2012.

We questioned 301 individuals born between 1950 and 1959, and 615 young people born between 1980 and 1985 who had been living in Beijing for at least six months at the time of the survey. The sample was constructed based on data from the 2010 Beijing population census (BNS, 2012). To ensure that this sample was as representative as possible of the Beijing population, I stratified it according to the following variables: age, gender, level of education and residence booklet (*hukou*) (see Table 3.1 for a detailed view of the sample). The respondents took part in the survey voluntarily. As a gesture of thanks, they were given a small gift at the end of the interview, which lasted for an average of 1 h 30 min.

Case study and method

This chapter examines the employment trajectories of the respondents born between 1980 and 1985 ($N = 615$). To compare life-course sequences of about the same size, only sequences from the age of 16 to 27 are considered, since part of the sample data is missing after that age (the youngest respondents were born in 1985 and were aged 27 in 2012). The average age of the respondents is 28.7 years. The distribution of the gender ratio and of the *hukou* registration place has been respected. In the sample, 41 per cent of the post-1980s have a Beijing *hukou*. If for all other stratification criteria the sample distribution is good, there is, however, a slight over-representation of individuals with a high level of education (especially master's and higher), and, correlatively, a minor under-representation of individuals with a low level of education,[5] irrespective of gender.

Table 3.1 Characteristics of the sample

Gender				Hukou		Place of Hukou registration in 2012		Education level		
				Urban	Rural	Beijing	Not Beijing	Low level	Medium level	High level
Female	N		290	215	75	120	170	106	80	104
	% Total number of female			74.14%	25.86%	41.38%	58.62%	36.55%	27.59%	35.86%
	% of column total	47.15%		49.09%	42.37%	47.81%	46.70%	46.29%	49.69%	46.22%
Male	N		325	223	102	131	194	123	81	121
	% Total number of male			68.62%	31.38%	40.31%	59.69%	37.85%	24.92%	37.23%
	% of column total	52.85%		50.91%	57.63%	52.19%	53.30%	53.71%	50.31%	53.78%
Column total	N		615	438	177	251	364	229	161	225
Column total / N=615 (%)		-		71.22%	28.78%	40.81%	59.19%	37.24%	26.18%	36.59%

Hukou		Beijing	Not Beijing	Low level	Medium level	High level
	Urban	N	438	125	121	192
	% Total number of urban			28.54%	27.63%	43.84%
	% of column total			54.59%	75.16%	85.33%
	Rural	N	177	104	40	33
	% total number of rural			58.76%	22.60%	18.64%
	% of column total			45.41%	24.84%	14.67%

As this chapter considers informal employment to be "employment that is not stable or secure, that lacks a written agreement or contract, and that does not provide social insurance or benefits" (Gallagher *et al.*, 2011, p. 2), the analysis focuses on workers who lack formal labour contracts or agreements and who are not entitled to social insurance benefits. It also considers working time, as informal work conceals different categories of situations. For instance, some people may be self-employed, some may be "dispatched workers" (agency workers); some may work full-time, and others part-time. For this purpose, the analyses focus on variables 35, 36 and 52 of the life-course matrix:

> V35: Over your life-course have you ever had a labour contract? Could you please tell me when and what kind of contract (long-term contract, fixed-term contract, short-term contract, dispatched workers, no labour contract[6])?
> V36: Please tell me how many hours per week have you been working over your life-course (less than 10 hours, less than 20 hours, less than 30 hours, less than 40 hours, less than 50 hours, less than 60 hours, more than 60 hours)?
> V52: Considering your whole life-course, could you please tell me the periods when you were insured (medical insurance[7])?

I use multichannel sequence analysis (MCSA) to describe heterogeneous individual trajectories on several dimensions simultaneously (Gauthier *et al.*, 2010).[8] It is based on optimal matching analysis (OMA) and takes it a step further. Like OMA, it takes "the entire sequences of status held by individuals over a given period of time as the analytical unit to find chronological patterns of stability and change" (Gauthier *et al.*, 2013, p. 247).[9] But MCSA does not only describe one trajectory followed by the individual; it can take into account multiple trajectories/channels by means of specific alphabets (Gauthier *et al.*, 2010). For instance, as there is interdependence between the type of employment and the fact of being insured or not, I use these two channels in the MCSA.[10] The employment trajectories of the respondents are coded using a six-category code scheme: long-term contract, fixed-term contract, short-term contract, dispatched workers, no labour contract, and not employed. A three-category code scheme is used for health trajectories: do have insurance, do not have insurance, and do not know; and working time is coded into a four-category code scheme: not employed, T<40 hours, 40 hours<T<50 hours, T>50 hours. By the means of MCSA, I run a cluster analysis on the inter-individual distance matrix using PAM's method[11] to reveal groups of similar sequences of individual trajectories.

Informal employment as a state strategy

Informal employment and the 1994 National Labour Law

In the first phase of the reforms (1978–1992), in order to attract foreign investment, local governments turned a blind eye to the continuous growth of informal employment. In 1986, the central government tried to implement the Temporary

Regulations on the Labour Contract System. Despite this attempt, labour-intensive enterprises, whose competitive advantage was low-cost labour, favoured workers' flexibility at the expense of labour security and social benefits that would be framed by a written contract (Gallagher, Dong, 2011).

During the second phase of the reforms, starting in 1992, the Chinese authorities considered informal employment as both a problem for social stability and a solution to the unemployment crisis mostly resulting from the dismantling of SOEs. As developed by Gallagher and Dong (2011), even if the National Labour Law passed in 1994 offered, for the first time since the reforms, many protections for workers and uniform regulations across sectors and enterprises, this legal reform was mostly in favour of labour flexibility and enterprise autonomy.

It helped to push SOE reform further by replacing nationwide the lifetime employment practice by individualised labour contracts. This broke the Maoist social pact, and urban workers lost their right to employment. The new legislation introduced different contract categories entitling different levels of social protection. Only long-term contracts provided workers with social insurance and benefits on the basis of an employer–employee contribution (social insurance for illness, accident, retirement, unemployment, maternity leave). With fixed-term contracts and short-term contracts for a specific mission, workers had to pay their social insurances themselves (LDF, 1995).

The lack of ability of the central government and unwillingness of local governments to enforce the National Labour Law, as well as the massive lay-off of state workers and the growing number of migrant workers, had nonetheless induced a steep increase in informal employment across sectors (Peng, 2009; Gallagher, Dong, 2011; Park, Cai, 2011). Friedman and Lee point out that in 2007 "only about 50 per cent of all enterprises [had] signed contracts with their employees, and the rate among non-state firms was only 20 per cent [however, this sector had outgrown the state sector in term of employment]. Among the labour contracts that were signed, 60–70 per cent were short-term contracts under one year. [And only] 12.5 per cent [of migrant workers had] signed contracts" (Friedman, Lee, 2010, pp. 509–510).

In the 1990s and early 2000s, informalisation was a strategy used by some employers to meet their needs for labour flexibility and profitability, which allowed them not to sign a contract with their employees or contribute towards social insurances. The trend was even towards a "formalisation of informalisation" or a "permanent temporariness", according to some scholars, especially due to the increased use of subcontracting agencies dispatching temporary workers and apprentices (Gallagher *et al.*, 2011; Swider, 2011). These agencies barely provided social insurances to their dispatched workers (Friedman, Lee, 2010).

Informal employment of the post-1980s generation in Beijing

In order to examine work trajectories from age 16 to 27[12] of urban and rural youths living in Beijing at the time of the interview in 2012–2013, the respondents were asked whether or not they were working, and under what kind of labour contract, specifying any changes over their life-course. They could choose among the following answers: long-term contract, fixed-term contract, short-term contract, dispatched workers, no labour contract. Moreover, for each period, they had to stipulate the number of hours they were working, and whether or not they had social insurance.

First of all, using MCSA, I considered together work and insurance status trajectories of each individual. Four main groups of trajectories were found by cluster analysis (Figure 3.1).

They are named according to their main characteristics: Group 1 as "Formal employment with long-term contract"; Group 2 as "Informal employment"; Groups 3 and 4 illustrate the high proportion of respondents in the sample having precarious employment. The differences between these two groups are that there are mostly people with a level of education between senior high school and community college in group 3, and mostly people with a level of education above bachelor's and a *hukou* registered in Beijing in group 4. These two groups were, thus, named "Precarious employment with medium level of education" and "Precarious employment with high level of education", respectively. In practice, the residence booklet not only divides the population between urban and rural, but also creates a social hierarchy between local people and people coming from outside (Wang, 2005). It is thus striking to see that in this sample, the type of *hukou* (urban or rural) does not have a significant impact on the chance for a youth born in the 1980s of belonging to one of these clusters. What matters is the place of *hukou* registration and, mainly, the level of education (Table 3.2).

In the sample, people who do not have a labour contract tend mainly not to have insurance. As shown by Figure 3.1, nearly 18 of every 100 respondents are in this situation (Group 2 in Figure 3.1). In regard to the total sample, they comprise 16 per cent of the women and 20 per cent of the men, and relatively speaking, they mostly have a rural *hukou*. For instance, in regard to the total sample, 29 per cent of the respondents with a rural *hukou* belong to the group "Informal employment" (Group 2), whereas 14 per cent of the interviewees with an urban *hukou* belong to this group (Table A3.3).

To understand which variables could best explain the propensity to be part of this group, we computed a logistic regression using SPSS software. We considered the group "Informal employment" (Group 2) as a categorical dependent variable, and the *hukou* (rural/urban), the place of the *hukou* registration at the time of the interview (Beijing/outside Beijing), sex, matrimonial status (married/other)[13] and level of education (low level/medium level/high level) as predictors. The results indicate that people with a level of education no higher than community college (*daxue zhuanke*) and a *hukou* not registered in Beijing have a far greater probability of having informal employment characterised by no formal work agreement and no social insurance protection (Table A3.3), whereas only 1 per cent of the respondents with a bachelor's degree and above belong to this group (Table A3.3).

According to the findings, the lower the level of education, the higher the odds for a youth to belong to the group "Informal employment" (Group 2). For instance,

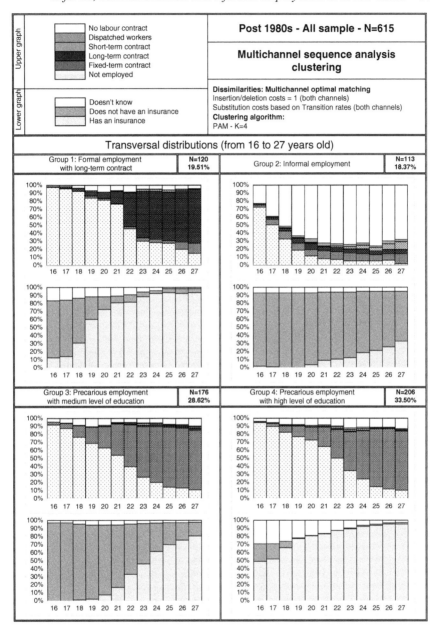

Figure 3.1 Transversal distribution of work and insurance status trajectories.

all other things being equal, the respondents with a level of education no higher than specialised secondary school – *zhongzhuan* – in the sample have the highest probability of working informally (Group 2) (Table 3.2). Moreover, even before starting their first employment, most of them did not have social insurance (Figure 3.1).

Table 3.2 Logistic regressions on cluster from MCSA on work, insurance status and working-time trajectories

Variables	Work and insurance status trajectories				Work and working-time trajectories		
	Group 1	Group 2	Group 3	Group 4	Group 1	Group 2	Group 3
Sex							
Male (ref.)	1	1	1	1	1	1	1
Female	1.136	0.684	1.057	1.058	1.594**	0.689	0.717
Type of hukou							
Rural (ref)	1	1	1	1	1	1	1
Urban	0.809	0.796	0.840	1.398	1.254	0.697	1.011
Place of hukou registration							
In Beijing (ref.)	1	1	1	1	1	1	1
Not in Beijing	0.994	5.947***	0.829	0.536**	0.695*	0.890	2.114**
Education							
High education (ref.)	1	1	1	1	1	1	1
Medium education	0.619*	13.701**	2.041**	0.514**	2.091**	0.257***	9.832***
Low education	0.163***	74.876***	1.426	0.390***	0.820	0.077***	63.687***
Marriage							
Not married (ref.)	1	1	1	1	1	1	1
Married	0.907	1.132	1.050	0.840	0.779	0.894	1.729*
Chi-square	46.165***	194.231***	12.842*	48.209***	42.101***	130.057***	229.913***
Df	6	6	6	6	6	6	6
Cox & Snell R Square	0.072	0.271	0.021	0.075	0.066	0.191	0.312
N	615	615	615	615	615	615	615

Notes
* p < .05 (Wald test),
** p < .01,
*** p < .001.

Table A3.3 Repartition, expressed in percentage, of the sample into the four types of trajectories (work and insurance status trajectories)

Gender

Female

	Group 1	Group 2	Group 3	Group 4	Total
N	59	47	85	99	290
%	20.34%	16.21%	29.31%	34.14%	100.00%

Male

	Group 1	Group 2	Group 3	Group 4	Total
N	61	66	91	107	325
%	18.77%	20.31%	28.00%	32.92%	100.00%

Hukou

Urban

	Group 1	Group 2	Group 3	Group 4	Total
N	91	61	120	166	438
%	20.78%	13.93%	27.40%	37.90%	100.00%

Rural

	Group 1	Group 2	Group 3	Group 4	Total
N	29	52	56	40	177
%	16.38%	29.38%	31.64%	22.60%	100.00%

Education

Low level

	Group 1	Group 2	Group 3	Group 4	Total
N	16	96	67	50	229
%	6.99%	41.92%	29.26%	21.83%	100.00%

Medium level

	Group 1	Group 2	Group 3	Group 4	Total
N	35	15	60	51	161
%	21.74%	9.32%	37.27%	31.68%	100.00%

High level

	Group 1	Group 2	Group 3	Group 4	Total
N	69	2	49	105	225
%	30.67%	0.89%	21.78%	46.67%	100.00%

(continued)

Table A3.3 (Continued)

Rural hukou / low level	Group 1	Group 2	Group 3	Group 4	Total
N	9	43	35	17	104
%	8.65%	41.35%	33.65%	16.35%	100.00%

Rural hukou / medium level	Group 1	Group 2	Group 3	Group 4	Total
N	9	9	15	7	40
%	22.50%	22.50%	37.50%	17.50%	100.00%

Rural hukou / high level	Group 1	Group 2	Group 3	Group 4	Total
N	11	0	6	16	33
%	33.33%	0.00%	18.18%	48.48%	100.00%

Urban hukou / low level	Group 1	Group 2	Group 3	Group 4	Total
N	7	53	32	33	125
%	5.60%	42.40%	25.60%	26.40%	100.00%

Urban hukou / medium level	Group 1	Group 2	Group 3	Group 4	Total
N	26	6	45	44	121
%	21.49%	4.96%	37.19%	36.36%	100.00%

Urban hukou / high level	Group 1	Group 2	Group 3	Group 4	Total
N	58	2	43	89	192
%	30.21%	1.04%	22.40%	46.35%	100.00%

Group 2

N= 113   18.37%

Gender	Female	Male
N	47	66
%	41.59%	58.41%

Hukou in 2012	Urban	Rural
N	61	52
%	53.98%	46.02%

Hukou in 2012	Beijing	Not Beijing
N	14	99
%	12.39%	87.61%

Education	Low level	Medium level	High level
N	96	15	2
%	84.96%	13.27%	1.77%

Marital status	Married	Other
N	76	37
%	67.26%	32.74%

	Urban	Rural	Urban	Rural
N	25	22	36	30
%	22.12%	19.47%	31.86%	26.55%

Therefore, Figure 3.1 and Table 3.2 highlight that the higher the level of education, the higher is the probability for the youths to have a work contract and social insurance. As illustrated with the "Formal employment" group (Group 1) and the "Precarious employment with high level of education" group (Group 4), once they are admitted to college or university at around 18–20 years old, the school provides them with social protection (Figure 3.1). The odds ratio is higher for someone from Beijing to be in the group "Precarious employment with high level of education" (Table 3.2, Group 4). Most of those with a medium level of education (Group 3 in Figure 3.1) only have insurance once they start working. It is, however, hard to tell whether they pay for it themselves or share the burden with their employers. So, we can expect that there may be some people in this group who do not have formal employment.

Furthermore, the analyses reveal an overwhelming tendency of employers to sign fixed-term contracts with their employees, especially unskilled workers, instead of long-term contracts (Figure 3.1, Groups 3 and 4, and Table 3.2). Nearly 60 per cent of the respondents do have fixed-term contracts, and close to 18 per cent do not have any work agreement during their life-course. These results highlight a trend towards employment precariousness. In addition, Gallagher and Dong point out that the length of these contracts tends to become shorter and shorter. They state that "whereas labor contracts of three to five years were more common in the mid-1990s, by the early 2000s most companies in China signed one year contracts with their regular employees, offering to long-term contracts to their more highly valued and scarce-skilled technicians and managers" (Gallagher, Dong, 2011, p. 40).

Ultimately, the reforms brought by the 1994 Labour Law have led to more labour deregulation and "widespread employment insecurity" for the majority of Chinese workers (Gallagher, Dong, 2011, p. 40). It is striking that only about 20 per cent of the respondents do have long-term contracts (Figure 3.1, Group 1), and that only a very slight minority who belong to the group "Informal employment" (Group 2) manage over time to get out of informality by signing a labour contract entitling them to social benefits.[14] So, even if among the people who have not signed a formal work agreement there might be some people having their own shops or enterprises (*getihu* or *siyingqiye*), it seems that a prolonged period of informality over the life-course, or a sort of "permanent temporariness", is pretty common for the most vulnerable youths living in Beijing – i.e. rural and urban migrants with a low level of education.

The three clusters we computed, using MCSA and considering together the work and working-time trajectories of each individual, show that the youths who have not signed a labour contract tend to work longer than the other segments of the active population (Group 3 in Figure 3.2, named "Informal employment").

Even if the 1994 Labour Law sets out a standard of eight hours a day, 44 hours a week, overtime limitations and at least one day off per week, according to our interviews, the youths working in Beijing without a labour contract or as temporary workers on fixed-term and short-term contracts tend to work more than 50 hours per week (art. 36 to 42, §4, LDF, 1995).

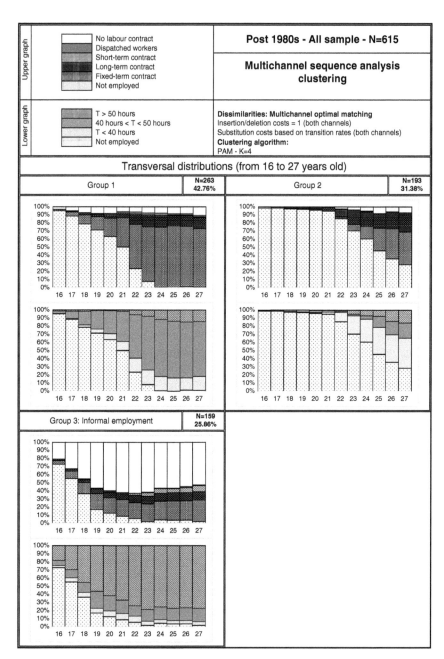

Figure 3.2 Transversal distribution of work and working-time trajectories.

The logistic regression we computed, taking the group "Informal employment" (Group 3) as a categorical dependent variable and the *hukou* (rural/urban), the place of *hukou* registration at the time of the interview (Beijing/outside Beijing), sex, matrimonial status (married/other) and level of education (low level/medium level/high level) as predictors, points out that working time is very strongly correlated with the level of education: the lower the level of education, the higher the odds for a youth of working over 44 hours a week (Table 3.2).

These informal workers are sometimes referred to as "temporary workers" (*lingshigong*) in Chinese media. The term comes from the planned economy era, when labourers were sometimes hired by SOEs to accomplish a specific task. They are mostly unskilled, yet they can be found in any sector of the economy today (state sector, private sector, collective sector, etc.). Not only do these workers represent a flexible means for companies and state agencies to adjust to the needs of the neo-liberal economy, but also they are relatively inexpensive, and they can easily be held responsible in the case of mistakes, pointing at their low level of "quality" (*suzhi*) instead of employers' responsibilities.

Since the end of the 1980s, this concept has been increasingly used by the party-state in order to promote a market economy. Some scholars have pointed out that the use of the "quality" rhetoric by the Chinese authorities echoes the neo-liberal discourse found elsewhere in the world and aims to shape reflexive individuals (Jacka, 2007, p. 122; 2009, p. 525; Anagnost, 2004; Yan, 2003; Greenhalgh, Winckler, 2005). According to Yan, Anagnost and Sigley, this discourse is also a means used by the government to conceal and legitimise the socio-economic disparities in post-Maoist China (Yan, 2003; Anagnost, 2004; Sigley, 2009).[15] Since the reforms, the power of the Chinese state is becoming more diffuse; using the channel of various institutions, it instils its discourse on "quality", which suggests that social success can be reached by all individuals if they make efforts to improve themselves and consume material goods (Jacka *et al.*, 2013, p. 193). But this rhetorical tool is not sufficient to contain the strengthening of voices denouncing the lack of social justice in post-Maoist China.

Informal employment and social peace

The Informal employment group and the Precarious employment with a medium level of education group (Groups 2 and 3 in Figure 3.1) also reveal that before 2007 and the implementation of the Labour Contract Law, the respondents aged between 16 and 21 years old at that time, and who were working either as dispatched workers or on fixed-term contracts, mostly did not have social insurances. The situation of these informal workers highlights the institutional incapacity and/or willingness of the central and local governments to implement the 1994 Labour Law standards and to protect workers' rights. Instead, they mostly used the law to end lifetime employment and increase labour flexibility.

Since the reforms of the early 1980s, social inequalities have strongly increased in Chinese society, resulting in growing social unrest (Jacka *et al.*, 2013). According to China's Public Security Ministry, in 2003 there were more than 58,000 "major incidents of social unrest" in China, and this number jumped to 87,000 in 2005. According to one report, "recent protest activities have been broader in scope, larger in average size, greater in frequency, and more brash than those a decade ago" (Lum, 2006, pp. 1–2).

Fearing the spread and the intensification of social protests all over the country that might challenge its political legitimacy and the pace of socio-economic reforms, the Hu-Wen administration proclaimed its willingness to work for the building of a harmonious society. The legislative efforts made in 2007 by the central government to enhance the protection of workers' rights with the Labour Contract Law have to be understood in this context. On paper, write Gallagher and Dong, "these new laws are in a model of greater social protection, less mobility, and decreased flexibility. [...] But, because the implementation period of these laws coincided with the onset of the global economic crisis in 2008 and new government concerns about employment, the implementation of these new laws has been more contentious and fraught with the competing concerns of the state, capital, and labor" (2011, p. 45).

Nonetheless, our data show that the new regulations aiming to increase employment security for fixed-term contracts and dispatched workers had had a positive impact for some of the respondents. It appears that after 2007, when they were aged between 22 and 27 years old, most of the respondents, who were working on fixed-term contracts without social protection, became insured (Figure 3.1, Group 3). This is obviously one of the consequences of the new Labour Contract Law, since the law mandates companies and labour service companies to pay for the social insurances of their full-time precarious workers. The Labour Contract Law (2008) also stipulates that companies have to turn fixed-term contracts into open-ended contracts after two consecutive fixed-term contracts. In addition, the legislation restricts the probation period, which was used by companies to reduce labour costs, and last but not least, it empowers trade unions (LDF, 2008).

Conclusion

Neo-liberalism and flexible accumulation of capital have spread worldwide over the last 30 years. And post-Maoist China has not been exempt from this phenomenon, as the rise of informal employments illustrates.

In this chapter, I have shown, through the case study of Beijing, that following a process of individualisation, individuals in post-Maoist China have been emancipated and disembedded from the collective institutions, such as the work units, that prescribed their social conduct and relations. They have become responsible for their individual destinies, for the chances and risks they encounter over their life-courses. But, as stated by Bauman, "[...] individualization is a fate, not a choice; in the land of individual freedom of choice, the option to escape individualization and to refuse participation in the individualizing game is emphatically not on the agenda" (2011 [2002], p. xvi). Then, in continuity with the individualisation theory and relying on the results of the empirical research conducted in Beijing, the chapter has argued that labour flexibility and the level of informal employment have been continuously growing in post-Maoist China, less as a result of individuals' strategies than as a result of corporate strategies, endorsed by the state to increase the country's economic global competitiveness. Furthermore, this chapter has tried to highlight the fact that state interests in China are heterogeneous on two levels. On the one hand, the post-Maoist party-state is balancing between the economic growth of the country facing the challenge of movable capital and its continuing demand for a cheap and flexible labour force, and better worker protections that would help avoid social unrest and threaten its political legitimacy. On the other hand, there are the specific interests of provincial and local governments, who, since the fiscal decentralisation and the economic slowdown, need economic growth in their localities in order to balance their budgets. So, despite some legislative efforts by the party-state to provide some degree of employment security and to reduce informal employment that is all too often permanent, the law still lacks stronger regulations that would guarantee its enforcement nationwide.

Acknowledgements

I am thankful to the Ernst & Lucie Schmidheiny Foundation and the Geneva-Asia Association, which supported this research. I am also grateful to Tong Xin in Peking University, the students who helped me collect the data in Beijing, to all the respondents who agreed to share their lives with us, and to Jean-Marie Le Goff and Nandan Nawn for their comments on an earlier version of this chapter. Any opinions, findings and conclusions expressed in this chapter are those of the author.

Notes

1 It divides the population into agricultural and non-agricultural households.
2 There are two definitions of the Cultural Revolution. Strictly speaking, it is the period from May 1966 to April 1969, during which Mao, with the armed wing of the Red Guards, restored his power. In the broad sense (the definition given by the party-state), the period of the Cultural Revolution extends from 1966 to 1976, the later date embodying the death of Mao and the fall of the Gang of Four.
3 See Barry Naughton for an exhaustive explanation of this mechanism (Naughton, 1995, pp. 85–110).
4 An experiment to legislate into law the labour contract system was already undertaken in 1986 with the "Provisional Regulations on Institution of Labour Contract System in State-Owned Enterprises" (国营企业实行劳动合同制暂行规定 1986 (Guoying qiye shixing laodong hetong zanxing guiding 1986).
5 In the analyses, levels of education were combined into three groups: "Low level" (primary school – *xiaoxue*, junior high school – *chuzhong*, and specialised secondary school – *zhongdeng zhuanye xuexiao*), "Medium level" (senior high school – *gaozhong* – and community college – *daxue zhuanke*) and "High level" (College – *daxue benke*, master's – *shuoshi* – and above).
6 *Wu guding qixian laodong hetong, guding qixian laodong hetong, yi wancheng yiding gongzuo renwu wei qixian de laodong hetong, laowu paiqian, wu laodong hetong.*
7 *Yiliao baoxian.* I decided to ask only about medical insurance, not all social insurances, to avoid confusion during the data collection. The same questionnaire was used to

collect data on the life-course of the 1950s and 1980s birth cohorts. Medical insurance is a good indicator because it could also be identified in Maoist China, whereas unemployment insurance or retirement pensions could not.

8 The MCSA are performed using TraMineR, a package of the R software, developed by G. Ritschard, A. Gabadinho, M. Studer and N. Müller (Gabadinho *et al.*, 2009).

9 For further details on how OMA works, see Gauthier *et al.*, 2010, pp. 4–5.

10 In the inter-individual distance matrix computed, insertion or deletion cost = 1, and substitution cost = transition rate.

11 Partitioning around Medoids (PAM). After evaluating various quality indicators (average silhouette width [ASW], point biserial correlation [PBC], Hubert's C coefficient [HC], Hubert's gamma [HG]) for a different number of clusters, as well as different cluster algorithms and the clusters produced, I chose the method of PAM – in four groups for the work and insurance status trajectories, and in three groups for the work and working-time trajectories – to form the clusters. Although the value of the coefficient for the measurement of ASW quality indicates that the quality of the clusters could be superficial ($0.25 < ASW < 0.5$), the values of the other quality indicators are acceptable (Studer, 2012). For more details, please see R Graphical Manual.

12 According to China's Labour Law, art.15 §2, working before 16 years old is not legal (LDF, 1995).

13 The other category includes not married, cohabiting and divorced.

14 As illustrated by the longitudinal representation of these very same clusters.

15 Between 1980 and 2010, the Gini coefficient, which measures income inequality, increased from 0.25 to 0.50 (Jacka *et al.*, 2013, pp. 220–221).

References

Anagnost, A. (2004). The Corporeal Politics of Quality (Suzhi). *Public culture*, 16(2), pp. 189–208.

Angeloff, T., Lieber, M. (Eds). (2012). *Chinoises au XXIe siècle. Ruptures et continuités*. Paris: Editions La Découverte.

Bauman, Z. (2001). *The Individualized Society*. Cambridge: Polity Press and Blackwell Publishers.

Bauman, Z. (2011) [2002]. Individually, Together. In U. Beck and E. Beck-Gernsheim (Eds), *Individualization*. London: SAGE.

Beck, U. (2008) [1986]. *La société du risque. Sur la voie d'une autre modernité*. Paris: Flammarion.

Beck, U., Beck-Gernsheim, E. (2010). Varieties of Individualization. In M. Halskov Hansen, R. Svarverud (Eds), *iChina. The Rise of the Individual in Modern Chinese Society*. Copenhagen: Nordic Institute of Asian Studies.

Beck, U., Beck-Gernsheim, E. (2011) [2002]. *Individualization. Institutionalized Individualism and its Social and Political Consequences*. London: SAGE Publications.

BNS. (2012). 北京市2010年人口普查资料 *(Beijing shi 2010 nian renkou pucha ziliao), Tabulation on the 2010 Population Census of Beijing Municipality*. Beijing: China Statistics Press.

Bonnin, M. (2004). *Génération perdue. Le mouvement d'envoi des jeunes instruits à la campagne en Chine, 1968–1980*. Paris: Editions de l'Ecole des hautes études en sciences sociales.

Bray, D. (2005). *Social Space and Governance in Urban China. The Danwei System from Origins to Reform*. Stanford: Stanford University Press.

Cheng, Y. (2009). *Creating the "New Man". From Enlightenment Ideals to Socialist Realities*. Honolulu: University of Hawai'i Press.

De Beer, P., Rocca, J.-L. (1995). *La Chine à la fin de l'ère Deng Xiaoping*: Paris: Le Monde-Editions.

Fairbank, J.K., Goldman, M. (2010) [1992]. *Histoire de la Chine. Des origines à nos jours*. Paris: Editions Tallandier.

Friedman, E., Ching Kwan Lee (2010). Remaking the World of Chinese Labour: A 30-Year Retrospective. *British journal of industrial relations*, 48(3), pp. 507–534.

Gabadinho, A., Ritschard, G., Studer, M., Müller, N.S. (2009). *Mining Sequence Data in R with the TraMineR package: A User's Guide*. Geneva: Department of Econometrics and Laboratory of Demography, University of Geneva.

Gallagher, M.E., Baohua Dong (2011). Legislating Harmony: Labor Law Reform in Contemporary China. In M.E. Gallagher, Ching Kwan Lee, S. Kuruvilla (Eds), *From Iron Rice Bowl to Informalization*. New York: Cornell University Press.

Gallagher, M.E., Ching Kwan Lee, Kuruvilla, S. (2011). Introduction and Argument. In M.E. Gallagher, Ching Kwan Lee, S. Kuruvilla (Eds), *From Iron Rice Bowl to Informalization*. New York: Cornell University Press.

Gauthier, J.-A., Widmer, E., Bucher, P., Notredame, C. (2010). Multichannel Sequence Analysis Applied to Social Science Data. *Sociological methodology*, 40(1), pp. 1–38.

Gauthier, J.-A., Widmer, E., Bucher, P., Notredame, C. (2013). Multichannel Optimal Matching: A Multidimensional Approach to Sequence Analysis. In R. Levy, E. Widmer (Eds), *Gendered Life Courses: Between Standardization and Individualization. A European Approach Applied to Switzerland*. Zürich: Lit Verlag.

Giddens, A. (2015) [1991]. *The Consequences of Modernity*. Cambridge: Polity Press.

Giele, J.Z., Elder, G.H. (Eds). (1998). *Methods of Life Course Research. Qualitative and Quantitative Approaches*. Thousand Oaks, California: SAGE Publications.

Greenhalgh, S., Winckler, E.A. (2005). *Governing China's Population. From Leninist to Neoliberal Biopolitics*. Stanford, California: Stanford University Press.

Hurst, W. (2009). *The Chinese Worker after Socialism*. Cambridge: Cambridge University Press.

Jacka, T. (2007). Population Governance in the PRC: Political, Historical and Anthropological Perspectives. *The China journal*, 58 (July), pp. 111–126.

Jacka, T. (2009). Cultivating Citizens: Suzhi (Quality) Discourse in PRC. *Positions: East Asia cultures critique*, 17 (3), pp. 523–535.

Jacka, T., Kipnis, A., Sargeson, S. (2013). *Contemporary China. Society and Social Change*. New York: Cambridge University Press.

LDF. (1995). 中华人民共和国劳动法 (zhonghua renmin gongheguo laodong fa, Le droit du travail de la RPC).

LDF. (2008). *中华人民共和国劳动合同法 (zhonghua renmin gongheguo laodong fa, Le droit du travail de la RPC)*.

Lin, Kun-Chin. (2011). Enterprise Reform and Wage Movements in Chinese Oil Fields and Refineries. In M.E. Gallagher, Ching Kwan Lee, S. Kuruvilla (Eds), *From Iron Rice Bowl to Informalization*. New York: Cornell University Press.

Liu, Zhiqiang (2005). Institution and Inequality: The Hukou System in China. *Journal of comparative economics*, 33, pp. 133–157.

Lü, Xiaobo, Perry, E.J. (Eds). (1997). *Danwei. The Changing Chinese Workplace in Historical and Comparative Perspective*. New York; London: M.E. Sharpe.

Lum, T. (2006). *Social Unrest in China*. Washington, DC: Congressional Research Service.

Monteil, A. (2010). *Emploi informel et gestion des inégalités sociales en Chine urbaine. Les politiques de promotion de "l'emploi communautaire" parmi les "groupes vulnérables" à Chengdu* (2006–2009). Doctorat, Socio-économie du développement, Ecole des Hautes Etudes en Sciences Sociales.

Naughton, B. (1995). *Growing out of the Plan: Chinese Economic Reform (1978–1993)*. Cambridge: Cambridge University Press.

Naughton, B. (2007). *The Chinese Economy. Transitions and Growth*. Cambridge: Massachusetts Institute of Technology.

Park, A., Fang Cai (2011). The Informalization of the Chinese Labor Market. In M. E. Gallagher, Ching Kwan Lee, S. Kuruvilla (Eds), *From Iron Rice Bowl to Informalization*. New York: Cornell University Press.

Peng, Xizhe (彭希哲) (2009). *2006 中国非正规就业发展报告：劳动力市场的再观察 (zhongguo feizhenggui jiuye fazhan baogao: laodongli shichang de zai guancha, Report on China's informal Employment Development: Survey on the Labor Force Market)*. 重庆 (Chongqing): 重庆出版社，Chongqing chubanshe.

Perry, E.J., Selden, M. (Eds). (2010) [2000]. *Chinese Society. Change, Conflict and Resistance*. Oxon: Routledge.

Peter, A., Chan, A. (2004). Does China Have an Apartheid Pass System? *Journal of ethnic and migration studies*, 30(4), pp. 609–629.

Sigley, G. (2009). Suzhi, the Body, and the Fortunes of Technoscientific Reasoning in Contemporary China. *Positions: East Asia cultures critique*, 17(3), pp. 537–566.

Studer, M. (2012). *Étude des inégalités de genre en début de carrière académique à l'aide de méthodes innovatrices d'analyse de données séquentielles*. PhD, Faculté des sciences économiques et sociales, Université de Genève (SES-777).

Swider, S. (2011). Permanent Temporariness in the Chinese Construction Industry. In M.E. Gallagher, Ching Kwan Lee, S. Kuruvilla (Eds), *From Iron Rice Bowl to Informalization*. New York: Cornell University Press.

Tong, Xin (佟新) (2009). 总结 (zongjie, Conclusion). In Xin (佟新) Tong 中国劳动关系。Eds. 调研报告 *(zhongguo laodong guanxi. Diaoyan baogao. Les relations de travail en Chine. Rapport de recherches empiriques)*. 北京 (Beijing): 中国言实出版社 (zhongguo yanshi chubanshe).

Walder, A. (1986). *Communist Neo-Traditionalism: Work and Authority in Chinese Industry*. Berkeley: University of California Press.

Wang, Feiling (2005). *Organizing through Division and Exclusion. China's Hukou System*. Stanford: Stanford University Press.

Whyte, M.K. (Ed.). (2010). *One Country, Two Societies. Rural-Urban Inequality in Contemporary China*. Cambridge, Massachusetts: Harvard University Press.

Yan, Hairong (2003). Neoliberal Governmentality and Neohumanism: Organizing Suzhi/ Value Flow through Labor Recruitment Networks. *Cultural anthropology*, 18(4), pp. 493–523.

Yan, Yunxiang (2010). The Chinese Path to Individualization. *The British journal of sociology*, 61(3), pp. 489–512.

Zhang, Lu (2011). The Paradox of Labor Force Dualism and State-Labor-Capital Relations in the Chinese Automobile Industry. In M.E. Gallagher, Ching Kwan Lee, S. Kuruvilla (Eds), *From Iron Rice Bowl to Informalization*. New York: Cornell University Press.

国营企业实行劳动合同制暂行规定 1986 (Guoying qiye shixing laodong hetong zanxing guiding 1986, Provisional Regulations on Institution of Labour Contract System In State-Owned Enterprises 1986). http://www.pkulaw.cn/fulltext_form. aspx?Db=chl&Gid=2905 (Accessed 26 May 2015).

Part II
Law in formalising informal workers

4 A new international labour standard for formalising the informal economy? A discussion of its desirability

Claire La Hovary

Introduction[1]

The International Labour Organization (ILO) has, quite naturally, long hosted discussions regarding informal economic activity. As a tripartite organisation that uniquely brings together on an equal footing Employer, Worker and Government representatives from all of its 186 member states, the ILO is clearly an important actor with regard to questions of informality. Indeed, the ILO's focus and role with regard to improving working conditions are clearly relevant to the many concerns that informality raises in this regard. The notion of an "informal economy" evokes for most observers images of workers suffering from poverty, exploitation, precarity, vulnerability and discrimination, for example, and it is generally agreed that an immense number of individuals are affected by such difficulties. Tackling these issues is of key policy relevance for the agenda of the ILO, and informality is a notion which it has linked with the principle of decent work for all.

The ILO is, furthermore, *the* international organisation that introduced the notion into global development debates,[2] thereby launching its "meteoric career in the world of policy" (Peattie, 1987, p. 853). At the same time, the difficulties surrounding the definition, or understanding, of informality have always been acknowledged within the ILO. As has been explained in the introduction to this volume, the concept of the "informal sector" was first introduced in the ILO in 1972 in order to describe certain types of work that were not being captured by official government statistics on employment. From this quite limited focus, the Organisation's use of the term has developed into an all-encompassing concept, termed the "informal economy", regrouping, as suggested by the ILO's International Labour Conference (ILC) in a resolution adopted in 2002, "all economic activities by workers and economic units that are – in law or in practice – not covered or insufficiently covered by formal arrangements" (ILO, 2002, p. 25/3, para. 3). The concept has, moreover, been the object of significant attention from ILO statisticians (who offer definitions of the "informal sector" and "informal employment", but not of employment in the "informal economy"), and the concept has been directly alluded to, in various ways, in some international labour standards (ILS).

As the introduction to this book highlights, the understanding of informality is, in general, clearly abstract; it means different things to different people, and it is a concept which carries layers of contradictory assessments as to its causes and the measures needed to address it: so much so, that many have even questioned the usefulness of the concept (Guha-Khasnobis *et al.*, 2006, pp. 1–2; Peattie, 1987; ILO, 1991). In light of all this, the decision taken by the Governing Body of the ILO in 2012 to put on the agenda of the ILC the adoption of a recommendation on "facilitating gradual transitions from the informal economy to the formal economy" – which was subsequently adopted by the June 2015 ILC[3] – is surprising, as the concept – and therefore that of "formalisation" – is considered extremely fluid.

The theme also poses many challenges from a legal perspective. Indeed, in the legal sphere, the *concept* – but not the numerous underlying issues it raises – has not been of central concern for scholars. Rather, the "informal economy" is an economic term that has developed apart from legal debates. As a result, the problems raised by the existence of an "informal economy" have mostly been addressed from a very precise angle – determining which workers are excluded from the scope of the law and attempting to suggest measures to bring them back into the scope of protection, as well as seeking to increase the protection afforded when it is insufficient, for example.[4] Moreover, the reality of workers escaping, *de facto* or *de jure*, the protection of the law has usually been approached by analysing the regulation of "non-standard" work and, more generally, through the lens of the crisis of application and of concept of domestic labour law (Davidov, Langille, 2006, 2011; Fudge *et al.*, 2012; Teklè, 2010; Stone, Arthurs, 2013 – this last book doesn't mention informality, for example). As a result, from a legal perspective, the notions of informality that overlap with current labour law concerns may be difficult to grasp.

This contribution focuses on the ILO and its 2015 Recommendation and the challenges of tackling the topic from a legal perspective. It will start by analysing, from a legal perspective, various understandings of the informal economy and the conceptual challenges they raise, highlighting how, as Trebilcock argues, the concept does not sit well in law (2006, p. 65). The second part of the chapter reviews the political and other circumstances surrounding the decision to put formalisation on the agenda of the ILC, and ultimately questions the desirability of formalisation as an objective within the context of the ILO's overall aim of promoting decent work for all.

The concept of informality and its legal aspects

The ILO 2002 understanding of the informal economy, which was retained in Recommendation No. 204, is certainly not uniformly accepted, and informality – like formality – means different things to different people. Indeed, many coexisting understandings or definitions of informality[5] are adopted at the national and international levels by academics, statisticians and policy-makers. To a certain extent, different definitions will reflect different underlying concerns – weak labour and human rights enforcement, tax evasion, unfair competition between formal and informal firms, poverty reduction, and so on – as well as the different approaches to measuring informality. The ILO's main concern, however, is improving working conditions for all. One of the ways it strives to achieve this is through the adoption of ILS.[6]

ILS apply generally to all workers (Trebilcock, 2004, pp. 588–592),[7] and the term "workers" is understood in the ILO to be much broader than "employees" and extends to all forms of work, including self-employment, domestic work, part-time work, contract labour, and so on. Fundamental rights at work in particular famously apply to all, and so does, more broadly, the concept of decent work. The problem is not so much the scope of ILS as their application in practice, in both the formal and the informal economy (Trebilcock, 2004, pp. 588–589) – this certainly raises questions as to whether and how some ILS should be revised.

The concept of informality has been referred to specifically in only some ILS and in some pronouncements of the ILO supervisory bodies. Its meaning remains extremely fluid, however, and the notion tends to refer to national understandings of informality rather than to the ILO's 2002 understanding.[8]

International labour standards, the ILO supervisory bodies and the informal economy

Only a few ILS refer explicitly to the informal sector/economy. These include Convention No. 150 on Labour Administration of 1978,[9] the Recommendation on Employment Policy (Supplementary Provisions) (No. 169) of 1984[10] and the more recent Recommendation No. 195 on Human Resources Development of 2004. This last Recommendation, for example, does not give a definition of the informal economy. However, by stating that members should "promote access to education, training and lifelong learning for ... workers in small and medium-sized enterprises, in the informal economy, in the rural sector and in self-employment", it does presuppose a distinction between these four categories. Far from clarifying concepts, then, ILS referring to informality are more a reflection of the debates surrounding the various understandings of "informality".[11]

The pronouncements of the Committee of Experts on the Application of Conventions and Recommendation (CEACR) have, as a consequence of the various understandings of informality at the national level, not clarified things, even if, according to a 2010 ILO publication, the CEACR has addressed issues of the informal economy in a more systematic manner since the 2002 discussion at the ILC (ILO, 2010, p. 13). Many of the CEACR's comments remain quite circular if one reads them with the 2002 understanding in mind: e.g. "the full benefits of the Convention rarely reach the informal economy" (ILO, 2010, p. 15) is not very helpful, as it is clear that, under the ILO's 2002 understanding of informality, the law by definition is not reaching the informal economy. Other comments, such as "labour law applies to very few workers because 95 per cent of workers are in the informal economy", are equally circular (ILO, 2010, p. 16).[12] The CEACR has, however, made a majority of its comments on "informality" in the context of child labour, and, to a lesser extent, regarding employment policy (ILO, 2010, p. 13).

In general, then, it could be claimed that the CEACR has not dealt with informality in a systematic manner. It should be recalled, though, that the CEACR will normally only mention the informal sector or economy if the government has mentioned it in its report. Moreover, supervisory bodies do deal with the issue of the national scope of the law when it does not correspond to a ratified convention, without mentioning that this implicitly concerns "informality".[13] Since 2009, however, the CEACR has requested that governments provide information on the application of ratified conventions in the "informal economy".[14] As a result, some states – such as Senegal, for example, mentioned in the 2014 ILO report – have replied that their labour code applies to workers in the "informal economy" when, in fact, the labour code does not mention the informal economy but simply states that it applies to "all workers and employers" (Art. L1, Labour Code, Law no. 97-17 of 1997).

Some conceptual difficulties in approaching informality from a legal perspective

As the introduction to this volume states, the law is often seen as a defining factor of informality. It is sometimes seen as a cause of informality – the law may be deemed too burdensome, or may even be seen as responsible for keeping workers out of the "formal economy", for example.[15]

It is also sometimes seen as a solution, or part of it – by extending the scope of national law and ensuring its implementation through effective labour inspection and labour administration, or by redefining its content to make the legislation less burdensome, adapt it to its environment, expand *or* lower the protection it affords, for example. These different views on the role of the law vis-à-vis informality have triggered enormous unresolved debates in economics and development studies, largely shaped by ideology. But while the law certainly intervenes at many levels of the informality debate, and connects to broader debates about the desirability of labour regulation from an economic perspective (e.g. Sengenberger, 2005), this section will limit itself to analysing the definition of informality from a legal perspective. It will point out its shortcomings, which include: (1) a mismatch between national statistics definitions and national scope of the law; (2) the fact that the ILO's 2002 understanding of informality may be too broad to be useful in terms of the situations it covers, the effect on workers' conditions, or the root causes of informality; (3) the various possible interpretations of the 2002 understanding; (4) the fact that the use of the word "informal" may be undermining the law; and (5) the fact that formalisation should also focus on the content of the law.

The whole formal/informal debate has happened mostly without the involvement of lawyers, despite the law often being at the centre of the definitions adopted (and the issues raised by the informal economy debates being, of course, at the centre of labour law scholars' preoccupations). As Daza states, "[e]fforts to define the informal sector in legal terms have been rare" (2005, p. 34).[16] The various definitions that exist at the national level, for example, are often developed for statistical purposes and are more often than not established without any consideration of the actual scope or content of national legislation. Incoherencies are consequently frequent, resulting in a mismatch between the national scope of the law and the national definition(s) of informality. Many workers labelled as "informal" under various definitions may, in fact, be covered by the law, which might even be applied in practice. For example, certain definitions of informality (ILO, 2013e) consider all workers in firms of fewer than 5 or 10 workers to be informal, when workers in such firms may, in fact, be covered, in law and in practice, by labour and social security laws (exclusions from labour legislation based on the size of the enterprise are, in fact, infrequent; Daza, 2005, p. 23). Other definitions consider all domestic workers to be informal when again, in some countries, domestic workers are covered by the law, which is applied in practice. The same problems also occur with regard to casual workers, who may be included in the scope of labour law but are also included in the national statistical definition of informality. As Trebilcock points out, "even an 'informal' enterprise can have 'employees' under national legislation governing the employment relationship, with resulting rights and duties for both the employer and the employee" (Trebilcock, 2004, p. 590). The actual scope of the national law is thus not systematically taken into account by statisticians and policy-makers, impeding the formulation of informed policies and measures to tackle "informality".

On the other hand, the ILC's 2002 understanding, which is less precise than many national definitions, has been considered to be much too broad and therefore problematic for legislators, labour lawyers and policy-makers (Trebilcock, 2006; Davidov, 2006, p. 3). It covers an extremely wide spectrum of situations, with very different outcomes. For example, an international consultant who escapes the application of the law, someone who is working in an export processing zone where labour and social security law is typically not applicable or not enforced, someone working for a big *or* for a small enterprise which is not registered, an illegal migrant working clandestinely, or a child working in dangerous situations could all potentially be classified as informal. Each of these workers may, however, have extremely different working conditions, going from the absence of any rights to the absence of a few rights. Moreover, an informal worker might be unregistered, under-registered, a disguised worker, an ambiguous worker, in a triangular relationship, in a precarious situation, or in a situation that is not covered by the law. Finally, an informal worker may be working informally because it suits him or her – for example, for the purpose of tax evasion – or, much more probably, because of lack of choice (see, generally, ILO, 2013e). All these situations call for different policy responses, something the ILO acknowledges when it states that there is no "one-size-fits-all" solution to formalisation (ILO, 2007a, para. 20).

The situations covered by informality may also present very different triggering factors or root causes. The concept, however, does not distinguish between the various potential underlying reasons – sheer poverty or inadequate attribution of state resources (which then leads to inadequate labour administration systems, insufficient labour inspection, and a deficient justice system), inadequate redistribution of state resources (which leads to poverty and lapses in education), lack of adequate legal instruments (which may be cumbersome, incoherent, not broad enough or not adapted to the reality), competition based on prices (which encourages firms and employers to overlook certain labour standards in order to survive and/or make profits), weakened states, exploitation, unemployment leading to illegal migration, and so on. There is, therefore, arguably not much added value in categorising most work situations in the informal economy as belonging to this category from a root causes perspective and, therefore, from a policy perspective. Indeed, this masks the origins of the problem, the available ways to improve the situation, and the very different impact on the precarity, vulnerability and working conditions of the workers involved.

A further difficulty relates to the benchmark that the ILO's 2002 understanding uses to identify formality. The formulation "not covered or insufficiently covered by formal arrangements" is not straightforward and may give rise to various interpretations. It is unclear whether it refers to all the various protections afforded by a legal regime or to only some of them. Certainly, labour law generally offers a balance between universal and selective components, and certain workers may benefit either partially, or after a length of time has elapsed, from certain provisions (for a recent analysis, see Davidov, 2014). This is particularly the case concerning access to social security.

The 2002 understanding of informality suggested by the ILO also poses a further challenge in that it tends to blur two extremely important issues at national level. The first one is the *scope* of the law – something that is decided by politicians, policy-makers and lawyers for reasons that one might or might not consider justified – and which could amount to violations of ratified ILO conventions. The second one is the *non-application* of the law (or non-compliance with the law), when workers are legally entitled to benefits but do not enjoy them in practice, which is a problem of enforcement and amounts to an unlawful act (Davidov, 2006; Daza, 2005). The limited scope of the law and the non-application of the law identify two completely different legal situations with, again, very different triggering factors. Davidov argues that the 2002 understanding is "misleading" precisely because it does not make the distinction between these two situations (2006, p. 4). According to Davidov – and this shows the difficulties that many lawyers have with the concept of informality – the ILO is downplaying the important difference between non-application in law and non-application in practice: neither has anything to do with "informality" – in one case, workers are excluded from the scope of the law, while in the other, the law is not respected. When the law is not respected, it creates not only a civil liability but a criminal one, and it is inappropriate to describe this as a mere situation of "informality", just as it would be inappropriate to describe theft as an "informal property arrangement" (2006, p. 7). Certainly, as Justice has remarked while discussing "informality", "[b]ecause the term sounds benign, it can make work carried out under appalling conditions sound acceptable" (Justice, 2002, p. 7). In other words, it de-responsibilises actors in cases where informality can directly be linked to their (in)action with regard to domestic and international law, including obligations stemming from ratified international conventions.

A final point concerns the emphasis that the ILO's 2002 understanding of informality places on the scope of the law as a defining factor, particularly in relation to formalisation. When one considers the law, it is important to take into account not just its scope and its implementation, but also its *content* – i.e. the protection it affords. From a legal standpoint, the concept of informality as expressed at the 2002 ILC only looks at the first *two* issues – the scope of the law (whether a worker is covered or not) and its implementation (*de facto* or *de jure* exclusion) – and seems to assume that the law provides sufficient protection.

The *content* of the law should be fundamental to the discussions about formalisation, however, particularly as many formal workers are not enjoying the same labour or social security rights as they did in the past, although they remain within the scope of the law and the law is applied to them. Indeed, as is well established, "atypical" does not necessarily mean "precarious" (Rodgers, Rodgers, 1989, p. 1). However, today, "typical" does not necessarily mean "non-precarious", and there has undeniably occurred a formalisation of precarity, whereby "precariousness is no longer, if it ever was, an exclusive feature of 'atypical' work, but rather a dynamic, a trend, ... that is increasingly affecting a vast range of personal work relations, both dependent and autonomous, and both typical and atypical" (Kountouris, 2012, pp. 21–22; Fudge, 2012, p. 10).

The fact that "formal" may be becoming less and less "decent" certainly puts a damper on the goal of "formalising", particularly from the ILO's key perspective of improving conditions of work for all. It is the fact that workers are precarious or lacking protection that is the issue, rather than the fact that they are formal or informal, as this does not have a causal effect on their precarious status (used here in the broadest sense of the term) – precarious work may be found in situations of both formality and informality. All workers could be formalised but with very few rights granted to them. Seen from this perspective, as glorifying the standard employment relationship might be a false goal (Albin, 2012–2013, p. 9), it is important not to glorify formality as the answer to all labour problems. Instead of focusing on who is formal and who is informal, the major concern should, perhaps, be about who is in need of protection (Justice, 2002, p. 9). Ultimately, this is the real challenge that the ILO has always faced.

An ILO Recommendation on formalising the informal economy

In 2007, a report on enabling transition to formalisation was discussed within the ILO's Governing Body. It was admitted that although "[f]ormalization and transition to the mainstream economy are desired goals ... different views exist as to what is meant by formalization and how to achieve it" (ILO, 2007b, para. 45). The report went on to say that "generally, these perceptions have not been sufficiently articulated" (ibid.). There has been no breakthrough as to what is meant by formalisation since 2007, however, whether outside the ILO or within, or how to tackle it. Indeed, the fact that "different views exist about what is meant by formalization and how it can be achieved" was highlighted in the report prepared for the discussions about a possible recommendation (ILO, 2014a, para. 100). In order to understand why a new recommendation was put on the ILC agenda, and subsequently adopted in June 2015, it is necessary to understand the underlying politics of the ILO.

The geopolitics of the new Recommendation

The decision to place an item on the agenda of the tripartite annual ILC, which ultimately adopts ILS, is taken by the tripartite Governing Body.[17] A topic is usually suggested to the Governing Body by Employer, Worker or Government representatives, all of whom have a say in the Organisation's decisions. The possibility of adopting a recommendation on "facilitating gradual transitions from the informal economy to the formal economy" was initially suggested by the Employers' group (the Employers) and proposed to the Governing Body in November 2012, with the support of the Workers' group (the Workers) obtained during informal tripartite consultations held in September 2012 (ILO, 2012b, para. 23). The proposition was discussed and approved by the Governing Body in March 2013 (ILO, 2013b), and a Tripartite Meeting of Experts (ILO, 2013c) was held in September 2013. Once it is decided to put a topic on the agenda of the ILC for standard setting, a two-year process involving Governments, Employers and Workers usually starts. In accordance with the double discussion procedure, a review of national legislation and a questionnaire was subsequently prepared by the Office and sent to the ILO's member states (ILO, 2014c, 53–66). Ninety-seven governments answered the questionnaire after consultation with the most representative national Employers' and Workers' organisations.

The initiative for a recommendation, suggested by the Employers and supported by the Workers, was presented by the Office as being "especially timely and relevant" (ILO, 2012b, para. 27) to the needs of the constituents and as, *inter alia*, providing "guidance to constituents in their efforts to address the informal economy in a comprehensive manner and to encourage transitions to formality", as, although ILS are not restricted in scope to the formal economy, "none of them provide the kind of broad policy guidance that is required". The recommendation was therefore seen to address "a major gap in ILO standards" (ILO, 2012b, paras. 28, 30, 32, 34). At the same time, it is odd that the Employers pushed for a recommendation, as they clearly have an ambivalent view of ILS. Generally, they hold the opinion that (overly) regulating working conditions has adverse effects on economic growth, and are resistant to the idea of adopting new standards granting more protection to workers.[18]

The answer to this paradox lies in the current ILO-related geopolitics. Historically, one of the main reasons motivating Employers' support for the adoption of ILS was the fear of communism, and this disappeared with the fall of the Berlin Wall (e.g. Maupain, 2013, pp. 43–44). This development has led to major tensions within the ILO, with Employers increasingly voicing their opposition to the ILO supervisory bodies' pronouncements having an impact outside the

ILO and "expanding" ILS through their interpretations. This opposition, which has particularly materialised around the issue of the right to strike, escalated in June 2012, when the Employers paralysed the proceedings of the ILC (e.g. La Hovary, 2013).

This crisis is still very much unresolved, and the Employers' support for yet another ILO standard granting more or better protection for workers is, therefore, highly suspicious. The Employers have made quite contradictory statements about the new Recommendation, with the Employer vice-chairperson, for example, expressing support for the proposal on formalisation, but also stating that "its content needed to be approached differently" at the 2012 Governing Body meeting, where the issue was first raised (ILO, 2012c, para. 9). Despite the fact that the proposal did not achieve unanimity,[19] the decision to place the item on the agenda of the ILC can be seen as maintaining a continuing dialogue between Employers and Workers, something Workers were keen to support. Certainly, the Worker vice-chairperson strongly endorsed the presentation made by the Office regarding the timeliness and relevance of such an instrument (ILO, 2012c, para. 15).[20]

The legal case for adopting a new instrument

While conventions are binding on states when ratified and create legal obligations in international law, recommendations provide guidelines and are not open to ratification. They do, nevertheless, generate legal effects and are key to applying conventions and developing policies: for example, paving the way when a convention is not (yet) desired, when it is not appropriate for the topic at hand, or to secure consensus among constituents. They are important instruments that can shape future ILS and influence decisions inside and outside the ILO. Recommendations, once adopted, become subject to the ILO supervisory system (*ILO Constitution*, Art. 19(6)(d)).

Reviewing the initial position of the Employers is particularly revealing, as they are in a position of strength in the ILO after the events of June 2012, which have shaken the equilibrium between workers and employers in favour of the latter, and they might, therefore, have more leeway to impose their views. At the same time, in order to understand the non-political reasons for the Employers' interest in "formalisation", it is important to remember the different underlying reasons why one might want to "formalise informality". While workers might want to formalise to improve working conditions, employers within the ILO are likely to be looking to reduce what they perceive as unfair competition between formal and informal firms – informal enterprises do not pay taxes or benefits, which means that they compete unfairly with other formal enterprises.[21] When seen from this perspective, it is perhaps not surprising that the International Organisation for Employers (IOE) – which provides support for Employers in the ILO – while stating its position with regard to the recommendations questionnaire set out by the Office, declared that it did not want discussions to include informal employment in formal enterprise; rather, it wanted to limit the formalisation debate to informal enterprises only (IOE, 2013, p. 6). This is clearly motivated by a desire to level the competition between firms and lower costs for enterprises in the formal economy, which has little to do with the immediate welfare of the workers concerned.

Employers were effectively rejecting the 2002 ILC understanding of informality when they "expressed great concern at the conflation of non-standard forms of employment and the informal economy, which the Employers strongly rejected" (ILO, 2012c, para 83). On the other hand, the International Trade Union Confederation (ITUC), which provides support for Workers in the ILO, suggested that the 2002 understanding of the *informal economy* should be replaced by the 2003 International Conference of Labour Statisticians (ICLS) definition of *informal employment* (ITUC, 2013; ILO, 2013c, para 94), thus abandoning the aim of directly addressing informal enterprises. Although the need for a clearer understanding has been voiced by both the ITUC and the IOE, their initial positions were at opposite ends of the spectrum. This may also reflect the fact that the 2002 understanding might be too all-encompassing to be useful. However, as a tripartite entente was settled in 2002, it would have been difficult to move away from it, even if many of the issues discussed in the past were being put on the table again. This was pointed out during the Tripartite Experts meeting of September 2013 (see Workers' position: ILO, 2013c, paras 50, 60, and 69). Despite some questioning of the definition of the informal economy, notably by the European Union and its member states, the 2014 discussions pointed towards a retention of the 2002 understanding, as the text of Recommendation No. 204 confirms.

Certainly, progress has been made towards improving the condition of workers at the national level – including enlarging the scope of the law when it excludes certain workers, expanding coverage of social security, allowing the establishment of new organisations defending the rights of informal/atypical/self-employed workers, and so on – and this is what the ILO wanted to consolidate in a recommendation (for examples of national good practices, see ILO, 2013a). At the same time, however, the Recommendation also potentially offers a platform for a different sort of change. The IOE was adamant that at the national level "law must change" (IOE, 2013, pp. 11–12). Indeed, during the discussions preceding the adoption of the Recommendation, the IOE insisted that existing laws at the national level may be responsible for the informal economy – which is something that the ILO has recognised. However, the IOE's insistence on this and on the need to assess existing laws before enforcing compliance to ensure that they are "sound and practical" (IOE, 2013, p. 9) is at the same time putting into question the validity of national laws at a time when workers are not in a position of strength. As the Employer spokesperson reiterated during the 2013 Tripartite Meeting of Experts, the "[n]ational legislative framework had to be more flexible" (ILO, 2013c, para. 33).

As international labour lawyers are well aware, international human rights apply to all, and, similarly, most ILS apply *de jure* to all workers. It is, therefore, telling that while it had been preliminarily decided to refer in the preamble of the proposed recommendation to only a few ILS in relation to formalisation – the fundamental conventions (relating to freedom of association and collective bargaining, discrimination in employment, forced labour, child labour), Recommendation

No. 202, Convention No. 122 on Employment Policy, and Recommendation No. 198 on job creation in small and medium-sized enterprises[22] – Employers have insisted that the preamble must be the "only authoritative reference with regards to relevant instruments", rejecting any additional annex in this regard.[23] The adopted Recommendation does, however, have an annex which refers to a number of relevant international instruments – not because they are applicable to the informal economy, but, rather, because they "provide guidance in specific policy areas" (paragraph 7(g)).

The adopted text: Recommendation No. 204

The resulting Recommendation, adopted in June 2015, is an amalgam of numerous propositions for broad measures, and it is unclear how it will provide clear and practical guidance to states. This in part reflects the fact that "informality" has such broad and diverse causes, but also suggests a lot of confusion as to the realistic aims of this instrument. Most importantly, however, from the perspective of this contribution, the Recommendation has some very unfortunate language, which is problematic from an international legal perspective.

It is particularly alarming to read paragraph 16 of the Recommendation, which states that "Members *should* take measures to … respect, promote and realize the fundamental principles and rights at work for those in the informal economy" (emphasis added) when members *have*, according to the 1998 Declaration, an "obligation" to respect, promote and realise these principles and rights, and ratifying states have, of course, an obligation to enforce fundamental conventions to *all workers*, including those in the informal economy. Such obvious softening of hard obligations is difficult to understand from an international legal perspective. Similar use of "should" is used to refer to hard obligations, for ratifying states, throughout the text. The indication in paragraph 41 that "[n]othing in this Recommendation should be construed as reducing the protection afforded to those in the informal economy by other instruments of the [ILO]" is, of course, especially welcomed in these circumstances.

This Recommendation, which was adopted with 484 votes in favour, one against and five abstentions, does show clear consensus. Indeed, despite challenging discussions in 2014,[24] an informal tripartite agreement was reached after the informal consultations which took place before the 2015 ILC, and constant reference to this informal agreement made discussions during the 2015 ILC relatively easy. We can only hope that this instrument will be of some use to guarantee decent working conditions to all workers.

Conclusion

The notion of informality raises numerous and conflicting views.[25] Introduced by the ILO into global development debates in the early 1970s, the concept of the informal sector has developed within the Organisation into a broader and all-encompassing notion, now designated as the informal economy, which describes "all economic activities by workers and economic units that are – in law or in practice – not covered or insufficiently covered by formal arrangements". Despite the law being at the centre of this understanding, the debates have evolved – inside and outside the ILO – without much interaction with the legal field.

Partly as a result, ILS and the ILO supervisory bodies' comments do not provide much in the way of clarification with regard to the concept. Rather, the ILO supervisory bodies' comments tend to deal mainly with the scope of national legislation vis-à-vis the scope of ILS. While this is, of course, extremely relevant to analysing the informal economy, it is not an issue that is widely considered within debates on informality, which have effectively left the legal perspective behind. This is, for example, evident in the way the national scope of the law is often disregarded by statistics.

Moreover, the ILO's 2002 understanding of the informal economy, which has been retained in the 2015 Recommendation No. 204, does not properly distinguish between the various impacts that "informality" may have on workers' conditions and their various root causes, and the way the term "informal" is used often tends to de-responsibilise actors. Most importantly, however, it obscures the fact that in the final analysis, "formalisation" should first and foremost be concerned with the content of the law, and not only its scope and application.

It has often been overlooked that if informality means different things to different people, so does "formality" and, therefore, formalisation. The last, in particular, has, for example, been seen as a way to alleviate poverty and empower workers through the implementation of universal social protection and the consolidation of decent work practices, but also as a means of allowing fair competition between firms through the dismantling of constraining levels of social protection for workers. Either way, however, ILS has to be at the centre of such debates, making the ILO a central focus of interest.

In many ways, however, focusing on informality may be a misleading target from the perspective of working conditions. Certainly, the main message conveyed by Guha-Khasnobis *et al.* is that "we need to move beyond formality and informality to make progress in understanding the realities of economic activities in poor countries, and to design policies to benefit the poor" (2006, p. 2). This has been echoed in the legal field,[26] where it can clearly be seen that the concept of informality is both too broad and unclear, whether with regard to its causes or to the remedies needed to address it. The confusion surrounding the issue means that opinions are by no means uniform in relation to the role that ILS can, or should, play.

Seen from this perspective, the breadth of issues stemming from informality means that it was clearly going to be difficult to adopt a precise – and, one may even say, useful – instrument on the issue, even though the concept is in serious need of clarification. The resulting Recommendation is disappointing in this regard.

But perhaps most troubling is the fact that the discourse promoting formalisation is occurring in a context of increasing formalisation of precarity. Ultimately, the aim of formalisation only makes sense if it is embedded in a broader concept of decent work for all – formalisation alone is not good enough, especially in a context where Employers are questioning concepts such as decent work or precarity (IOE, 2013, pp. 5–6), or established rights such as the right to strike, and are seeking to push a very particular vision of formalisation. Indeed, their position became very clear during the 2014 ILC, when the Employers stated that while "Enterprises and workers both must transition to the formal economy, … incentives or provisions guaranteeing workers' rights would not help that process" (ILO, 2014b, para. 1340; also IOE, 2015, p. 3).

Considering the broader political circumstances, both within and outside the ILO, perhaps the best we could have hoped for with regard to the Organisation's Recommendation concerning the transition from the informal to the formal economy is that it did not attack the existing corpus of ILS or try to reformulate it (this is something that should be carried out in another setting); although it does not attack them directly, it seriously undermines them. A better solution might be to abandon the concept of "informality" altogether, and focus on the underlying nature of work instead.

Notes

1 This article draws partly on Claire La Hovary, "The Informal Economy and the ILO: A Legal Perspective", *The international journal of comparative labour law and industrial relations*, 30 (2014).
2 As the ILO's director general has remarked, "One of the ILO's most distinctive contributions to development thinking has been the concept of the "informal sector" (ILO, 1991, p. 3).
3 Recommendation No. 204 of 2015 concerning the transition from the informal to the formal economy.
4 As Davidov states, "[w]ho is covered by labour law? And who should be covered by labour law? These are among the most contentious and crucial questions in the field" (Davidov, 2014, p. 1). These questions extend to social security law – see in particular Filali Meknassi (2005–2006). My comments exclude, of course, the attention given in India to the "unorganised sector".
5 Terms such as "informality", "informal employment", "informal sector", "informal economy", "black" or "underground" market, "self-employment", "microenterprise", and "casual work", among others, are often used interchangeably (Rakowski, 1994, p. 502). Daza, however, warns about interchanging terms whose use depends on context and on possible legal implications (Daza, 2005, p. 7). See also Chen (2012).
6 ILS, comprising conventions and recommendations, are central to the primary aim of the ILO, which is the pursuit of social justice through the improvement of labour conditions for all. Since 1919, the ILO has adopted 189 conventions and 204 recommendations on a wide range of issues, of which 67 and 84, respectively, as well as six protocols, are currently considered up to date.
7 See also ILO (2006) for the application of freedom of association by the Committee on Freedom of Association to agricultural workers (para. 241), self-employed workers (para. 254), domestic workers (para. 267) and workers in export processing zones (para. 264), for example. These workers are considered to be "informal" under various definitions.
8 We do not examine here which ILS is relevant to the informal economy – this has been done elsewhere: Trebilcock (2004); ILO (2013a).
9 C150 provides for the extension "of the functions of the system of labour administration to include activities … relating to the conditions of work and working life

of appropriate categories of workers who are not, in law, employed persons, such as … (a) tenants who do not engage outside help, sharecroppers and similar categories of agricultural workers; (b) self-employed workers who do not engage outside help, occupied in the informal sector as understood in national practice; (c) members of co-operatives and worker-managed undertakings; (d) persons working under systems established by communal customs or traditions". This invocation of the informal sector refers to a national understanding of the term, and excludes from its scope certain workers (in categories (a), (c) and (d)) who might be included in the 2002 understanding of the informal economy.

10 R169 encourages the "progressive transfer" of workers from the informal to the formal sector (para. 9), understands "jobs of the informal sector" to mean "activities which are carried on outside the institutionalised economic structures" (para. 27) and distinguishes these from "illegal employment", which is understood as "employment which does not comply with the requirements of national laws, regulations and practice" (para. 8). Understood in this way, "illegal employment" would be included in the 2002 understanding of the "informal economy".

11 Furthermore, the "informal economy" is mentioned in the preamble of the 2008 Declaration on Social Justice for a Fair Globalisation (it cites "the growth of both unprotected work and the informal economy" as effects of global economic integration) and Recommendation No. 202 on social protection floors of 2012 mentions "transitions from the informal to the formal economy" without defining either term.

12 Furthermore, as the statistics are probably compiled according to a national definition and not the ILO's 2002 understanding, we do not really know who is included in the "informal economy".

13 There are abundant examples – see the observation concerning Uganda, Convention No. 98 on Collective Bargaining, 2009; the "informal economy" is not mentioned in this observation, but the scope of the law is. This example was given, with many others, in the 2014 ILO report preparing the discussions at the ILC, giving the false impression that the CEACR is explicitly mentioning the informal economy when it is simply dealing with the scope of national legislation, as it has always done (ILO, 2014a, para. 49).

14 In relation to Convention No. 87, the CEACR has requested information on "the nature and extent of the informal economy in the country, including percentage of women, percentage of migrants" as well as "any initiatives taken to ensure either in law or in practice the realization of the rights under the Convention to those in the informal economy" (ILO, 2009, p. 52).

15 The World Bank has held that "[l]abour market policies – minimum wages, job security regulations, and social security – are usually intended to raise welfare or reduce exploitation [b]ut actually work to raise the cost of labour in the formal sector and reduce labour demand … increas[ing] the supply of labor to the rural and urban informal sectors' (World Bank, 1990, 63). See also Perry *et al.*, who state that "excessive labor costs, whether arising through labor legislation – exaggerated minimum wages, severance costs, labor taxes, or unrealistic union demands – depress the number of jobs in the formal sector' (2007, p. 125).

16 Few countries define "informality" in their labour legislation. Daza identified Tanzania as one of the few countries to have a legal definition of the informal sector (2005, p. 13).

17 Both conventions and recommendations in the ILO are adopted following the same procedure (ILO, 2012a).

18 See Rodgers *et al.* (2009), p. 24. Indeed, the discussions that took place in 1997 and 1998 in view of adopting an instrument on the theme of contract labour (workers dependent on an employer but not defined as employees) was abandoned because of Employers' resistance or, in their own words, "implacable opposition to the adoption of any instrument on the subject of contact labour" (ILO, 1998, 16/3). The Home Work Convention, for example, did not get the support of Employers, who even withdrew

from the discussions of this instrument (see Vosko, 2004, p. 140). Moreover, most of the abstentions and the votes against the Convention on Domestic Workers came from Employers (ILO, 2011, 30/42–7).

19 While the Africa Group supported the initiative, the IMEC (Industrialized Market Economy Countries) group and other governments, including China and India, would have preferred the topic to be the object of a general discussion.

20 Moreover, Workers have the strategy of adopting one instrument a year (ILO, 2013d, para. 7), and they may have considered this as an opportunity to increase workers' protection.

21 Employers' concerns were the same in 2014 as in 2002 (Trebilcock, 2005, p. 1).

22 The ITUC, for its part, had suggested to its members that the preamble refers to several other ILS, including minimum wage, social security and home work (ITUC, 2013, p. 1).

23 ILO (2014b), paras 1552, 1555 – as a result, the issue will be revisited in 2015.

24 ILO (2015), para.11.

25 This has again been exemplified during the Tripartite Meeting of Experts in September 2013 (ILO, 2013c, paras 93–111) and at the 2014 ILC.

26 As Judy Fudge has noted, "It is important … not to reify the distinction between formal and informal employment" (2012, p. 9).

References

Albin, Einat (2012–2013). Introduction: Precarious Work and Human Rights. *Comparative labor law and policy journal*, 34, pp. 1–20.

Chen, Martha (2012). *The Informal Economy: Definitions, Theories and Policies.* WIEGO Working Paper No. 1.

Davidov, Guy (2006). Enforcement Problems in Informal Labor Markets: A View from Israel. *Comparative labor law and policy journal*, 27, pp. 3–26.

Davidov, Guy (2014). Setting Labour Law's Coverage: Between Universalism and Selectivity. *Oxford journal of legal studies*, 34, pp. 543–566.

Davidov, Guy, Langille, Brian (Eds). (2006). *Boundaries and Frontiers of Labour Law.* Oxford: Hart.

Davidov, Guy, Langille, Brian (2011). *The Idea of Labour Law.* Oxford: OUP.

Daza, Jose Luis (2005). *Informal Economy, Undeclared Work and Labour Administration.* Dialogue Paper No. 9. Geneva: ILO.

Filali Meknassi, Rachid (2005–2006). Extending Social Security in the Developing Countries. *Comparative labor law and policy journal*, 27, pp. 207–223.

Fudge, Judy (2012). Blurring Legal Boundaries: Regulating for Decent Work. In Judy Fudge, Shae McCrystal, Kamala Sankaran (Eds.). *Challenging the Legal Boundaries of Work Regulation.* Oxford: Hart.

Fudge, Judy, McCrystal, Shae, Sankaran, Kamala (Eds). (2012). *Challenging the Legal Boundaries of Work Regulation.* Oxford: Hart.

Guha-Khasnobis, Basubed, Kanbur, Ravi, Ostrom, Elinor. (2006). *Beyond Formality and Informality, in Linking the Formal and Informal Economy.* Oxford: OUP.

ILO Constitution (1919). Geneva: ILO.

ILO (1991). *The Dilemma of the Informal Sector.* ILC, 78th Session. Geneva: ILO.

ILO (1998). *Records of Proceedings. Vol. 1.* ILC, 86th Session. Geneva: ILO.

ILO (2002). *Conclusions concerning Decent Work and the Informal Economy, Records of Proceedings.* ILC, 90th Session, Geneva: ILO.

ILO (2006). *Digest of Decisions and Principles of the Freedom of Association Committee of the Governing Body of the ILO.* Geneva: ILO.

ILO (2007a). *The Informal Economy: Enabling Transition to Formalization, Background Document*. Geneva: ILO.

ILO (2007b). *The Informal Economy*. GB.298/ESP/4. Geneva: ILO.

ILO (2009). Report III (Part I A). *Report of the Committee of Experts on the Application of Conventions and Recommendations*, ILC, 98th Session. Geneva: ILO.

ILO (2010). *Extending the Scope of Application of Labour Laws to the Informal Economy*. Geneva: ILO.

ILO (2011). *Record of Proceedings*. ILC, 100th Session. Geneva: ILO.

ILO (2012a). *Handbook of Procedures relating to International Labour Conventions and Recommendations*. Geneva: ILO.

ILO (2012b). *Agenda of the International Labour Conference*. GB.316/INS/4. Geneva: ILO.

ILO (2012c). *Minutes of the 316th Session of the Governing Body*. GB.316/PV. Geneva: ILO.

ILO (2013a). *The Informal Economy and Decent Work: A Policy Resource Guide*. Geneva: ILO.

ILO (2013b). *Agenda of the International Labour Conference*. GB.317/INS/2(Rev.). Geneva: ILO.

ILO (2013c). *Report of the Tripartite Meeting of Experts on Facilitating Transitions from the Informal Economy to the Formal Economy*. GB.319/INS/14/6. 16–20 September 2013. Geneva: ILO.

ILO (2013d). *ILO Workers' Group Priorities (2011-2014)*, ACTRAV. Geneva: ILO.

ILO (2013e). *Measuring Informality: A Statistical Manual on the Informal Sector and Informal Employment*. Geneva: ILO.

ILO (2014a). Report V(1). *Transitioning from the Informal to the Formal Economy*. ILC, 103rd Session. Geneva: ILO.

ILO (2014b). *Provisional Records No. 11(Rev.)*. ILC, 103rd Session. Geneva: ILO.

ILO (2014c). Report V(2). *Transitioning from the Informal to the Formal Economy*. ILC 103rd Session. Geneva: ILO.

ILO (2015). *Reports of the Committee on the Transition from the Informal to the Formal Economy: Summary of Proceedings, Provisional Records No10-2*. ILC, 104th Session. Geneva: ILO.

IOE (2013). *Proposed New ILO Standard(s) – Informal Economy*. Geneva: IOE.

IOE (2015). *IOE Report – 104th Session of the International Labour Conference, 1–13 June 2015*. Geneva: IOE.

ITUC (2013). *Suggestions of Responses to the ILO's Questionnaire*. http://www.ituc-csi.org/IMG/pdf/no_32_-_app_-_questionnaire.pdf (Accessed 20 January 2016).

Justice, D.W. (2002). Work, Law and the "informality" Concept. *Labour education*, 127, pp. 5–10.

Kountouris, Nicolas (2012). The Legal Determinants of Precariousness in Personal Work Relations. *Comparative labor law and policy journal*, 34, pp. 21–46.

La Hovary, Claire (2013). Showdown at the ILO? A Historical Perspective on the Employers' Group's 2012 Challenge to the Right to Strike. *Industrial law journal*, 42, pp. 338–368.

La Hovary, Claire (2014). The Informal Economy and the ILO: A Legal Perspective. *The international journal of comparative labour law and industrial relations*, 30, pp. 391–411.

Maupain, Francis (2013). *The Future of the International Labour Organization in the Global Economy*. Oxford: Hart.

Peattie, Lisa (1987). An Idea in Good Currency and How It Grew: The Informal Sector. *World development*, 15, pp. 851–860.

Perry, Guillermo E., Maloney, William F., Arias, Omar S., Fajnzylber, Pablo, Mason, Andrew D., Saavedra-Chanduvi, Jaime, Bosch, Mariano. (2007). *Informality: Exit and Exclusion.* Washington: World Bank.

Rakowski, Cathy A. (1994). Convergence and Divergence in the Informal Sector Debate: A Focus on Latin America. *World development,* 22, pp. 501–516.

Rodgers, Gerry, Rodgers, Janine. (1989). *Precarious Jobs in Labour Market Regulation.* International Institute for Labour Studies. Geneva: ILO.

Rodgers, Gerry, Lee, Eddy, Swepston, Lee, Van Daele, Jasmien (2009). *The International Labour Organization and the Quest for Social Justice, 1919–2009.* Geneva: ILO.

Sengenberger, Werner (2005). *Globalization and Social Progress: The Role and Impact of International Labour Standards.* Bonn: Friedrich Ebert Stiftung.

Stone, Katherine, Arthurs, Harry (Eds). (2013). *Rethinking Workplace Regulation.* New York: Russell Sage.

Teklè, Tzehainesh (Ed.) (2010). *Labour Law and Worker Protection in Developing Countries.* Oxford: Hart.

Trebilcock, Anne (2004). International Labour Standards and the Informal Economy. In Jean-Claude Javillier, Bernard Gernigon, Georges Politakis (Eds), *Les normes internationales du travail: un patrimoine pour l'avenir.* Geneva: ILO.

Trebilcock, Anne (2005). *Decent Work and the Informal Economy.* Discussion Paper No. 2005/04, EDGI-WIDER.

Trebilcock, Anne (2006). Using Development Approaches to Address the Challenge of the Informal Economy for Labour Law. In Guy Davidov, Brian Langille (Eds), *Boundaries and Frontiers of Labour Law.* Oxford: Hart.

Vosko, Leah (2004). Standard Setting at the International Labour Organization: The Case of Precarious Employment. In J.J. Kirton, Michael J. Trebilcock (Eds), *Hard Choices, Soft Law: Voluntary Standards in Global Trade, Environment and Social Governance.* Aldershot: Ashgate.

World Bank (1990). *World Development Report – Poverty.* Washington: World Bank.

5 When informal work becomes litigious in a labour courtroom

Roberto Fragale Filho

Introduction

The figures are quite impressive. Brazilian labour judiciary has had more than three million new cases every year since 2011, and in 2014 it reached a peak of 3,472,861 new cases (TST, 2015). Actually, since 1994, Brazilian labour judiciary has been averaging more than two million new cases on an annual basis. They deal with many different aspects of the workplace, such as unfair dismissals, overtime, wages, health and safety, and sometimes, informal work. Basically, all of the former already have a formal labour contract as a starting point, while the last (i.e. informal work) has to overcome the preliminary question of whether a labour contract does exist in the informal arrangement being discussed in court. As a matter of fact, informality comes to labour courts in the quest for the recognition of a formal labour contract. As the existence of labour rights relies on such recognition, litigants, lawyers and judges concentrate in such cases all their efforts in trying to make facts fit into the formal frame provided by labour law.

As a labour judge, I have repeatedly undertaken, on an almost daily basis, such an exercise, and the analysis in this chapter draws on my more than two decades of bench experience, half of it in the labour court of São João de Meriti, a working-class dormitory city near Rio de Janeiro. I will present three vignettes of informal labour circumstances as they could have been argued in the courtroom. They are not literal reproductions of cases that I have heard, but, rather, a *bricolage* of countless claims that I have examined throughout the years. They will be used here as ideal types to analyse how informality and Brazilian labour law interact in a courtroom. Yet, before presenting them, I shall explore what informality means in a labour court and how it can (or cannot) be framed under the Brazilian labour law. Examining concrete circumstances related to informal work from such a perspective will give visibility to two dichotomous perspectives – formal vs. informal and legal vs. illegal – which frame the whole debate, despite not being "able to catch up with the issues of informal workers", as Routh and Borghi point out in the introductory chapter to this volume. The outcome will show that legal coding translates the formal vs. informal approach into a legal vs. illegal equation, eliminating any room for judicial creative answers. Thus, going beyond such coding becomes a must in order to integrate informality in a better and more performative way in the workplace.

Framing the debate

Informality has been an object of interest for academic studies as evidence of many different economic phenomena, such as: (a) contemporary economic reorganisation, (b) labour market insecurity and precariousness, (c) transition towards a service society, (d) rigidity in labour regulation, and (e) occupational (as opposed to professional) development (Krein, Proni, 2010). Regardless of this variety, the analytical frames mobilised to explain informality always seem to be structured in a dichotomous perspective, as modern and traditional work were previously conceptualised as opposites in explaining modernisation and urbanisation processes. As a matter of fact, informality is a concept mostly defined by what it is not, i.e. *formality*, as thoroughly outlined in the introductory chapter of this book. Informality could, then, be thought of as a characteristic of occupations that struggle to be recognised as professions in the formal world, or as the simple lack of an official recognition of validity, a necessary condition for the exercise of most labour and social rights (Santos, 1979; Carvalho, 2001). Additionally, informality can also be perceived as something more complex, unrelated to formality or legality, once one starts to think of the informal economy as a concept covering both a kind of work present in economically non-structured areas as well as a kind of work also present in economically structured areas (Cacciamali, 2000; Moretto, Capacchi, 2006; Barbosa, 2009).

However, this conceptual opening does not resist a juridical understanding of informality, which still reasons in a very strictly dichotomous way: labour law protection is reserved for those registered in the formal labour world, and everybody else, who is outside of it, is denied such rights (Souto Maior, Gnata, 2013). Although attempts have been made to reason differently, pledging, for instance, the unionisation of informal workers (Frangi, Routh, 2014), formality seems to be still basically accessible through a labour contract which grants workers an employee status. It is an inside and outside situation: some are protected by this legal umbrella of employment contract and some are left out of it, unprotected against the hazards of life.

Thus, for someone to step into the legal formal world of social rights and get protection from the abovementioned umbrella, the signing of a labour contract remains as the main entrance door. But what keeps people from stepping into this formal world? Economic logic is mostly put forward as the main reason for not following such a path. Costs related to the maintenance of the social rights umbrella are high, and sometimes unaffordable by small employers or independent workers. Informal arrangements are often the outcome of this lack of compliance, and they usually work fine until some unexpected circumstance triggers a (labour) dispute. Quite often, such a dispute ends up in a labour court.

Thus, a common path for informal workers to access such rights is through labour courts, where they usually litigate for the recognition of a formal labour contract. These are winner-takes-all claims in which litigants, lawyers and judges are incapable of looking at the legal controversy from the informal perspective but, on the contrary, concentrate all their efforts on trying to make it fit into the formal frame, which is perceived as the only possible grammar to explain the facts (Nobre, Rodriguez, 2011). The following three vignettes of informal labour circumstances as they could have been presented in a labour dispute may help us to understand how this legal coding operates.

Vignette 1: Informality at its most extreme

The courtroom is ambiguously austere and imposing. Unlike in American movies, the judge is already there, looking at his daily package of 15 labour cases which are about to be heard. Litigation during an existing labour contract is rare. As usual, all cases deal with past labour relationships, sometimes formally recognised through a labour contract. Understandably, there is some tension in the waiting halls as former employees meet their previous employers. As the officer of the court announces the case, a small group of five people in the courtroom witnesses the entrance of the two ladies and their lawyers. They take their place at the table, employee on the left side and employer on the right side of the table. The tension noticed outside moves to the courtroom, and rises when the judge asks about conciliatory possibilities. Face to face, the two ladies keep quiet. They seem to be ashamed to be there, to have to discuss their problems with unknown people. Their lawyers reply almost simultaneously, repudiating any chance of conciliation. They are there to litigate, and their clients want their day in court. There is no alternative left, and the case is to be heard. Here are the facts. Mary used to work in an informal beauty salon without a formal labour contract. It was informality at its most extreme: an informal enterprise with informal workers. She set up her working hours according to her domestic duties and the school hours of her five-year-old child. A haircut and style would cost $10–25, and she would retain 40 per cent of this price for herself. Hair highlighting services ranged from $30 to $60, and her share would be 60 per cent. Finally, cosmetic treatment of hands and nails had a fixed price of $15, and her percentage was set at 70 per cent. The salon rent and other expenses were paid by the owner, John, who was also the supplier of cosmetics and beauty products. Credit cards and bank cheques were unknown to the business. Everything was paid in cash. Mary was satisfied with her labour arrangements, as John paid her for 30 days' holiday and the 13th salary every employee is entitled to at the end of the year. This arrangement lasted for three years, and collapsed when Mary was invited to work in a neighbouring beauty salon. Linda, the owner of the rival business, had offered her a 10 per cent rise for all services she provided. Mary did not hesitate to change jobs. Yet, everything remained informal. Linda did not offer Mary a formal labour contract, and her beauty parlour was as informal as the one run by John. From day one, Mary was extremely satisfied with the 10 per cent rise she got from her move to Linda's business. Her happiness was shaken six months later when James, Linda's abusive and violent husband, trashed the beauty salon and threatened her with death. Scared, Linda ran away to a distant city where she felt safe, leaving Mary and her colleagues running the business. By the end of the year, Linda was still on the run. Her mother would stop by the beauty salon every now and then to pick up some money and forward it to her. The decision to pay Mary and her colleagues the 13th salary and holiday pay was left to the workers themselves, and they decided not to do it. Unsatisfied, they kept running the place until a few months later, when Linda decided to close down the salon. She explained to Mary and her colleagues that this was necessary to break all the links she still had with her former husband in order to restart her life and to claim custody of her children, who had stayed with their abusive father. Unemployed, Mary went on to find a job in a third beauty parlour in the same neighbourhood, with the same labour arrangement she had formerly had with John, that is, no formal labour contract. She had engaged in similar informal contracts three times. Still, she felt Linda had not been fair to her, as she had not paid a 13th salary or holiday pay. After discussing her situation with a lawyer, she decided to sue Linda for the recognition of a formal labour contract between them. As a consequence of such recognition, she would be entitled not only to a 13th salary and 30 days' holiday pay, but also 30 days' prior notice of dismissal, payment of an indemnity equivalent to 40 per cent of all deposits made in her Fundo de Garantia de Tempo de Serviço (Time Service Guarantee Fund (FGTS)) plus the withdrawal of the deposits themselves, overtime payment after eight daily and 44 weekly working hours, and quite a few other rights. She did not seem to be bothered about these supposedly withheld rights, as she kept limiting her claim to denial of the 13th salary and holiday pay. Each party had the chance to speak and present their case. Each brought two witnesses to corroborate their respective stories. A final attempt to conciliate was rebutted by both of them. Now, it was all up to the judge to decide.

Mary's story offers us a concrete context in order to appreciate the nature and problems of informality and informal relations in economic activities. Was there a labour contract, and therefore, was she an employee? A glimpse at the *Consolidação das Leis do Trabalho* (Brazilian Labour Code (CLT)) might be useful. As a matter of fact, CLT does not establish a legal definition for a labour contract. A legal definition thus has to be extracted from the characterisation, offered by article 3, of who is to be considered an employee: "Employee shall mean any person who performs services other than casual services for an employer under the direction of the employer and in return for remuneration." From its wording, three different elements must be present for one to be considered an employee: continuity (as opposed to the eventuality present in casual services), subordination (which is to be extracted from compliance with the employer's commands) and economic dependence (monetarily expressed through a salary payment).

Continuity, in legal labour jargon, is to be understood as a characteristic of a (labour) relation that continues over time, which does not necessarily correspond to a permanent relation. The debate over what is a continuous relation in a domestic environment is a good illustration of such a distinction: is a domestic worker who for the last five years has worked eight hours twice a week cleaning one's house to be considered in a continuous labour relation? Courts have unsuccessfully struggled to offer an answer to this question (TST, RR 59300-54.2007.5.03.0060, 19 October 2012; TST, RR 502-08.2012.5.01.0246, 27 February 2015). One, two, three, four days a week: what constitutes continuity? The Rio de Janeiro State Labour Court established in 2011 that a domestic worker is not be considered an employee if he or she works up to three days a week for the same supposed employer, even if he or she has done so for countless years (TRT-RJ, Statement 19, 17 May 2011). Precedent is here established under the assumption of an absence of continuity, apparently assuming that work to be continuous has to be done on an almost daily basis.

As for subordination, it can be thought of from different perspectives: technical, economic or juridical, for instance. As a matter of fact, the prerogative given to an employer to direct and supervise an employee's activity expresses a technical subordination, while disciplinary powers are related to a juridical subordination. Economic subordination is somehow related to the third characteristic extracted from the legal definition of a Brazilian employee – economic dependence – which finds its expression through the payment of wages. A labour contract does not need to be in a written format, and can be extracted from the sole presence of the three legal characteristics inscribed in CLT's article 3. Brazilian legal doctrine (Süssekind *et al.*, 2002 [1957]) calls it a *reality contract*, echoing the *reality principle*, establishing that a labour contract is to be extracted from the daily execution of work activities regardless of the legal jargon used to define it.

Formality is thus assured by labour contracts which entitle employees to a whole set of legal rights, all of them inscribed in the Brazilian Constitution: protection against unfair dismissal, minimum wage, a 13th salary payment at the end of year, payment for overtime hours at a rate of at least 50 per cent more than normal working hours, an annual 30 days' holiday with an additional payment of one-third of the employee's normal salary, maternity leave for 120 days without employment and salary prejudice, and a minimum 30 days' notice for dismissal. It also caps working hours at eight hours per day and 44 hours per week. Every employee is entitled to an individual FGTS account, to which the employer is required to contribute a monthly deposit equivalent to 8 per cent of the employee's salary. Once the employee is dismissed, the employer is required to make an additional deposit equivalent to 40 per cent of all deposits previously made, and the employee is allowed to withdraw all the savings from his FGTS account. The employee is also entitled to unemployment insurance, which may last from three to six months depending on the duration of his last labour contract.

However, if termination is due to "just cause" (an employee's serious misconduct), none of these three benefits (additional employers' deposit, FGTS account withdrawal, and unemployment insurance) are available. A temporary job guarantee is available to union leaders from the time they present their candidacy until one year after their term if they are elected, to pregnant women from the time of conception until five months after the birth, and to victims of work accidents from the accident until one year after their full recovery as attested by the social security services (Fragale Filho, 2013).

A court dispute over the existence of a labour contract is, thus, a quarrel about being (or not being) eligible to this wide set of rights. Yet, the present proceeding is a winner-takes-all dispute, and Mary's sole focus on the 13th salary payment and holiday pay, as described in the first vignette, seems, in that sense, extremely limited. If the court recognises her as an employee, she will be entitled to the whole set of rights linked to her labour contract. Legal reasoning pertaining to labour does not allow this selective approach, even if this is the litigants' desire.

Reverting to our dispute under discussion, manicuring has been recognised as a professional activity since the enactment of the Federal Statute n. 12,592, of 18 January 2014. Originally composed of only six articles, the statute grants workers performing capillary, aesthetic, facial and corporal beautification, and hygiene activities on clients the professional status of cosmetologists, such as hairdressers, barbers, beauticians, manicurists, chiropodists, epilators and make-up artists. Accordingly, these professionals must comply with sanitary norms, such as sterilisation of materials and instruments used on clients, and are entitled to a national day – every 18 January – celebrating their profession. Dispositions on who could undertake such activities were inscribed in the remaining two articles, which ended up being vetoed by the president. As explained in the veto message, according to the Brazilian Constitution, only professions which may cause harm to society admit limitations on their exercise, and this was supposedly not the case for cosmetologists.

Yet, transition from an occupation to a profession is not what Mary seemed to be after. Her move to Linda's beauty parlour was clearly motivated by the 10 per cent increase in remuneration, even though it was not quite clear how things would be regarding the 13th salary and holiday pay. As part of their informal arrangement, they would probably discuss both circumstances when these rights became due: at the end of the year (December) and after she completed 12 months of work, respectively. But they never got the chance to discuss them, as Linda had to run from her violent husband. As Mary brings her dissatisfaction to the court and it gets translated into legal grammar, it is no longer about what seemed to bother Mary at the time; it is all about the lack of formality and of a labour contract. As the object of their disagreement has been transformed, conciliation ends up being the only way for them to refocus their discussion on the two originally controversial aspects.

As a matter of fact, this is possible because, through conciliation, their dissent is no longer a legal one; it is transformed into economic figures. If their conflict remains a legal one and has to be adjudicated, this economic grammar no longer applies, and there is no room for the judge to come up with some kind of intermediate equity-based decision. A judge's decision is supposed to decide between winners and losers, between who pays and who does not. The outcome of a judge's work – adjudication – is about the law expressing how people are supposed to behave and what they are supposed to endure for not complying with this. Finally, as adjudication reframes facts into law, it establishes precedents and gives guidance for future actions, but what it forgets is that people's social interactions are not necessarily law-driven. Here is another vignette to help us think of informality.

Vignette 2: Informality in a domestic environment

Patricia has had no formal education beyond the primary years, and most of her professional experience comes from domestic jobs, some formally recognised and duly inscribed in her labour booklet, and others absolutely informal. After her marriage, she stopped working and had been unemployed for a little over a year. At first, she was fine with this, as it allowed her to stay home with her newly born child, James. Still, income has been a family problem, as her husband Joseph does not make enough for them to live on. When Elizabeth, her previous domestic employer, invited her to come back, she did not hesitate to take the job, as her family was facing financial problems, and even the minimum salary offered by Elizabeth would be a great help. As her husband works all day, caring for baby James became a problem. She then asked her sister Barbara, who lived nearby and used to spend part of the day chatting with her at her house, to look after her child during the day, and offered to split her minimum salary between them. Although they did not establish a formal labour contract, she split with her sister all of her gains, including the 13th salary she was paid at the end of the year and her 30 days' holiday pay, and when she stayed with her baby, Barbara's work was not necessary. This arrangement suited everybody, as she was able to add half a minimum salary to her family's income and provided half a minimum salary to her sister for doing something she was, in a way, already doing. Life went on like this for 18 months, until Elizabeth decided to move to another city and Patricia's work became no longer necessary. Patricia was then dismissed and got all the indemnities related to her dismissal: 33 days' prior notice for dismissal and payment of an indemnity equivalent to 40 per cent of all deposits made in her FGTS plus the withdrawal of the deposits themselves. As Barbara had been of great help throughout the whole period Patricia was working for Elizabeth, Patricia decided the fair thing to do would be to split her dismissal indemnities, too, with her sister. Barbara gladly took the money from her sister, but could not refrain from complaining that she had not been paid a minimum salary throughout the 18 months. Although Patricia could not hide her discomfort, she decided to ignore her sister's remark. Months later, Patricia was notified by the Labour Court to present her defence on a labour suit brought against her by her sister, who was claiming the existence of a labour contract between them in which her employer – her sister Patricia – had failed to comply with the law, as she was not paid the minimum salary and her labour contract was not formally recognised. The two sisters, who had not spoken to each other since the suit was filed, met again in the courtroom, accompanied by their lawyers. They did not bring any witnesses, as there was no dispute over the facts. Actually, their disagreement is over the interpretation of the facts: Barbara claims the existence of a labour contract between them, while Patricia states that their relation was due to family ties, and the payments she made were a way of sharing gratitude for their mutual aid. Each party got the chance to speak and present their case. Two conciliatory attempts were made, but were rejected by both of them. Once again, now, it was all up to the judge and his decision.

Domestic work is quite common in Brazil, and has seen different regulations since the 1916 Civil Code. Until recently, it was regulated by Federal Statute n. 5,859, of 11 December 1972, which defined a domestic employee as "any person who performs services of continuous nature and not for profit for an individual or a family in its residence" and granted the following basic rights: prior notice of dismissal, 20 working days' holiday and the 13th salary payment. The 1988 Federal Constitution enlarged domestic workers' rights to include minimum wage, 120 days' maternity leave, five days' paternity leave, a weekly day off and retirement, but it was only through the Constitutional Amendment n. 72, of 3 April 2013, that the whole set of constitutional labour rights became available to domestic workers. However, a few more months would be necessary for the enactment of the Complementary Federal Statute n. 150, of 1 June 2015 regulating the exercise of all of these rights.

While legislative debate over the Constitutional Amendment n. 70 was still in progress, society echoed this discussion, focusing on the impact of this increase of rights on informality. Claims arguing that domestic work (1) was no longer the main occupation of feminine workers, (2) had seen its costs (including wages) skyrocket and, therefore, (3) had been continuously declining and would disappear in the near future or be replaced by independent day workers, despite the lack of any consistent empirical evidence of their validity, were forwarded as truisms in the debate (Magalhães, 2015). Clearly pointing out the unsuitability of classical Taylorist and Fordist practices for domestic work, controversy also arose over how to control working hours and how to validate any chosen type of control. This debate, as Magalhães (2015) wrote, revealed the archaic and deeply rooted character of the Brazilian social structure.

Yet, considering that this new legal framework for domestic work is in its earliest stages, it is quite unclear what its real impact will be on a domestic labour market composed of 6.6 million workers, a figure lower only than that of India, which has a population six times bigger than the Brazilian population. On the other hand, what is quite clear is the unchanged dichotomy that distinguishes formal and informal domestic work based on the continuity characteristic of the labour contract, as explained before. Thus, as labour activities performed in both formal and informal domestic work are the same, one could think of them as two concentric circles, the former having a smaller radius than the latter. Moving from the exterior circle to the interior one and stepping into formality requires the recognition of an existing labour contract. Nothing disallows an employer from recognising the existence of a labour contract with a domestic worker who works less than three times a week.

But, if no recognition is offered and parties do litigate, like Barbara and Patricia in our second vignette, the continuity characteristic is to be examined. Once again, as litigants come to an impasse and are unable to settle their case, a judge must adjudicate guided by the law and legal precedent, which, in this situation, is established as the three-times-a-week rule. Is Barbara, then, to be considered as entitled to a formal labour contract? Apparently, yes, as she worked for more than three times a week. Indeed, this undisputed fact is the basis of the reality from which the labour contract characteristics are supposed to be extracted. One may ask, then, whether these supervening facts modify what seemed to be their original intention of mutual help without any consideration of the legal frame. The dichotomist legal approach does not allow anything in between these two extremes: formality or informality. Definitely, it is all or nothing, and it falls to a third party – a labour judge – to decide.

Both vignettes suggest a zero-sum situation in which informality was at its peak: the lack of a labour contract was combined with a total lack of any kind of formal agreement. But informality can also be extracted from situations in which some written formal contract has established a different legal frame for the work developed by the parties themselves. This is exactly the case for our third and last vignette.

Vignette 3: A crossover of informality and formality

It is 5 am, and William is already at the gate of Quick Deliveries, a local transportation company that delivers goods for a big food supermarket chain. It is a big enterprise, whose truck fleet is composed of 60 enterprise-owned vehicles driven by direct employees accompanied by at least one driver's helper and 20 independent drivers who drive their own trucks. The latter do not have any driver's helper hired by Quick Deliveries. On a daily basis, they hire people like William, who gather every day in front of the company's gate. Usually, they leave the loading area by 5:30 am, when helpers are called on an order of arrival basis. As independent drivers get acquainted with helpers, preference may be accorded to any one of them regardless of their order of arrival. Driver's helpers are truck's merchandise loaders, as they are described in the Brazilian Occupational Code (CBO). William does not worry any more about being one of the earliest to arrive, as for the last 11 months, he has been continuously picked up by David as his helper. Actually, the only occasions on which he is not picked up are when he does not show up for work, something he does not do very often, as he does not get any payment whenever that happens. David pays William on a daily basis according to the amount of goods delivered: for a truck load under 100, between 100 and 200, and above 200 boxes, payment is $25, $30 or $35, respectively. William is the breadwinner for his family, which is composed of his wife and his five-year-old boy. Of course, William does not pay social security dues, as this would dramatically affect his family budget. Although, as an independent driver, David has a formal contract with Quick Deliveries, his labour conditions are somewhat similar to those of William. As a matter of fact, David gets paid on a similar scale: for a truck load under 100, between 100 and 200, and above 200 boxes, payment is $100, $120 or $140, respectively, and payment is made on a weekly basis for days effectively worked. Prices are fixed by Quick Deliveries, and David's contract can be terminated without prior notice if he fails to show up for 10 days in a month. Likewise, David does not pay social security dues, for the same reasons: it would dramatically affect his family budget and jeopardise his and his wife's living. Still, all these labour circumstances seemed fine by both of them, as they had no other choice. One day, while doing a delivery for Quick Deliveries, the truck collided with a bus and unfortunately, they both died. Both families fell into total disarray, as they had lost their breadwinners. Desperate, both wives sued Quick Deliveries for the recognition of the alleged labour contracts of their deceased husbands. Once they showed up in the courtroom, one could feel their anxiety, as Quick Deliveries had told them the company had no liability whatsoever for the tragedy they were going through. This discourse was reproduced in the courtroom, with an addendum: if anyone was liable, it was the deceased David, because he was the one who had hired William. Witnesses were heard, and all controversy about facts got elucidated with all litigants remaining attached to their convictions. After a long hearing, no conciliatory agreement could be reached. Once again, now, it was all up to the judge and his decision.

William and David are workers who bring light to what David Weil (2014) has designated as the "fissured workplace". As he wrote, "workplace fissuring arises as a consequence of the integration of three distinct strategic elements, the first one focused on revenues (a laser-like focus on core competency), the second one focused on costs (shedding employment), and the final one providing the glue to make the overall strategy operate effectively (creating and enforcing standards)". This combination, indeed, makes the classical scheme of employment an exception, and puts enormous economic pressure on independent contractors such as David to lower compliance levels that would make his work financially unviable.

Thus, informality becomes part of a formal arrangement, in which Quick Deliveries' responsibility seems unreachable. But life does not necessarily work according to people's desires, and unexpected circumstances have brought all parties together to the courtroom, where any kind of conciliatory agreement seems completely out of reach. This fragmented work environment highlights how informality, understood as the lack of legal formalisation, may be combined with formality through different layers of work. As a matter of fact, it is the kind of circumstance that demonstrates, on the one hand, how formality may be combined with precarity and, on the other hand, how informality does not essentially differ in result from formality. The vignette shows how blurred the outcome may be once concepts such as atypical, decent and/or precarious work are integrated into the formal/informal dichotomy.

The outlook: Legal coding – a binary hypothesis?

How do all of these translate into the dichotomist perspective found in the legal qualification of the labour contract? The trajectory from the first vignette, in which informality was presented at its most extreme (both enterprises and workers were informal), to the last vignette, in which different layers of formality and informality may result in an undifferentiated work environment as far as social protection is concerned, passing through the second vignette and its specific domestic circumstances, shows us the limits of the legal binary coding. The vignettes described above must actually be decided by a legal classificatory analysis of facts trying to place them into one of the extremities of the reasoning line presented in Figure 5.1. There is no room for a partial analysis, for a creative use of the legal coding. Different situations from the labour world are to be placed closer to either one or the other extremity according to the similarity of their circumstances to

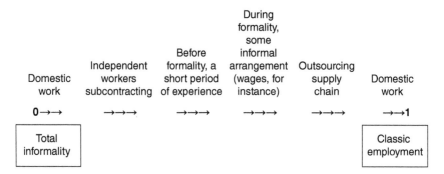

Figure 5.1 From informality to formality.

the classical figures of formal employment or informality. The intermediate areas of the reasoning line, in which blurred circumstances of subcontracting and outsourcing may be found, suggest layers of informality over formality that are only supposed to be decoded by the legal binary grammar.

While the labour world circumstantially moves from one extremity to another, labour judges are supposed to reason in a classificatory system that does not recognise whatever lies between the two extremities. It is a frustrating context, in which legal reasoning for labour matters seems incapable of figuring out a way out of this dilemma. As a consequence, one may inquire whether or not labour judges are to be condemned for never going beyond the classical structure of a labour contract and accepting precarity as something inherent in these new workplace arrangements. Should they be condemned to think of the labour world in an abstract manner while still having to face its harsh conditions? What is judging actually all about? Is it about framing concrete circumstances into an abstract world?

Whatever the circumstances may be, as millions of cases are presented one after the other to the Brazilian labour courts, all parties involved in labour disputes come to realise that there are more grey areas between formality and informality than anyone would expect. Judging can be straightforwardly done once it limits itself to its binary coding. Still, if the focus is to be on workers and seeking to improve their condition, overcoming the limited and strict legal concept of formality becomes a necessity. Informality, as polysemic as the concept may be, cannot be treated just as a lack of (something), and its legal examination has to place workers at the top of its concerns. Judging informality is, thus, all about navigating these uncharted waters, focusing, as suggested by La Hovary in her contribution to this volume, on the underlying nature of work, and thus trying to figure out how to make the workplace a more integrated and better place for everyone.

References

Barbosa, Alexandre de Freitas. (2009). *De "setor" para "economia informal": aventuras e desventuras de um conceito*. São Paulo: USP (mimeo). http://www.fflch.usp.br/centrodametropole/antigo/v1/texto_sem_2009_barbosa.pdf (Accessed 20 July 2015).

Cacciamali, Maria Cristina. (2000). "Globalização e processo de informalidade", *Economia e Sociedade* 14, pp. 153–174. http://www.eco.unicamp.br/docdownload/publicacoes/instituto/revistas/economia-e-sociedade/V9-F1-S14/06-Cacciamali.pdf (Accessed 20 July 2015).

Carvalho, José Murilo de. (2001). *Cidadania no Brasil. O longo caminho*. Rio de Janeiro: Civilização Brasileira.

Fragale Filho, Roberto. (2013). Resolving Disputes over Employment Rights in Brazil. *Comparative labor law and policy journal*, 34, pp. 929–947.

Frangi, Lorenzo, Routh, Supriya. (2014). From Employee to *Homo Faber*? Considerations about Union Renewal and Informal Workers in Brazil and India. *Just labour: A Canadian journal of work and society*, 21, pp. 42–67. http://www.justlabour.yorku.ca/volume21/pdfs/03_frangi_routh_press.pdf (Accessed 29 May 2015).

Krein, José Dari, Proni, Marcelo Weishaupt. (2010). *Economia informal: aspectos conceituais e teóricos* (série Trabalho Decente no Brasil, Documento de Trabalho n. 4).

São Paulo: Escritório da OIT no Brasil. http://www.oitbrasil.org.br/sites/default/files/topic/employment/pub/economia_informal_241.pdf(Accessed 4 April 2015).

Magalhães, Henrique Júdice. (2015). *Seria bom se fosse verdade – Cinco mitos sobre a trajetória recente e as perspectivas do trabalho doméstico no Brasil* (article published 7 April 2015 at www.resistir.info). http://resistir.info/brasil/trabalho_domestico.html (Accessed 15 June 2015).

Moretto, Cleide Fátima, Capacchi, Maristela A. (2006). A (in)formalidade e o setor (in)formal para além do ilegal. In Cleide Fátima Moretto (Ed.), *Trabalho e .trabalhadores: significados e significâncias*. Ijuí (RS): Unijuí.

Nobre, Marcos, Rodriguez, José Rodrigo. (2011). "Judicialização da política": déficits explicativos e bloqueios normativistas. *Novos estudos CEBRAP*, 91, pp. 5–20. http://www.scielo.br/pdf/nec/n91/a01n91.pdf (Accessed 10 July 2015).

Santos, Wanderley Guilherme dos. (1979). *Cidadania e Justiça. A política social na ordem brasileira*. Rio de Janeiro: Campus.

Souto Maior, Jorge Luiz, Gnata, Noa Piatã Bassfeld. (2013). *Trabalhos Marginais*. São Paulo: LTr.

Süssekind, Arnaldo, Maranhão, Délio, Vianna, José de Segadas, Teixeira, João de Lima. (2002 [1957]). *Instituições de Direito do Trabalho* (20ª edição). São Paulo: LTr.

Tribunal Superior do Trabalho (TST). (2015). *Série Histórica da Movimentação Processual – 1941/2015*. http://www.tst.jus.br/justica-do-trabalho2 (Accessed 10 July 2015).

Weil, David. (2014). *The Fissured Workplace. Why Work Became So Bad for So Many and What Can Be Done to Improve It*. Cambridge, Massachusetts and London, England: Harvard University Press.

6 Informal employment in China

Analysis of labour law

Aiqing Zheng

Introduction: the meaning and emergence of informal employment in China

"Informal employment", increasingly accepted by academic researchers, is not yet a term officially used in China. Since 2001, the Chinese government prefers to use "flexible employment (*ling huo jiu ye*)" instead of "informal employment". The Labour Institute on Labour Science, attached to the Ministry of Human Resource and Social Security, in its research report of 2001,[1] defined flexible employment as all kinds of employment which are different from the traditional, dominant employment in working time, working place, remuneration, labour relations and social insurance. Regarded as the official understanding of flexible employment, this definition obviously includes employment in both formal and informal sectors. But academic opinions are divergent on the meaning and the scope of the two terms – informal employment or flexible employment. Some experts, both Chinese and foreign, see no difference between the two concepts (Shi Meixia, 2007, p. 11; He Ping, Hua Yingfang, 2008, p. 2; Fang Lee Cooke, 2011, p. 101), while others believe that flexible employment denotes a broader meaning than informal employment, including all kinds of informal jobs and some formal jobs executed in a flexible way (Ren Yuan, Peng Xizhe, 2007, p. 7). In fact, lack of consensus on the understanding of the concept has negative impacts on the adoption of policy or law in the field, and this also makes it difficult to obtain accurate statistics on the scale of informal employment.[2]

For practical reasons, here we also use the two terms without distinctions, and we adopt the common view of many Chinese authors and a few foreign authors (Shi Meixia, 2007, p. 11; He Ping, Hua Yingfang, 2008, p. 2; Fang Lee Cooke, 2011, p. 102) in that we consider the following three types of employment as informal employment. First, it includes some employees working in a flexible manner but covered by labour law, such as part-timers, temporary workers and dispatched workers. Second, it involves persons who work in informal sectors, such as in residential communities, families, micro-enterprise, or individual commercial households (*ge ti hu*). Finally, it indicates self-employed persons in all kinds of free professions and odd jobs, such as individual businessman, individual translator, computer repairman, street businessman, etc. The last two kinds of employment are not yet covered by labour law.

So, we should insist that our comprehension of informal employment is a little broader than the understanding of foreign experts, for whom informal employment has nothing to do with labour law coverage. For instance, in China, as we mentioned above, jobs in an enterprise which are exercised in a flexible manner, such as part time, or done by agency workers, are also considered as informal, but already covered by labour legislation. We think that the emergence of informal employment on a large scale in China is mainly linked with three principal circumstances: reform policy, market-direction development and urbanisation. The first background is the implementation of the reform and opening-up policy of 1978, which began to permit multiple types of property. Private sectors began to be legitimised in the 1980s. The first groups of persons who were engaged in informal employment were young people who returned from the countryside to the cities at the beginning of the 1980s.[3] As victims of the Maoist policy that they should learn from peasants after high school in the 1970s, they were faced with big difficulties in finding a job after their return to the cities, in the context of already serious unemployment in urban areas, caused by the planned economy. Encouraged by the employment policy of "three combinations (*san jie he*)",[4] many of them began to work as self-employed in informal activities, especially engaged in the form of individual commercial households (*ge ti hu*). The second circumstance is the massive lay-off (*xia gang*) policy during the process of reform of state-owned enterprises (SOEs) from the mid-1990s to 2005, which caused nearly 50 million workers to lose their jobs.[5]

To deepen the reform of SOEs by restructuring these enterprises into independent market entities according to the modern company model, the redundant workers, who were mostly recruited during the planned economy era, were necessarily laid off. The great majority of this huge number of unemployed people were later re-employed in informal sectors[6] in the context of government encouragement[7]. The term "informal employment" was first used in 1996 by the Shanghai municipal authorities in a document titled "Several Opinions to Encourage the Laid-off Workers to Be Reemployed in Informal Employment". The third background for the emergence of informal employment is the acceleration of urbanisation since the end of the 1990s, which attracts a big flow of the rural population to cities every year. According to the last national survey, among the total number of 260 million migrant workers, the majority of them are involved in informal employment in cities.[8]

Generally speaking, against these three backgrounds, people, whether returned youth, laid-off workers or migrant workers, were mainly obliged to do informal jobs for survival. This means that informal employment before 2004 was not a voluntary choice for Chinese people. Furthermore, it was not yet encouraged by the central government. From the perspective of personal internal connotations, the Chinese traditional mentality on employment well explains the non-voluntary choice to do informal jobs. Traditionally, Chinese people have a strong sense of collectivity, and they are likely to work in formal work units full-time with a stable unit–worker relation, such as the "iron rice bowl". So we observe that discriminatory views against migrant workers in cities or against people in odd jobs in urban areas existed for a long time, especially from the 1990s to the mid-2000s.

Furthermore, some self-employed persons also regarded themselves as the "second class" in society. From the perspective of the external environment, the central government, before the early 2000s, seemed to have no incentive to initiate informal employment, and it only changed its attitude due to the later need to redirect the massive number of laid-off workers.[9] At this stage, there were no economic policies encouraging the development of small businesses, just as many economists pointed out that tax and finance measures were not sufficiently encouraging, and that small or micro-enterprises were often under a heavy tax burden and had great difficulty in obtaining loans (Hu Angang, Yang Yunxin, 2001; Guo Zhengtao, Zhao Yuandu, 2007).

Nevertheless, since 2004, with more and more gradual administrative and financially preferable measures, and also with the expansion of the Internet and the deep social transition, more individuals have come to be engaged voluntarily in informal jobs.[10] Nowadays, young people engaged in informal jobs are no longer obliged to do so by the need for survival, but have gone into them by voluntary choice: one of the most striking pieces of evidence is that the number of online stores is rising at a crazy rate in China,[11] and another piece of evidence is also significant: people engaged in private enterprise and individual commercial households (*ge ti hu*) occupied 35.4 per cent of the total active population in 2005. This rate reached 45.7 per cent in 2011.[12]

Furthermore, the latest All-China Federation of Trade Unions (ACFTU) survey in 2012 reveals that every year, an additional 150 million persons go into informal jobs.[13] We think that this increase of people engaged in informal employment is possible only because Chinese society is becoming economically and socially more and more open, which offers a favourable environment for people to make their own choice of profession. The great increase of informal employment can be confirmed by comparing the following two figures: the Fifth Survey of Chinese Workers of 2002 shows that temporary workers (including part-timers and seasonal workers) accounted for 8% of the total urban active population, while the Seventh Survey of Chinese Workers of 2012 indicates that informal employment already comprises 40% of the total urban active population.[14]

In the face of this rapid development of informal employment, are both the central government and local governments ready to provide the necessary protections to people engaged in informal employment, especially the protections of labour and social security law? Moreover, labour legislations have developed remarkably in the last two decades, along with the trend of informal employment; therefore, it is necessary to study the attitude of labour legislation towards informal employment. Put more precisely, what are the influences on informal employment resulting from (1) the Labour Law of 1994 (LL), the first comprehensive labour legislation, and (2) the Labour Contract Law of 2007 (LCL), the specific legislation on labour contracts, and (3) what problems have the other labour regulations brought to informal employment?

The impact of the Labour Law of 1994

The original purpose of the LL of 1994 was to protect the legal rights of labourers by confirming the concrete labour rights of workers and the legal obligations of employers. However, (a) the LL did not reach its original target due to its legislative flaw on labour contract terms. In addition, (b) the reform policies, rather than the provisions of the LL, were implemented during the process of deepening SOE reform in the decades of 1990s, which caused the serious problem of a massive number of laid-off workers.

Defective provisions of the LL and its indirect role in the emergence of informal employment

The LL of 1994, regarded as a milestone in Chinese labour legislation history, was the first protective labour legislation to be nationally implemented, providing basic labour protection to all workers in all kinds of enterprises. This law initiated the legal regulation of the labour relationship by confirming specific labour rights of workers and imposing obligations on the employer,[15] which had never before been precisely confirmed by law. Numerous facts showed that the labour protections enjoyed by the workers in the planned economy era began to be eroded during the two decades of SOE reform in the 1980s and 1990s.[16]

This prompted the adoption in 1994 of the LL, which was regarded as the first national law to protect the legal rights of labourers and which established a series of basic legal labour systems for the labour market. For these reasons, we do not agree with the opinion which considers this law to be a deregulation measure, and hence the ensuing opinion, which views the period of the 1980s and the early 2000s as a stage of deregulation (Fang Lee Cooke, 2011, p.101), cannot be completely correct. For us, the SOE reform policy is deregulatory in nature, but not the Labour Law of 1994.

Despite its historical role in labour legislation, two shortcomings of the LL regarding the labour contract are obvious: no sanctions to guarantee the written labour contract and no limits to the recourse of the fixed-term contract. First, according to art. 19 of the law, the labour contract should be signed in written form, but this statutory obligation was not accompanied by sanctions. So, in practice, the rate of conclusion of written contracts was very low. Second, concerning the choice of contract term, this law followed effectively the principle of freedom of consent. It allowed the parties to choose the fixed-term contract freely and imposed just one condition on the choice of open-term contract.[17] In fact, this allowed enterprises to freely choose a fixed-term contract with a term ranging from a few months to several years. Being inclined to more flexible employment, the enterprises preferred to sign a very short-term contract with workers, which led to the trend for short-term contracts, just as is observed by Sandra V. Constantin in Chapter 3.

These two problems (the lack of written labour contracts and the tendency for short-term contracts), both signs of the increase of informal employment, were clearly reported by the NPCSC vice chairman H.E. Luli in 2005 at the 19th Congress:[18] "problems such as low conclusion rate, short contract term and nonstandard content exist in labour contract. The conclusion rate of labour contracts is less than 20% in small and medium-sized non-public enterprises and even lower in individual economic organisations. Some employers would not like to enter into a long-term contract with workers in order to avoid statutory obligations. Most of the labour contracts are concluded with a term no more than one year, reflecting an evident short-term trend."

In fact, workers in short-term contracts easily became temporary workers. This meant high precariousness of their employment: a high chance of losing the job after the expiration of this short term. This is described by some sociologists as a kind of "informalisation" strategy by employers to meet their needs for labour flexibility and profitability, just as is argued by Sandra V. Constantin in Chapter 3.

Furthermore, without a written contract with the enterprise, their labour rights, instead of being protected by labour legislation, were settled according to civil law, obviously less favourable for workers. Numerous cases demonstrated that their labour disputes with the enterprises, without a written labour contract, were legally treated according to civil contract law.[19] Although they should theoretically have been protected by labour law, in reality they were exempt from it and were left in a kind of informal situation.

These defective provisions are, in fact, due to two principal reasons: lack of labour contract experience and incorrect legislative guidelines on the labour contract system. The LL of 1994 marked the first national introduction of a labour contract system. Without enough experience in implementation of labour contracts, the provisions were stipulated in a rather simple manner, such as the provision of written contracts without any sanctions. The legislator of LL in 1994 completely applied civil contract theory to labour contracts, so that chapter III of LL on labour contracts expressed much more civil contract freedom of the two parties, without paying attention to the protection of the vulnerable party – the workers – in the labour contract relationship, such as adopting an attitude of free choice between fixed-term contract and open-ended contracts, and the permitted clause on breach liability by negotiation. Regarding the labour contract as a kind of civil contract, without considering their core difference, this incorrect legislative orientation marked the lack of correct comprehension of labour contracts at that stage in China. Consequently, led by the incorrect legislative direction, the defective provisions of the LL have led indirectly to the rise of informal jobs in reality.

The non-implementation of the LL, the massive layoff of workers in the 1990s and the intensification of informal employment

The LL of 1994 stipulates, in art. 27 and 28, the strict conditions for redundancy, its procedures and the compensations to the laid-off workers.[20] But these articles were not effectively implemented. The massive number of laid-off workers from the mid-1990s to the early 2000s were not legally treated according to these articles, because this latter measure constituted a reform campaign for SOEs in order to remove the heavy staff burden which had accumulated in the planned economy stage. It was the governmental reform policy rather than the labour law which was carried out. At the beginning of this "official" redundancy, a great number of laid-off workers were not compensated in time, which even led to numerous demonstrations by workers.[21] It was not until the end of the 1990s, realising that the difficulties of their survival would pose a threat to public security, that the central government began to issue protective policies to guarantee their minimum subsistence.[22]

In fact, under the guidance and encouragement of central government to develop informal jobs, the majority of this massive number of laid-off workers were obliged to engage in informal jobs to survive,[23] which led naturally to the explosion of informal jobs in China. The Shanghai Model[24] was introduced to all the provinces as a characteristic and efficient measure to absorb the huge number of laid-off workers, which, indeed, yielded very significant results in dealing with this problem.[25]

Hence, we agree with the conclusion of Sandra V. Constantin in Chapter 3, that the early development of informal employment is more a result of official economic strategy in the stage of deepening reform – to make the SOEs more profitable – than a natural result of individual choice.

But we do not agree with her opinion in Chapter 3 about the deregulation resulting from the LL of 1994. Even if we consider the trend towards short-term labour contracts and the defective protection of the massive number of laid-off workers as a kind of deregulation of the labour market, compared with the all-round protection of workers in the era of the planned economy, this deregulation does not directly result from the LL of 1994, but from the SOE reform policies. Unfortunately, the flaws of the LL served indirectly to permit employers to legally pursue flexibility, and its provisions, indeed, received bad implementation in the special context of SOE reform, which powerfully drove the SOEs to pursue profitability.

The impact of LCL on informal employment

The defective provisions of the LL of 1994, mentioned above, were clearly corrected by the LCL of 2007, especially with the two obligations imposed on the employer: the first is the obligation to sign a written labour contract, with specific sanctions imposed on the employer in case of the breach of this obligation; the other is the obligation to sign an open-ended labour contract under three circumstances stipulated in article 14,[26] whose target is to prevent the trend towards short-term contracts. Apart from these improvements, the LCL, regarded as more protective to workers, is the first national labour legislation which directly concerns informal employment, with the provisions of chapter V on part-time job and labour dispatch. What we can draw from these provisions is the flexibility arranged by the legislator on the regulation of labour relationships concerned with (a) part-time jobs and (b) labour dispatch.

Part-timers: legally differently treated from full-timers

Although local regulations on part-time jobs had existed since 2002,[27] the LCL of 2007 set up national rules for part-timers for the first time. From these provisions, the conclusion is obvious that part-time work is regarded by legislators as a kind of flexible employment, with more flexible formalities in the conclusion and termination of contracts compared with the provisions concerning full-time jobs.

First, the conditions of conclusion and termination of labour contracts in regard to full-timers and part-timers are quite different. The provisions are comparatively lax towards part-time contracts. For a full-time labour contract, it is obligatory to conclude a written contract, whereas for a part-time job, an oral contract is permitted.

Second, the termination of a labour contract for a full-timer should be legally justified and with notice in advance, accompanied by termination compensations in some circumstances. By contrast, the employer can terminate the labour contract of a part-timer at any moment, with no justification or compensation.

Third, the social insurance of part-timers is also differently arranged. For full-timers, the enterprise is obliged to pay each month a percentage of the payroll to the social insurance funds for employees for five kinds of social insurance (retirement insurance, illness insurance, unemployment insurance, professional accident insurance and maternity insurance), while the employee is also obliged to contribute a percentage of his salary for three kinds of social insurance (retirement, illness and unemployment), which is legally deducted monthly by the employer. But for part-timers, the employer is not obliged to pay their social insurance; it is the part-timer himself or herself who has to pay some kinds of social insurance, according to a different rate. For instance, for retirement, a full-timer in Beijing pays a monthly 8 per cent of his salary and his employer pays 20 per cent for him, while a part-timer pays a monthly 20 per cent of his salary for his own retirement, directly to the social insurance funds. This different legal arrangement gives rise to the following question: does this kind of difference constitute a kind of discrimination against the part-timer?

Anyway, LCL provides a kind of minimum protection for part-timers in two ways: the guarantee of a minimum wage and the duration of payment of the wage. The pay should be superior to the local minimum wage and should be paid within 15 days.

Unfortunately, there are no national statistics on part-timers. Although the LCL provides flexible measures to encourage the employer to use part-timers, it seems that this kind of informal employment has not rapidly developed. Two reasons may explain this: on the one hand, this is due to the traditional recruitment mentality of the enterprises, which prefer to use a person on a full-time basis; on the other hand, the smart recourse to part-timers requires the enterprise to have a clear view on the distinctions between diverse jobs. We don't think that the majority of Chinese enterprises are happy about this latter condition.

Dispatched workers: theoretically better regulated by labour law, but always discriminated against and in a precarious situation

The dispatching of labour forces in China emerged in the mid-1990s in the context of massive layoffs of workers from SOEs and in combination with the flow of abundant rural labour forces to cities (Zhou Changzheng, 2007). Before the implementation of LCL, in the absence of any legal regulation, it was a common phenomenon that dispatched workers were regarded as "second-class citizens" in user-enterprises, discriminated against especially regarding salary and social insurance. The LCL of 2007 protected them for the first time with several provisions: insisting on the equality principle in labour rights for dispatched workers, generally concentrating the dispatched workers in temporary, auxiliary and replacement jobs; requiring financial conditions for the establishment of a service-dispatching company (*laowu paiqian gongsi*); and strengthening the legal responsibilities of both the user-enterprise and the service-dispatching company.[28] But in its 2007 version, because of the compromise,[29] LCL did not insist on its original strict attitude on this issue, and finally adopted some equivocal and tolerant provisions[30] which proved to be very badly implemented in practice. Four years' implementation of LCL demonstrated that these defective provisions on labour dispatch, accompanied by the provisions of the same law to promote the open-ended labour contract at the same time, triggered a resulting explosion of labour dispatch, totally contrary to the legislators' intention.

In all professions and all industries, whether public or private, labour dispatch was so widely used that it was intended to replace the traditional bilateral labour relationship.[31] This abusive use of labour dispatch caused severe problems of discrimination against the labour dispatched workers. For instance, a survey in Beijing shows that 85 per cent of dispatched workers face discrimination in salary, 47 per cent of them are not paid for their social insurance, 69 per cent of them are not allowed a weekly rest, and 59 per cent of them signed a labour contract for less than two years (Zhang Liya, 2011).

In the face of these problems, the ACFTU has been calling since 2010 for the LCL to be amended so as to strictly limit the recourse to labour dispatch. Finally, the amendment of LCL in 2012 reiterated the strict attitude towards the recourse of labour dispatch with the clarification that labour dispatch is only a subsidiary legal form of the labour market, which should be kept on a small scale so that it will not encroach on the traditional bilateral employer–employee relationship. Therefore, several more stringent provisions were adopted:[32] to strictly limit the use of labour dispatch only to temporary, auxiliary jobs or replacement jobs; to strengthen the financial conditions for the establishment of a dispatching company by 2 million RMB instead of 500,000 RMB; to emphasise the equality principle of labour treatment between dispatched workers and workers directly recruited by the enterprise; and finally, to impose more severe liabilities on violators.

Nonetheless, the principle of equal pay for dispatched workers still remains thorny, because the provision of LCL on this point is not detailed enough. Art. 63 of LCL stipulates that the user-enterprise should pay equally dispatched workers who work on the same job as other, directly recruited workers; in the case of absence of this pay reference in the user-enterprise, according to this article, the salary level of the same job or a similar job in the same region will be taken as the pay reference. Obviously, this provision is difficult for the user-enterprise to implement, and it is also difficult for the dispatched workers to control its implementation, because this pay reference is not open: who knows the pay level of such a job in the same region?

The average local salary can be found, but there is no open list of local salaries for every kind of job. Furthermore, with the weak role of the trade unions, who can help the dispatched workers to find a pay reference? Therefore, we conclude that article 63 only reflects a good theoretical wish of the legislator; without any further specific regulations or accompanying measures, it remains an empty rule in name only. In addition, two years' implementation of this amendment demonstrates inequality between dispatched workers and directly recruited workers regarding salary and the payment of social insurance (Zhang Jing, 2013, p. 73; Yang Guolan, Huang Aihua, 2014, p. 19; Han Xiaoli, 2015, p. 23).

Another problem is that the precariousness of the labour-dispatched workers still exists after the amendment of LCL. According to article 58 of LCL, without amendment, the term of the labour contract for dispatched workers is stipulated to be greater than two years. But it is not clear whether or not the employer, here referring to the service-dispatching company, should obey article 14[33] of LCL, which obliges the employer to sign an open-ended labour contract (more likely to be a permanent job for workers) in the case of labour contract renewal after the fixed-term labour contract has expired twice. In fact, without clear guidance on this point, the majority of service-dispatching companies conclude a fixed-term contract of two years twice with the dispatched workers, and after the second expiration of the term, their labour relationship terminates automatically, without any obligation to sign an open-ended labour contract.[34]

Generally speaking, it is true that the LCL has brought greater job stability, as confirmed by Sandra V. Constantin in Chapter 3, but this is only true for directly recruited workers,[35] not yet for dispatched workers.

The distinctive legislative arrangements for part-timers and dispatched workers, as described above, are no doubt for the purpose of flexible employment. However, it makes us question these differences: does this different arrangement mean a kind of discrimination against part-timers or dispatched workers? Based on what we know of European social law, this kind of difference should not exist.

The impact of other labour regulations on informal employment

With the implementation of a socialist market economy since 1993, in the context of more and more conflict in employment relationships, Chinese labour law began to develop by setting up precise protections for the traditional formal employment relationship in order to meet the need for keeping employers' and employees' power in balance. For this reason, labour regulations, designed first for the traditional formal employment relationship, only cover this relationship. We can naturally raise the questions: (a) apart from the two principal comprehensive legislations (the LL of 1994 and the LCL of 2007), are there any labour regulations specialising in informal employment? and (b) what is the impact of labour regulations on migrant workers, the principal contributors to the Chinese economy, and also a major section of the people engaged in informal employment?

Special labour regulations on informal employment: local colour and very limited protection on one or two items of social insurance

Generally speaking, the number of national labour regulations concerning informal employment is small. The first mention of self-employed persons in governmental document was a ministerial document on retirement insurance in 2001.[36] The first national labour regulation specially focused on flexible employment was issued in 2003, covering social insurance of part-timers.[37] The second special regulation, also released in 2003, provides the possibility for all people involved in flexible employment to integrate into the urban basic illness insurance.[38] In contrast to the rarity of national special regulations on this issue, there are a great number of local regulations; many provinces or big cities have issued local rules for informal employment. Generally, local regulations are more useful and accessible to them.

Furthermore, these local regulations concern just one or two items of social insurance: pension and illness insurance. Compared with the relatively high rate of coverage of five kinds of social insurance for formal employment,[39] only a very limited proportion of people in informal employment are covered by pension and illness insurance. They are almost completely excluded from professional injury insurance, unemployment insurance and maternity insurance. According to some academic studies, in 2011, for people in informal employment, the coverage rate of pension insurance was around 10 per cent, and the coverage rate of illness insurance was about 30 per cent (Zhao Chongping, Tan Yong, 2014, pp. 196, 257).

Academic research on informal employment also concentrates on pension and illness insurance. Much of it analyses the main reasons for this lower coverage for pension and illness insurance for informal employment (Deng Dasong, Yang Jie, 2007, p. 144; Cai Xiaoshen, Zhang Shu, 2008, p. 21; Ge Hongfei *et al.*, 2013, pp. 70–71). First, the payment rate for these two items is too high compared with the remuneration of people involved in informal employment. According to some local regulations, the payment rate is fixed according to a percentage of local average salary, which is calculated on the basis of formal employment, totally excluding reference to the remuneration level of informal employment. Second, unaware of the need to register for retirement or illness insurance, they prefer to put their money in the bank instead of paying for these insurances.

Finally, after registration and payment for these insurances, it is still difficult to transfer their registration record from one place to another if they change their jobs. In fact, the current pension and illness insurance system is not suitably set up for them. As has already been pointed out by many authors, the unsuitable payment rate for social insurance is the main reason for the low coverage or absence of social insurance for people involved in informal employment; therefore, they suggest setting up flexible rates for informal employment (He Ping, Hua Yingfang, 2008, p. 28; Xia Linlin, 2011, p. 221; Zhu Ze, Xie Zhanfeng, 2011, p. 6).

As for professional injury insurance, only 24 per cent of migrant workers are covered by it, and all other people in informal employment are excluded. Regarding unemployment insurance and maternity insurance, only a few cities or provinces have adopted special policies for them, such as the cities of Chongqing, Nanjing, Haerbing and Suzhou. Concerning unemployment insurance, there are even controversial opinions on the necessity of including people in informal employment in the unemployment insurance; if the answer is affirmative, the question is how to decide the protection level for them (Jiang Limei, 2010, p. 92; Zhao Chongping, Tan Yong, 2014, p. 343). Considering the absence of maternity insurance for them, we think that this indeed reveals total negligence by governments.

Social insurance problems for migrant workers

The number of migrant workers in cities has increased annually with the progressive urban reform and urbanisation since 1990s, and they are the main body of people engaged in informal employment. According to the survey of National Administration of Statistics of 2012, the total number of migrant workers had reached 263 million, especially concentrated in manufacture, construction, service, retail, transportation and the catering industries, and only 44 per cent of them had signed a labour contract with their employer. This means that 56 per cent of them were engaged in informal employment. In fact, the proportion of workers signing a labour contract is much higher than the percentage of workers doing so in 2006, when only 10 per cent of the workers signed labour contracts and 90 per cent of the migrant workers were engaged in informal activities (Ren Yuan, Peng Xizhe, 2007, p. 71). We think that this improvement results directly from the implementation of the LCL since 2008 – which provides more written labour contracts and job stability – as confirmed by the questionnaire in Chapter 3. However, migrant workers still constitute a major proportion of people engaged in informal employment. According to the Seventh Survey of Chinese Workers of 2012, 53 per cent of labour-dispatched workers are migrant workers, and 45 per cent of them work for individual commercial households.[40]

Migrant workers are underdogs in both political status and economic welfare (Zhang Xuedong, 2014, p. 52). Even for those with a signed labour contract, in formal employment, theoretically covered by all labour legislations, it is an open fact that their labour rights and interests are not yet protected as well as those of urban workers. The ACFTU describes their labour situation like this: low qualification of job, low stability of job, lack of professional promotion, unhealthy working environment, longer working day, and higher labour intensity.[41] In fact, as well as these problems, social insurance is also a problematic issue for them. The major problem regarding this issue, described by the term of "two low rates and one high rate", has already existed for a decade: low coverage rate of social insurance, low benefit rate from social insurance, and high rate of withdrawal from social insurance registration.

Generally speaking, according to national statistics, in 2011, the national coverage rate for migrant workers was around 14 per cent for retirement insurance, 17 per cent for illness insurance, 24 per cent for professional insurance, 8 per cent for unemployment insurance and 6 per cent for maternity insurance.[42] Comparing the statistics of 2011 with the statistics of 2005, we can confirm the stagnation of the coverage rate during the period from 2005 to 2011.[43] This stagnation illustrates well the very obvious phenomenon that many migrant workers who had already paid for social insurance have later withdrawn from it because they did not value the future benefits, which were proved to be at a very low level.

One of the reasons for the problems outlined above is the openly recognised absence of a reasonably well-designed system for them. There is no unified national social insurance for migrant workers; the situation still remains puzzling: multiple models without coordination and local colour without unification. Four models exist: only the first has links with the urban workers' system, while the other three are quite separate (Ren Lixin, 2009, p. 80). The first is the model of "integration", which integrates people in informal employment into urban workers' social insurance. For example, in Guangdong province, since 1994, migrant workers were gradually included in local retirement insurance, illness insurance, professional accident insurance and unemployment insurance. The second is the model of "low threshold", which provides for people in informal employment a special social insurance system with lower payment rate and lower benefits, such as the system of Zhejiang province since 2003. The third is the "comprehensive model", which combines all the items of social insurance into one special comprehensive social insurance system, and this model is found in Shanghai, later copied by several other cities. The fourth is the model of returning to the rural system, which means that all migrant workers exempt from the urban system should register in the rural social insurance system. None of the four models is coordinated with the current, existing urban social insurance system or rural social insurance, and the obstacles preventing the integration of migrant workers with stable jobs into the urban social insurance are not yet overcome.[44]

Conclusion

Informal employment in China is the natural result of both the state's economic strategy to reform SOEs and the process of urbanisation, rather than an individual choice. The LL of 1994 indirectly promoted the emergence and development of informal employment. The LCL of 2007 provides direct, but very limited, regulation of it. The special local rules on pension or illness insurance for informal employment still remain problematic. In the context of increasing development of informal employment in the future, enabled by the opening up of Chinese society, labour law is still far from ready to provide enough protective regulations. According to our calculation in 2004, Chinese labour legislation covered only 36 per cent of the urban active population. Actually, we could estimate

45 per cent.[45] This rate, which is still low, strongly reflects the fact that people in informal employment are formally excluded from the coverage of labour law.[46] We can conclude that, because of the absence of clear, close attention paid to informal employment at all levels of government and other important institutions,[47] the labour and social protections of people in informal employment will remain in the stage of stagnation or disorder.

Notes

1 This research report on flexible employment, conducted by the Labor Science Institute, is not published, but its main points have been well reported by the Chinese internal media.
2 Different percentages are quoted by different academic articles: some think 40 per cent, others 46 per cent, still others 51 per cent in 2011. According to the Seventh Survey of Chinese Workers, carried out by ACFTU in 2012, informal employment occupies only 40 per cent of the active population. The Seventh Survey of Chinese Workers, Press of Chinese Workers, 2014, p. 70.
3 Seventeen million young intellectual people were sent to the countryside during this movement.
4 The "three combinations" employment policy, adopted in 1980 to deal with serious unemployment, indicates: government guidance to jobs; creation of jobs by unions between individuals or between individuals and units; and self-employment by the individual.
5 According to the annual report of the Labour Ministry from 1997 to 2005 (1997: 6.9, 1998: 6.1, 1999: 6.5, 2000: 6.5, 2001: 5.2, 2002: 4.1, 2003: 2.6, 2004: 1.5, 2005: 0.7), in addition to numerous laid-off workers in 1995 and 1996, the total number of laid-off workers is nearly 50 million. The Seventh Survey of Chinese Workers of 2012 indicates that more than 47 million laid-off workers were aided to find jobs between 2002 and 2011. Press Chinese Workers, 2014, p. 70.
6 According to a comprehensive estimation of several provinces, 80–90 per cent of laid-off workers were re-employed in informal employment in the service industry. The Fifth Survey of Chinese Workers, carried out by ACFTU in 2002, published in 2006, Press of Chinese Workers.
7 The 10th Five-year Plan of 2001 promoted changes in employment mentality, and encouraged more part-time or seasonal jobs or other flexible jobs. The Report of the 16th Congress of the Chinese Communist Party of 2002 reiterated the emphasis on guiding the change of employment mentality, promoting different kinds of flexible jobs, and encouraging self-employment or the creation of jobs by entrepreneurs. The central government issued different kinds of preferential policy (tax, administration fee, loan, etc.) to encourage re-employment in the informal sector during the period from 1998 to 2005.
8 Survey Report on Migrant Workers of National Administration of Statistics in 2012. www.stats.gov.cn (Accessed 30 January 2016).
9 Ibid.
10 This trend can be proved by the increase of the number of registrations of individual commercial households (*ge ti hu*): according to the statistics of State Administration for Industry and Commerce, in 2004, there were 2,350 individual commercial households; in early 2013, this number reached 4,060. In 2013, there were more than 80 million people involved in individual commercial households. *People's Daily*, 16 February 2013.
11 According to the Seventh Survey of Chinese Workers carried out in 2012 by the ACFTU, the number of jobs online exceeded 10 million. Press of Chinese Workers, 2014, p. 37.

12 Chinese Labor Annual Statistic Book of 2006, 2012. Press of Chinese Labor and Social Security.

13 The Seventh Survey of Chinese Workers, Press of Chinese Workers, 2014, p. 70.

14 The Fifth Survey of Chinese Workers, Press of Chinese Workers, 2006, p. 35; the Seventh Survey of Chinese Workers, Press of Chinese Workers, 2014, p. 70.

15 Art. 3 of the law stipulates that workers enjoy the right of equality in access to jobs, the right of getting remuneration, the right of rest and vacation, the right of labour security and labour hygiene protection, the right of professional training, the right of social insurance and social welfare, the right of labour dispute resolution, and other statutory rights.

16 Report of Legal Committee of Permanent Commission of National People Congress for the adoption of Chinese Labor Law.

17 Art. 20 of the law stipulates that the term of a labour contract can be fixed-term, open-term or for a special job; for those whose seniority is more than 10 years, in the case of renewal of the contract, an open-term labour contract should be concluded if the worker wishes.

18 Report of NPCSC Law Enforcement Inspection Team on Inspection of the Implementation of Labor Law of 1994, submitted to the 19th Session of the 10th NPC, 28 December 2005. www.npc.gov.cn (Accessed 30 January 2016).

19 Study on Labor Dispute Resolution, edited by Beijing Labor and Social Security Law Society, Law Press, 2001.

20 Art. 27: during the stage of restructuring the enterprise according to bankruptcy law or in the case of severe difficulty in the operation of the enterprise, which proves the need to reduce the number of staff, the enterprise can dismiss the workers, after consultation with trade unions or workers' assembly, and report to local labour administration. The enterprise should recruit the dismissed workers as a priority if recruitment occurs within six months of this dismissal. Art. 28: workers dismissed according to art. 24, 26 and 27 should be compensated economically.

21 One meaningful example: collective labour disputes during 1996 and 2001 accounted for 26 per cent of the total number of labour disputes in Shanghai, according to the survey of Shanghai Federation of Trade Unions. See the Fifth Survey of Chinese Workers, Press of Chinese Workers, 2006.

22 Such as the "Opinion on the guarantee of laid-off workers' minimum life and their replacement" of the State Council in 1998, and the "Regulation on minimum guarantee of life in urban area" of the State Council in 1999.

23 According to the annual report of the Labour Ministry from 1997 to 2004, the number of laid-off workers is almost 40 million (1997: 6.9, 1998: 6.1, 1999: 6.5, 2000: 6.5, 2001: 5.2, 2002: 4.1, 2003: 2.6, 2004: 1.5, 2005: 0.7)

24 This model insists on the establishment of different kinds of informal labour organisation (such as community service units, self-relieved bases, etc.) to provide informal jobs for the unemployed (Ren Yuan, 2008).

25 According to the Chinese Labor Annual Statistic Book of 2007, at the end of 2006, these informal labour organisations absorbed 50.5 million laid-off workers.

26 Article 14 provides three circumstances under which the employer should conclude an open-ended labour contract with the employee. An employer and an employee may conclude an open-ended labour contract upon reaching a negotiated consensus. If an employee proposes or agrees to renew his labour contract or to conclude a labour contract in any of the following circumstances, an open-ended labour contract shall be concluded, unless the employee requests the conclusion of a fixed-term labour contract:

(1) The employee has been working for the employer for a consecutive period of not less than 10 years;

(2) when his employer introduces the labour contract system or the state owned enterprise that employs him re-concludes its labour contracts as a result of restructuring,

the employee has been working for the employer for a consecutive period of not less than 10 years and is less than 10 years away from his legal retirement age; or

(3) prior to the renewal, a fixed-term labour contract was concluded on two consecutive occasions and the employee is not characterized by any of the circumstances set forth in Article 39 and items (1) and (2) of Article 40 hereof.

This comes from conversations between the author and a few HR managers and lawyers of labour law during the spring of 2014.

27 The Labor Contract Regulation of Shanghai of 2002 was the first local regulation on part-timers.

28 See articles 57–67 of ECA of the 2007 version.

29 The draft of LCL was stricter than the version of 2007: for instance, in order to guarantee the salary payment of the dispatched workers, the draft required that the dispatching company should pay 50,000 RMB for every dispatched worker to a financial institution. This requirement was strongly opposed by all the dispatching companies. In the final version adopted in 2007, this requirement was cancelled.

30 The original objective was to strictly limit the dispatched workers to only three types of jobs: temporary, auxiliary and replacement jobs, but the expression of the adopted article – art. 66 – stipulated: "in general, labour dispatch applies on temporary, auxiliary jobs and replacement jobs". This is very equivocal regarding the use of labour dispatch in reality. In addition, the legislator was tolerant regarding the measure of a guarantee to workers, finally by the requirement of 500,000 RMB as registered capital for the establishment of a dispatching company in art. 57, instead of the original condition in its draft of the deposit of an amount of RMB from the dispatching company to the specific finance institution that would be calculated according to the number of workers dispatched.

31 According to a survey by ACFTU at the end of 2010, there were around 60 million dispatched workers in total. The percentage of dispatched workers reached 20 per cent of the total national workers. In some industries, the labour dispatch composed 70 per cent of the total staff, such as in the telecommunications industry; even in some SOEs, more than two-thirds of staff were dispatched workers. *Journal of economy observation*, 28 February 2011.

32 See articles 57–67 of LCL, 2012 version.

33 See note 26.

34 This comes from conversations between a few HR managers and lawyers of labour law during the spring of 2014.

35 The reason is that the employer should abide by article 14 and sign an open-ended labour contract with his workers.

36 Notification on policies of improving urban employees' basic retirement insurance, Ministry of Labor, 2001, stipulated that persons engaged in individual commercial households (*ge ti hu*) may pay monthly or yearly retirement insurance for themselves according to the provincial rate. Those with 15 years' payment can enjoy their pension at 60 years old.

37 Opinions on the Employment by Part-Time, Ministry of Labor, 2003, stipulated that part-timers should pay for their retirement and illness insurance themselves, and enterprises should pay accident insurance for those with whom the enterprises have established a labour relation.

38 Directive Opinions on Integration of Persons Engaged in Flexible Employment in Urban Area into the Basic Illness Insurance, Ministry of Labor, 2003.

39 It is an obligation for employers to pay social insurance for employees in formal employment. The statutory obligation and the dispute system guarantee the relatively high coverage of these employees by social insurance.

40 The Seventh Survey of Chinese Workers, conducted by ACFTU in 2012, Press of Chinese Workers, 2014, pp. 47, 61.

41 Ibid., p. 80.
42 Survey Report on Migrant Workers of National Administration of Statistics in 2012, www.stats.gov.cn (Accessed 30 January 2016).
43 Research Report of Chinese Migrant Workers, carried out by the research department of the State Council in 2005, Press of China Yanshi, 2006, p. 248; National Administration of Statistics in 2012, ibid.
44 The Seventh Survey, note 40 on p. 80.
45 Based on the annual labour statistics of the Ministry of Human Resources and Social Security. www.mohrss.gov.cn (Accessed 30 January 2016).
46 There are many discussions on extending the coverage of labour law to domestic workers, but there is still a fair way to go; Chinese labour law will need to mature.
47 Lack of attention by ACFTU and other trade unions to informal employment: the Seventh Survey of Chinese Workers conducted by ACFTU in 2012 only mentions the situation of informal employment in a few sentences.

References

ACFTU (All-China Federation of Trade Union) (2014). *The Seventh Survey of Chinese Workers*, Beijing: Chinese Workers Press.
Cai Xiaoshen, Zhang Shu (2008). Absence of Social Insurance of People in Flexible Employment and Analyses on its Reasons. *Reformation & strategy*, 24(8), pp. 20–22.
Deng Dasong, Yang Jie (2007). Situation of Social Insurance for People Engaged in Flexible Employment and Suggestions. *Statistic and decision-making*, 247(9), pp. 144–145.
Fang Lee Cooke (2011). Labor Market Regulations and Informal Employment in China, *Journal of Chinese human resources management*. 2(2), pp. 100–116.
Ge Hongfei, Yan Yaoting, Pan Yang, Tu Shengnan (2013). Summarization of the Studies on Social Insurance for Peoples Engaged in Flexible Employment. *Social sciences review*, 28(9), pp. 70–71.
Guo Zhengtao, Zhao Yuandu (2007). Research on Development of Informal Employment. *Taxation and economy*, 4, pp. 52–55.
Han Xiaoli (2015). *Studies of Legal Regulations on Labor Dispatch – Base on Investigation in Tianjin City*. Master's degree dissertation of Hebei Economic and Trade University.
He Ping, Hua Yingfang (2008). *Research on Social Security of Informal Employment Employees*. Beijing: China Labor and Social Security Press.
Hu Angang, Yang Yunxin (2001). Change of Employment Model: From Formal to Informal. *Management word*, 2, pp. 69–78.
Jiang Limei (2010). Analyses on the Reasons of Absence of Unemployment Insurance for Peoples Engaged in Flexible Employment. *Journal of Shijiazhuang Economy Institute*, 33(4), pp. 90–93.
Ren Lixin (2009). Social Security for Migrant Workers: Situation, Difficulties and Influencing Factors Analyses. *Social Science*, 7, pp. 79–85.
Ren Yuan (2008). Improve the Informal Employment: Reflections on Shanghai Model. *Social science*, 1, pp. 119–125.
Ren Yuan, Peng Xizhe (2007). *Report of Informal Employment in China in 2006*. Chongqing: Chong Qing Press.
Shi Meixia (2007). *Research on Labor Relations of Informal Employment*. Beijing: China Labor and Social Security Press.
Xia Linlin (2011). Research on the Retirement Insurance of Groups in Informal Employment. *Urban economy of China*, 2, p. 221.

Yang Guolan, Huang Aihua (2014). Satisfaction Degrees of Dispatched Workers to Their Jobs and Suggestions of Improvement. *Economist*, 6, pp. 19–21.

Zhang Liya (2011). The Situation of Labor Relationship for Dispatched Workers. *Human resources and social security of China*, 10, pp. 41–42.

Zhao Chongping, and Tan Yong (2014). *Research on the Social Security System for Persons in Flexible Employment*. Beijing: Guang Ming Daily Press.

Zhou Changzheng (2007). *Development and Legal Regulation of Labor Dispatch*. Beijing: China Labor and Social Security Press.

Zhu Ze, Xie Zhanfeng (2011). Reflections on the Reasons of the Low Registration of People in Flexible Employment to Retirement Insurance and Suggestions. *Labor and security world*, 10, pp. 4–7.

Zhang Jing (2013). Situation, Problems of Labor Dispatching and Suggestions of Improvement. *Academic exchange*, 232(7), pp. 73–76.

Zhang Xuedong (2014). Studies on the Protections to Migrant Workers in Informal Employment. *Agriculture economy*, 10, pp. 52–54.

7 Regulating informal work through consumocratic law

Empirical and theoretical insights from the RugMark/GoodWeave experience

P. Martin Dumas

Introduction

It is largely admitted that the latest wave of free trade, at the world level, has contributed to the destabilisation of various regimes of social protection, developed or supported at state level. An epitome of this phenomenon is the challenge posed to protective state law by the configuration of transnational production networks. Given that national laws have hitherto proved inapt to meet this challenge through an adequate apprehension of the complexity and diversity of transnational operations, increased attention has been directed to the role of other regulatory means. One of them involves consumers as agents endowed with extra-judicial regulatory power – *consumocrats*. With a view to enhancing the conditions of informal work transnationally, this chapter is intended to provide empirical and theoretical insights on the efficient functioning of consumocratic regulation by (1) identifying a number of characteristics peculiar to the consumocratic system, (2) describing a transnational governance scheme driven by consumocrats and designed to fight informal child labour in Southern Asia – RugMark (now GoodWeave), (3) examining institutional obstacles to increased transparency and rule changing under consumocratic law, and (4) discussing their implications for Global Administrative Law (GAL) and, possibly, for some policies of the International Labour Organization (ILO), if it is to participate, directly or indirectly, in the development of existing or future consumocratic regimes.[1]

Characteristics peculiar to the consumocratic system

When they act as consumers, adults, like children, are often regarded as the subjects of protective state regulation – potential, manifest or latent victims of corporate negligence, misrepresentations, price-fixing and abusive marketing. The status of consumers may change significantly, though, depending on whether or not the societal value of consumer goods is elicited through markets. Central in this process is the control over the diffusion of societal information on world consumer markets. Its understanding requires an examination of the regulatory regime through which citizens are invited to broaden their notion of a desirable good and exercise new forms of authority over private enterprises. This regime is said to be *consumocratic*,[2] in contrast with the more self-centred spirit of consumerism.

Consumocracy may be defined as a *system soliciting other-regarding dispositions in consumers, allowing them to exert more authority on market enterprises through broadened qualifications of desirable goods.* We have explained elsewhere (Dumas, 2012) that the consumocratic system may mark the development of modern societies in four notable ways: first, by effectively soliciting rational and other-regarding behaviour, while ensuring that instrumental reason does not obligatorily take precedence over finalities on the market place; second, by inviting the individual – i.e. the consumocrat[3] – to inject "meaning" into the socket of the liberal order itself, and offering an ordering of values in which the sense of indifference is posited below that of social responsibility, *prior to choice*; third, by giving politically disenchanted consumers the opportunity to exert new authority outside the traditional spheres of consumer influence, generally shaped by a deficient ideology – one under which *it is (wrongly) assumed that market mechanisms are* inherently *guided by the solicitation of consumers' individualistic concerns*; fourth, by concretely challenging the common perception that the failure by the state to correct economic externalities in markets leads to undesirable results that are inevitable. It is shown that a nascent consumocracy may be opening promising spheres of influence in the field of socio-environmental regulation, without direct state intervention – a state of affairs which may prove critical in the face of future social and environmental crises.

This is done, transnationally, through the operation of codes of conduct, the enforcement of which is signalled to consumers via a more or less transparent form of societal marketing. Societal labels are typically placed on the outside of products in order to signal the effects such products or production conditions may have on consumers, other people or the environment. Societal information may thus relate to the socio-environmental conditions under which goods are produced, and to activities undertaken to improve these conditions. The meaning of logos not accompanied by a text description must be conveyed through other media such as the Internet, wireless communication and television. A variety of impacts ensue, with a degree of directness the state could hardly approach.[4]

An increasing number of independent codes of conduct constitute, in this view, a body of rules, enforced through demand-side market-based mechanisms, and used as instruments of corporate governance (hereinafter referred to as *consumocratic law*[5]). As such, they do not fit well within the "soft law" regime of corporate voluntary initiatives. In contrast with citizens called to express, ex ante, their preferences for particular socio-economic plans through voting, consumocrats are, rather, called here to play a role ex post, and themselves pronounce on the desirability of certain goods in comparison to others, following a number of non-traditional criteria already embodied in labelled codes. Such criteria may pertain to the protection of ecosystems (air, water and soil) and animals, the downsizing of the military industry, the reduction of flagrant inequities, and the amelioration of the labour conditions in which vulnerable categories of employees find themselves – children in particular. One of the most sophisticated regimes of consumocratic labour law (on child protection and schooling) was developed by RugMark/ GoodWeave in Uttar Pradesh, India.

The RugMark/GoodWeave initiatives

The RugMark code was developed in 1994, by Indian carpet manufacturers and exporters along with many leading non-governmental organisations, under the guidance of carpet importers and the influence of consumers, and as a result of the failure by the Indian state to tackle its child labour problems alone. Intensive campaigns in Europe (and Germany more particularly) against the use of child labour had, indeed, led to a proposal to boycott the import of carpets from India.[6] In its attempt to progressively eliminate (informal) child labour in the Indian "carpet belt", RugMark now certifies to consumers that carpets bearing the RugMark label are child-labour free, rehabilitates former child weavers found by its inspectors, and manages free schools in Uttar Pradesh.[7] It is worth noting that exporters and weavers, typically, do not voluntarily join the RugMark network. Carpet importers (mostly from Europe and North America) have literally imposed their conditions on carpet exporters.[8]

In the summer of 2009, a new brand name was created ("GoodWeave"), indicating that RugMark intended to phase out its label and logo. The RugMark Foundation, India, resisted the change, as appears from its website.[9] In fact, the RugMark organisation has gradually split into two disconnected networks: RugMark India and the new GoodWeave, which encompasses the entire spectrum of the former network of organisations, with the exception of the local RugMark team based in India.[10] Since most of the facts on which this chapter is based were collected during or immediately before these changes, they will be considered as relating to the operations of RugMark, even though our conclusions also hold for the new GoodWeave.

The content of the RugMark code derives directly from two sources: the substantive obligations agreed to by export or import firms under RugMark licensing agreements as well as a series of commitments and contentions of RugMark, described and published on websites and made accessible to consumers.

Obligations provided under RugMark licensing agreements include observance of the RugMark International (RMI) Standard, in force since 1994, which engages all licensed exporters in RMI member countries: (1) to submit a list of all their loom manufacturing units and have them registered with RugMark; (2) to allow unannounced random inspections by RugMark inspectors; (3) not to illegally employ any person under the age of 14; (4) to pay minimum official wages to weavers and endeavour to pay "fair wages" to adult workers; (5) to remove children found working on looms or disengage the loom in the case that the loom owner does not comply with inspectors' orders; (6) to pay RugMark a 0.25 per cent royalty on the net export value of the carpets in order to cover the costs entailed in the inspection and labelling system. Non-compliance with the RMI Standard leads to a revocation of the licence to use the RugMark label and potential market losses.

The RugMark code also incorporates a series of official contentions described and published on websites and made accessible to consumers. One such commitment involves abiding with Indian state law. In particular, RugMark reassuringly expresses disapproval of *illegal* child labour. However, while the central message conveyed to consumers is that RugMark "offers the best assurance that no child labor was used in the manufacture of a carpet or rug", a more ambiguous message is to the effect that "[i]n the case of traditional family enterprises, children under 14 years of age helping their parents must attend school regularly" – a condition typical of the family or local community business context.[11] In principle, the RugMark code thus authorises the work of children who accompany their parents (or their uncles) – "family business" being excluded from the work interdictions posed under the code. In well-established weaving communities, several family members are typically involved in carpet weaving. Numerous children can invoke their family relationship with a distant uncle (*chacha*) to justify their work behind a loom.[12] This possibility is made stronger by the lasting influence of the professional caste system (i.e. the Hindu *jati* and Muslim *birādarī*) over the weavers and their profession. The *jati* that gathers the Hindu weavers of Uttar Pradesh has been formed, in general terms, by families of traders and farmers who joined this profession around the 1950s. By often turning a blind eye to state law, RugMark inspectors are said to favour a "realistic approach" and concentrate their efforts on combatting the worst forms of child labour and avoiding misguided consumer boycotts.[13]

Thanks to RugMark and its consumocratic regime, the illegality of child labour in the carpet belt has been progressively recognised, and thousands of deprived (working and non-working) children have had free access to a primary education of relatively good quality, many of them having subsequently engaged in higher studies. The RugMark initiative also spurred the development of similar organisations such as Step and Care & Fair in Northern India, Nepal, Pakistan and Tibet.

What becomes problematic, with a view to improving the RugMark regime, is the degree of transparency required in the diffusion of societal information when pursuing the double objective of preventing negative consumer sanctions and eliminating the worst forms of child labour. Several gaps were noted between RugMark's discourse and its concrete interventions. We adopt a pragmatic approach when analysing them, on the basis of our fieldwork accomplished between September 2006 and March 2007, with some update work in the winters of 2012–2013 and 2013–2014.[14] We note that studies on such initiatives have mostly consisted of describing the RugMark scheme (along the lines of the portrait presented by the organisation itself) within a general framework and a period of only a few days (Seidman, 2007; Diller, 1999; Hilowitz, 1998; DOL, 1997). Some authors, concerned with the lack of transparency in the operation of the RugMark scheme, have underlined the shortcomings of the existing literature in this respect (McDonagh, 2002).

Some synthetic observations must be made concerning the overall reaction of the RugMark Direction to these concrete gaps. Deviations relating to the inspection of carpet looms, the rehabilitation of child workers, and some discriminatory practices understandably embarrass the Direction. There is no doubt in its eyes that consumers should be made aware of the good news coming from the RugMark scheme, above all. The organisation would not be efficient if it openly blamed and shamed weavers, exporters and their intermediaries whenever the RugMark code is not enforced. The Direction maintains that its collaboration and persuasion efforts are in the interests of the children, and more efficient than adversarial measures. In private, the Direction does not hesitate to recognise the flaws in its achievements[15] as well as in its discourse.[16] It insists, though, on the importance of diffusing essentially *positive* field results, at the expense of transparency. It is aware of the intransigent attitude of Oriental and Occidental people vis-à-vis the child labour issue.[17] It fears that this attitude may trigger boycotts (or threats of boycotts)[18] should the organisation decide to expose its flaws or reveal all types of obstacles to its action. The "grey zones" in the RugMark scheme are thus said to be better left to knowledgeable local employees called upon to exercise their judgement. Characteristic examples of these grey zones include the decision of inspectors to rescue working children and to put pressure on employers to let them leave the workplace.

It is worth recalling at this stage that a critical mass of consumers may suffice to force national or transnational corporate entities to amend some of their practices. Few competitive organisations, indeed, can afford the luxury of abandoning a small though "critical" portion of their clientele under the significant pressures exercised on corporate profitability equations.[19]

Pre-constitutional obstacles to increased transparency and rule changing

The most important obstacles to increased transparency in the transmission of societal information by RugMark are combined in the form of substantive and procedural factors: the complexity of the context within which the organisation operates; the controversial character of the means used by the organisation to fulfil its mission; and the absence of mechanisms designed to translate this complexity to consumers and offer a framework for eventual exchanges with producers.

First, this regulatory problem would not be so critical if any work performed by a child under the age of 14 (outside the purview of a family business) was more detrimental than beneficial to the child, directly or indirectly; the original RugMark code would not suffer from any major deficiency. The mission of the organisation would simply consist of enforcing that code as well as possible and fighting any form of power abuse. Any contravention of the code would represent both a derogation of the principles promoted by its societal marketing and a menace to the well-being of weavers. Such is not the case, though. The evidence shows that the benefits which could be received, by a poor family, from the labour of a child – an *opportunity forgone* (i.e. the "opportunity cost", in economic language) – may be very high. It may draw the line between a healthy and an insufficient family diet, the administration of a vital medical treatment and its inaccessibility, the possibility and impossibility for some brothers and sisters to gain access to a college education, and so on. Such conditions are necessarily aggravated by the absence or insufficiency of basic services (such as education, health and financial services) and by the slowness of the political and economic reforms on which the adequate provision of these services often depends. The complexity of the context in which RugMark operates does not transpire from the recognition of these intervening variables as much as in the evaluation of their relative importance. To what extent should a problem relating to the safety, health, diet or finances of a family legitimise the work of a school-aged child? From a distance, without a detailed knowledge of the peculiarities of the daily life of some destitute families, this appreciation is hardly possible. Not to mention the fact that child labour does not necessarily encroach on the school schedule; it has been stressed that part-time work, before and after class, was a common occurrence within the carpet belt – an arrangement absent from the RugMark code.

Second, the unofficial means used by RugMark in the pursuit of its mission do lend themselves to polemics or criticism. The facility with which weavers can register one loom with RugMark, and another one with a competing organisation that does not perform inspections, is a typical illustration of this. The reputation of the organisation, no doubt, would be tarnished if it were revealed that the RugMark inspection system can so easily be circumvented by displacing children to a neighbouring loom, all else being equal. While the royalties paid to the organisation for each labelled carpet sold on the market do contribute to improving the welfare of poor families, the RugMark label does not always provide "the best assurance" that a carpet was woven by adults and that one can trace it back to the loom on which it was produced. Also, the appreciation by inspectors of the age of a child and his attachment to a family of weavers is conducted with a great deal of elasticity: so much so that while RugMark is said to condemn "illegal" child labour, this no longer refers to prohibitions found under Indian law, but to RugMark's own standards, unknown to the public. Under the pressure of carpet importers and their clienteles, these non-state standards are enforced with relative flexibility and secrecy.

Third, in the absence of mechanisms designed to translate this complexity to consumers and offer a framework for eventual exchanges with producers, RugMark regulators are exposing their organisation to the risks posed by the leaking of sensitive information towards a large, non-specialised audience. The absence of any communication mode between consumers and producers led to the boycott of Indian carpets in the early 1990s. Social labelling, standing for one fairly elementary mode of interaction between producers and consumers, is here confronted with a problem similar to that which gave birth to the RugMark organisation itself. The gap perceived between consumers' broader expectations and the harsh reality shaping the action of RugMark is at the heart of this problem. Consumers may have been reassured, more or less genuinely, with respect to the use of Indian child labour since the birth of RugMark. This comforting position, however, is fragile: the mere presentation of sensitive or controversial information to the targeted public would suffice, in the present context, to undermine the credibility of the organisation – not to mention the dire consequences likely to affect weavers as a result. Ultimately, one may conclude, the vulnerability of the RugMark system rests on the absence of a deliberation space between consumers and producers, under the risk of increased regulatory transparency, either enforced or unexpected.

A second major conclusion, then, resides in the recognition that it is impossible, from an instrumentalist point of view, to sensibly reform RugMark's institutional apparatus without endowing it with a (new) constitutional platform. One is led to acknowledge that the necessary contextualisation of societal information, within a more transparent framework, is bound to reveal the constitutional flaws of the organisation, and, by ricochet, to lead to calls for its constitutional reform. Such a platform would serve as a basis for the redistribution of (executive, legislative and interpretative) powers and functions which, until now, have been kept in the hands of a handful of people. An overview of the procedural and substantive elements of such a reform is offered below.

On the procedural level, one notes that RugMark's inspection system is based on an *inquisitorial* mode. It is, in effect, RugMark that takes the initiative in the monitoring, auditing and certification process in the handmade carpet industry by directly undertaking the information gathering required by its mission. Since its inception, this inquisitorial scheme has been deemed sufficient in responding to the informational demand of societal marketing. Yet the success of the RugMark mission necessitates the adoption of a supplementary, *accusatorial* mode of information collection – a more independent, complaint-based system, in other words. The main reasons supporting this conclusion are as follows.

First, the vast and hostile territory covered by the four inspectors poses a serious obstacle to access to the production sites.[20] Inspecting all carpet looms within a reasonable period is impossible under these conditions. Other hurdles include the difficulties attached to the identification of looms within villages as well as their inspection before and after regular office hours. A flagrant violation of the RugMark code may thus persist without any inspector having even the chance of intervening. In these circumstances, surprise inspections based on sampling procedures appear to answer a need for equality before the RugMark code more than a need for efficiency.

Second, the institutional flaws of the current regime drive potential sources of infractions outside the scope of the RugMark inspectorship. One flaw concerns the child labour *displacement effect* following a *selective registration* of carpet looms with RugMark. It has been shown that a community of weavers could very well register one (or several) loom(s) with RugMark while maintaining one (or several) unregistered loom(s) outside the purview of the RugMark code. The ensuing displacement of young workers towards such unregistered looms has created privileged and non-representative zones of direct RugMark influence, outside of which the child labour problem may be unintentionally moved. Another important flaw relates to the reputational risks incurred as a result of the non-correspondence between the series number displayed on a RugMark label and the registration number of the loom on which the carpet was produced, contrary to RugMark's official claims. In this context, a mention to the effect that the label signals the intervention of RugMark within a broader sphere of regulatory influence – as opposed to a collection of hardly traceable carpet orders – would be more likely to reassure informed consumers. And the use of external "antennas", more autonomous and decentralised, would prove necessary in this respect. Flagrant violations of the RugMark code could then be uncovered outside the more privileged zones created by the organisation.

Third, the inquisitorial mode does not lend itself well to the disclosure of internal, professional faults committed by RugMark inspectors and directors within or beyond the boundaries of their legitimate powers. Under the current regime, no victim of inspectors' negligence or zealousness, for instance, could effectively voice his complaints in seeking remedial action. Corruption and abuse of power may threaten the organisation, and although the latter finds its legitimacy in intervening in the operations of private enterprises, it does not necessarily welcome outside scrutiny of its own activities.

Fourth, the inquisitorial regime does not adequately support consideration of new facts in the course of its operations. It tends, on the contrary, to consolidate its regulatory agenda, to the exclusion of relevant facts and opinions more likely to enrich and safeguard the mission of the organisation. By contrast, a supplementary, complaint-based accusatorial system would open the door to a self-correcting dynamic fed by the influx of these novel elements. A consideration of the discrimination exercised against the Muslim and the *Dalit* communities in the administration of RugMark schools illustrates this point. Socio-religious discrimination issues are, indeed, absent from the RugMark code, and without the intervention of an outside party, it is doubtful whether they will be integrated into it. The desirability of this addition, in turn, calls upon an examination of the substantive aspects of the envisaged reform.

On the substantive level, it is clear that RugMark's regulatory system suffers principally from a lack of fundamental principles, that is, background rules intended to guide rules of a more particular nature. This deficiency manifests itself in the main zones of tension observed during fieldwork, whether within handmade carpet production units (e.g. between the interest of a parent and that of a child), more strictly domestic affairs (e.g. between the right to leisure and education, and the right to life and bodily health), or communities assembled in a village and its surroundings (e.g. the interests of the Hindu community and those of the Muslim community) (Dumas, 2015a).

Lastly, it is worth stressing the obvious point that a viable reform of RugMark presupposes that its body of rules be organised in a (minimally) hierarchical fashion. By establishing a constitutional platform for RugMark's code and operations, the current regime could, indeed, free itself from its fixed arbitrariness. A reform would require the arrangement of occasional constitutional reviews – legislative and judicial – by a constitutional board or a similar authority. In the absence of such reviews, the success of the rule-changing process contemplated above would be compromised, in the same way as state laws would remain unbalanced without the effective supremacy of a constitutional charter or its equivalent.

Implications for GAL and the ILO

Transparency is generally regarded as a key feature of GAL. In situations of legitimacy or democratic deficit, the development of GAL rests first of all on the realisation of the political ideal of accountability (Krisch, 2009). And since information and accountability are inseparable, transparency is said to occupy a central place in the set of "good governance values" promoted under GAL (Harlow, 2006, p. 199). One will have understood that a lack of transparency could, in principle, imperil or discredit the development of this body of non-state law.

Transparency may characterise not only the process of rule-making and decision-making but also, and more pertinently here, public outcomes reporting.[21] It is, indeed, from a consequentialist perspective that our research could shed light on the constraints and opportunities facing the modulation of transparency levels in the maturation of GAL. For it is in relation to the quality of a system's end results (in contrast to participation processes in the gathering of information or ideas) that we have suggested addressing relevant problems of legitimacy likely to affect the consumocratic system. In spite of the origin of the consumocratic system among non-state systems of governance, such constraints and opportunities could be re-envisaged as follows within the more sophisticated, though less sanction-oriented, framework of GAL.[22]

The primary lesson for GAL to be drawn from this research is that, under certain regulatory conditions, both transparency and opacity may serve its development positively, in line with consequentialist considerations. Perhaps paradoxically, it is suggested, too, that opacity as a regulatory tool could help consolidate GAL around the challenges of diversity and pluralism. This requires some explanation.

First, a transparency measure should not be applied within the framework of a general, blanket policy of transparency. This implies that well-designed transparency policies may require a constant search for the appropriate dosage of transparency and opacity in the diffusion of more or less context-sensitive information. For example, there are good grounds for stating that the ILO would be justified, following a pragmatic and consequentialist approach, in not drawing the world's attention to the work of some children employed under difficult (though arguably acceptable) conditions, even if apparently in breach of an ILO convention. It would be no less justified, surely, to expose state negligence towards kidnapped children engaged in forced labour.[23] In this spirit, a public report issued by the ILO could more clearly be the result of efforts to purposefully combine various shades of transparency or opacity in the presentation of data and administrative outcomes.

Second, in distinguishing between what should and what should not be revealed to the public, it is crucial, in the same vein, not to confuse the ultimate objectives of ILO action – likely universal[24] – and the means used to reach them – likely more controversial. Thus, the interdiction of child labour (i.e. a means to an end) should not be one of the decisive yardsticks against which the efficiency of government action is to be assessed by the ILO; the ultimate objective in this case is more certainly the improvement of the well-being of (working) children.[25] For, indeed, it is not certain whether the strict interdiction of child labour is always or necessarily conducive to that objective. Accordingly, an opacity measure aiming at attenuating the potentially undesirable effects (on children and their families) of an otherwise binding norm of international or local labour law is compatible here with a transparency measure designed to denounce the violation of a legal norm conducive, when sanctioned, to the improvement of children's conditions (e.g. the interdiction of forced labour through kidnapping and abduction).[26]

Third, it is often the case that behind controversies regarding the means used to accomplish ILO's mission lie differing cultural (or philosophical) conceptions of what is right and what is wrong. The debate over the interdiction of child labour is a case in point. There exists a major ideological gap separating the representations of those who consider child labour, in any form, as an abominable phenomenon, and those who more candidly regard the role of working children as "assisting" adults, in general.[27] This is worth stressing, because the quest for "good governance values" underlying the development of GAL (namely, transparency, among other "principles and values")[28] has been severely criticised for its Occidentalism and lack of regard for local diversity and pluralism (Harlow, 2006). As regards the principle of transparency, the occidentalisation thesis is founded on the assumption that it be applied uniformly, with no space for asymmetric treatment. A differentiated application of the principle of transparency in international public reports is, nonetheless, precisely what is realistically contemplated under the approach advocated above. Under this pragmatic approach, a number of polemics unfolding against the background of cultural and socio-economic diversity would more likely be subjected to relatively opaque measures. Locally legitimated cultural practices deemed contrary to (a certain interpretation of) "human rights values", under conditions to be determined by a competent authority, would thus not be condemned through official exposure, in a plausible development of global compliance measures.[29] It is in this sense that opacity as a regulatory tool could help consolidate GAL around the challenges of diversity and pluralism.

Fourth, such a modulation of transparency levels in the communication of official outcomes, in the same spirit, may require resorting to a minimalist – more functional than idealistic – human rights framework. This is arguably a condition for the ILO to benefit from possible developments in GAL, in agreement with a pragmatic approach to the difficult challenge of balancing pluralism and globalism. The ILO appears to be already *en route* towards achieving this condition. In effect, around the adoption of the "Declaration on Fundamental Principles and Rights at Work" in 1998, the ILO renounced founding its action primarily on legalistic assessments and sanctions of Convention violations; it is, instead, privileging the *promotion* of a select few and more "uncertain" labour principles and rights (La Hovary, 2009). In so doing, it seeks to promote a minimalist set of well-known "fundamental principles and rights at work", thereby establishing a hierarchy of norms among its 189 conventions.[30] Meanwhile, the ILO is changing its focus to adopt a less transparent and (even) more suggestive language in annual outcomes-reporting processes. While the organisation can be seen as attempting to smooth the passage from an asymmetrical world of rapid global integration and economic inequality towards one of "social justice" (Blackett *et al.*, 2008), it faces at least one important caveat in the process, as it is deprived of a "core convention" on the worst forms of *adult* labour. As minimalist as it may be, the new framework of fundamental principles and rights, though establishing a certain hierarchy of priorities, does so to the possible detriment of unorganised adults working under unsafe conditions.[31]

Finally, if information goes hand in hand with accountability, the significance of this premise should be clarified in light of the above. Is an organisation rendered less accountable, on the whole, by being more transparent in information gathering than outcomes reporting? What if it is compared with an organisation applying a more systematic policy of transparency? It is likely, from a deontological perspective, that the legitimacy of a more or less transparent organisation would be seriously contested.[32] And the problem is not simplified by the fact that, on a regulatory terrain occupied by several actors, what is considered fundamentally legitimate for one group may not be so for another. Not exposing the violation of a norm whose legitimacy is contested from within (e.g. by a group of regulators) poses the transparency problem in a more truly pluralistic perspective. We are invited, then, to attach primary importance to the possible difficulties deriving from the fact that organisations may have to satisfy a plurality of "legitimacy communities" and, in particular, that regulators and communities may respond in various ways to increased accountability and legitimacy demands – from defiance to acquiescence (Black, 2008). It is not denied here, either, that the accountability of a regime should ideally involve an assessment of the accountability of the outcomes of the regime as a whole (Stirton, Lodge, 2001). But it is also reaffirmed that a plurality of actors may generate contrasting messages of legitimacy and, as suggested earlier, that an appropriate dosage of transparency and opacity can help smooth difficulties raised by such diversity, however illegitimate this approach might appear from deontological angles. Revealing, perhaps, in this regard is the practice of some transnational organisations, when themselves exposed and questioned, to obfuscate these very issues.

Conclusion

Paths to improving the fate of informal young workers with the help of Indian state law face a variety of obstacles. Among them, arguably, is the balkanisation of social law in such a way as to isolate informal workers from the operations of labour laws. Whether they work for a micro-enterprise, a small family business, for themselves or without a formal contract, informal workers in India most often find themselves excluded from the scope of state labour law.[33] Such is the case of child weavers, who typically work for their parents or under similar conditions of informality.

We have suggested that consumocratic law may help overcome these difficulties, among others, by directly linking (formal and informal) production and purchasing chains. In fact, the "demand-side" character of consumer regulatory power is worth stressing in a context in which state protection measures, typically addressing the supply side of the economy, are often overruled by lobbying. This point is relevant to the extent that appropriate state intervention is lacking on the supply side of markets, that is, at the locus of production or along transnational distribution chains. The "demand-side" character of consumer regulatory power, by contrast, brings hope for informal workers and other targeted populations. Consumocratic law, in fact, provides *direct* incentives for producers to improve their products and practices along value chains and, in consequence, cannot in principle be overruled by suppliers or lobbyists. It is called on to supplement protective state law when the latter is inappropriately enforced, but also when it is inappropriately designed, whether the state is incapable or simply unwilling to protect these populations more efficiently.

Notes

1 In a remarkable analysis of the future of the ILO in the global economy, Maupain concludes that "interested governments, in the North and South both, might well be inspired to initiate the [consumocratic] scheme outside the ILO under an appropriate "orchestrator' […] this might ultimately be the best way to get the ILO involved in what may be the only plausible solution to make the 'rules of the game' really and quickly effective" (Maupain, 2013, pp. 241–242). Note that our results are based on the examination of *private* consumocratic regimes and that, in relation to international economic law, while the legal status of (government-sanctioned) *mandatory* labelling of goods differentiated on the basis of how they are produced remains uncertain under the General Agreement on Tariffs and Trade (GATT), the status of private programmes hinges more centrally on its likely impact on the targeted populations. See, in this regard, Dumas (2015a, forthcoming).
2 From *consummare* (Lat.), to consume, and *kratos* (Gr.), authority.
3 A *consumocrat* is a consumer who pays attention to the societal attributes of goods or services via societal marketing – for the well-being of others, ultimately.
4 In the works of regulatory cost–benefit analysis proponents, consumer choices do not, in fact, lay themselves wide open to bureaucratic inefficiencies, agency capture and paternalism – at least, not as openly as political action through voting does (Zamir, 1998).
5 For more details regarding the nature and operation of consumocratic law, see Dumas (2013). Legal pluralists are agreed that "'law' does not solely emanate from the state; just what it is and how it is distinguished from other forms of norm-based social ordering is still contested" (Black, 2002).
6 cf. http://www.rugmarkindia.org (hereinafter the "RugMark website") (Accessed 15 June 2015).
7 The RugMark organisation has gradually split into two disconnected networks: RugMark India and the new GoodWeave, which encompasses the entire spectrum of the former network of organisations, with the exception of the local RugMark team based in India. Since most of the facts on which this chapter is based were collected during or immediately before these changes, they will be considered to be relevant to the operations of RugMark, even though our principal conclusions also hold for the new GoodWeave. Even though the original RugMark and the GoodWeave networks extend beyond the frontiers of Uttar Pradesh (to reach Nepal, Pakistan and other parts of India), only facts collected in Uttar Pradesh are discussed in this chapter.
8 One should perhaps distinguish here between "voluntary" codes of conduct and those effectively linked to societal labelling programmes. Societal labelling was, indeed, perceived by key actors in the carpet industry as involuntary and dictated by the preferences of the buyers (cf. fieldwork notes (45C) 22 January 2007, pp. 126–127; (46) 23 January 2007, pp. 142–144; Sharma, 2004).
9 cf. http://www.rugmarkindia.org.
10 cf. http://goodweave.org/home.php.
11 RugMark website (I) (Accessed 15 June 2015). Among the four types of child labourers (i.e. family and local children – in principle targeted by RugMark schools – and migrant and bonded children – in principle targeted by the RugMark rehabilitation centre),

only family workers and local workers are allowed to both work and attend school (cf. fieldwork notes (17) 7 November 2006, p. 33; (46) 23 January 2007, pp. 142–145).

12 Fieldwork notes (51) 10 February 2007, p. 170.

13 Fieldwork notes (51) 10 February 2007, p. 169.

14 See for more details Dumas (2015b). Fieldwork was undertaken and completed with the financial support of generous fellowship plans – from the Commonwealth Foundation and the Fonds de recherche Société et Culture (Québec) in particular.

15 For instance, the Direction deplores that in matters of rehabilitation, it cannot do anything without parental consent.

16 Officially, RugMark is said to abide by Indian law in matters of labour inspection. In practice, the organisation ignores an October 2006 amendment of section 3 of the *Child Labour (Prohibition and Regulation) Act* under which any domestic child labour is forbidden. By turning a blind eye to child labour performed within a family unit, RugMark inspectors supposedly favour a non-state, "realistic" approach. A proviso to section 3 of the Act provided that the child labour interdiction "shall not apply to any workshop wherein any process is carried on by the occupier with the aid of his *family* [...]", meaning, in relation to an occupier, "the wife or the husband, as the case may be, of such individual, and the children, brothers and/or sisters of such individual".

17 A Varanasi human rights lawyer insisted in that regard that "the only thing an inspector should tolerate, in workplaces involving the presence of a learning child, is a child watching adults at work" (cf. fieldwork notes (50A) 9 February 2007, p. 162).

18 Such reactions allegedly forced the implementation of RugMark in the first place: "Intensive campaigns against the use of child labour led to a proposal to boycott the import of carpets from India. To avoid the negative consequences of such a step on workers [...] RugMark, the initiative against the use of illegal child labour in the carpet industry, was initiated in 1994 by Indian carpet manufacturers and exporters along with many leading non-governmental organisations" (cf. RugMark website (Accessed 1 June 2015).

19 See for more details Dumas (2013).

20 The core carpet belt extends to a triangle formed by the districts of Varanasi, Mirzapur and Bhadohi, and a hundred kilometres separate the marginal villages of this central region. Beyond this triangle, located in the south-east of the Uttar Pradesh State, other production centres are maintained or expanding in the states of Rajasthan, Jharkhand and Bihar, as well as in Koshambi, Allahabad and Agra, in Uttar Pradesh. Between 200,000 and 300,000 looms are scattered over a territory of 200,000 km², of which 45,000 km² are attached to the carpet belt. These estimations are based on the Indian census of 2001 and the author's fieldwork notes (#49) 2 February 2007, pp. 158, 164. See also Sharma *et al.* (2004, p. 37).

21 When affirming that its organisation "is committed to openness and transparency in all its operations, activities and decision-making processes" (Somavia, 2008), the former director general of the ILO suggested that outcomes reporting may equally be subjected to this policy.

22 It has been suggested that the frontiers of GAL be cautiously extended to the activities of some (inter/trans)national non-governmental bodies (Kingsbury *et al.*, 2005, p. 17).

23 This should be done while making sure, to the greatest possible extent, that such exposure would not trigger uncontrollable reactions from employers ready to find better caches for their young employees.

24 Universal peace through "social justice" may be viewed as the ultimate goal of the ILO. The Preamble to its Constitution opens with the following words: "Whereas universal and lasting peace can be established only if it is based upon social justice", which were restated in the opening section of the 1998 Declaration: "*social justice is essential to universal and lasting peace*". See Langille (2003) for an original re-reading of the ILO Constitution.

25 See, for instance, Meknassi (2006) for a comparable critique of "universal entitlements" in the extension of social security in the developing countries.

26 The quasi-universal acceptance of the Convention on the Worst Forms of Child Labour (Convention 182, 1999) is indicative of a closer and more efficient link, underlying this convention, between the objective in question and the means selected to reach it. To put it more bluntly, with a view to enforcing and developing consumocratic labour law, Convention 182 appears to be more useful than Convention 138 (on the minimum age for admission to employment).

27 See, for instance, Dessy and Pallage (2005) and Weiner (1991, 1998) for typical contrasting pro-work and anti-work positions. Note that pro-work authors generally point to the idea that there must be an economic change in the condition of a struggling family to free a child from the responsibility of working (World Bank, 2004).

28 Other such elements include the principle of legality and due process principles, the set of rule of law values, and other "good governance values" – such as participation and accountability – as well as human rights values (Davies, 2005).

29 It is implied, for example, that widely condemned practices, even if culturally legitimated in some parts of the world (e.g. the excision of girls, without restricting such considerations to violations of bodily integrity), would be more overtly denounced than practices less universally rejected (e.g. some forms of employment discrimination).

30 Twenty-seven of these conventions have been either shelved or withdrawn (see the ILO site at http://www.ilo.org/ilolex/english/subjectE.htm, accessed 6 July 2015).

31 See, in this regard, Alston (2004) for a rather aggressive formulation of the "anti-core rights" point of view, in which all "non-core rights" would be perilously relegated to a second-class status.

32 A deontological perspective can be defined as implying that "people are sensitive to moral duties (e.g., transparency) that require or prohibit certain behaviours, irrespective of the consequences" (Tanner *et al.*, 2008, p. 257).

33 See Routh (2014, pp. 48 *et seq.*) for a detailed examination of this question in the Indian context.

References

Alston, P. (2004). Core Labour Standards and the Transformation of the International Labour Rights Regime. *European journal of international law*, 30, pp. 457–521.

Black, J. (2002). *Critical Reflections on Regulation*. Centre for Analysis of Risk and Regulation (LSE), 1–27.

Black, J. (2008). Constructing and Contesting Legitimacy and Accountability in Polycentric Regulatory Regimes. *Regulation and Governance*, 2(2), pp. 137–164.

Blackett, A., Diller, J., and Langille, B. (2008). *The Future of International Labor Law*. Proceedings of the 101st Annual Meeting, American Society of International Law.

Davies, A.C.L. (2005). *Global Administrative Law at the International Labour Organization: The Problem of Softer Standards*. NYU Law School Seminar Series.

Dessy, S. and Pallage, S. (2005). A Theory of the Worst Forms of Child Labour. *The economic journal*, 115, pp. 68–87.

Diller, J. (1999). Responsabilité sociale et mondialisation: qu'attendre des codes de conduite, des labels sociaux et des pratiques d'investissement? *Revue internationale du travail*, 138, pp. 107–139.

Department of Labor (DOL) (1997). *By the Sweat & Toil of Children: Consumer Labels and Child Labor*. Washington DC: US DOL, ILAB.

Dumas, P.M. (2012). The Malaise of Modernity under Consumocratic Order. *Economics & sociology*, 5, pp. 75–92.

Dumas, P.M. (2013). Three Misunderstandings about Consumocratic Labor Law. *Comparative labor law and policy journal*, 35, pp. 67–92.

Dumas, P.M. (2015a). Filling the Institutional Void between Fundamental Rights and the Legal Purchase of Goods: What Role for Consumocratic Law? In Jean Allain, Ting Xu (Eds), *Property and Human Rights in a Global Context*. Oxford: Hart.

Dumas, P.M. (2015b). Thickening Soft Law through Consumocratic Law: A Pragmatic Approach. In Anne Trebilcock and Adelle Blackett (Eds), *Research Handbook on Transnational Labour Law*. Cheltenham: Edward Elgar Publishing.

Harlow, C. (2006). Global Administrative Law: The Quest for Principles and Values. *European journal of international law*, 17, pp. 187–214.

Hilowitz, J. (1998). *Labelling Child Labour Products*. Geneva: IPEC (ILO).

Kingsbury, B. (2009). *The Concept of "Law" in Global Administrative Law*. IILJ Working Paper 09-29, New York University.

Kingsbury, B., Krisch, N., and Stewart, R. (2005). The Emergence of Global Administrative Law. *Law and contemporary problems*, 68, pp. 15–61.

Krisch, N. (2009). *Global Administrative Law and the Constitutional Ambition*, LSE Working Paper Series (No. 10).

La Hovary, C. (2009). *Les droits fondamentaux au travail*. Geneva: The Graduate Institute.

Langille, B. (2003). Re-reading the ILO Constitution in Light of Recent Evidence on Foreign Direct Investment and Workers Rights. *Columbia journal of transnational law*, 42, pp. 101–113.

McDonagh, P. (2002). Communicative Campaigns to Effect Anti-Slavery and Fair Trade: the Cases of Rugmark and Cafédirect. *European journal of marketing*, 36, pp. 642–666.

Maupain, F. (2013). *The Future of the International Labour Organization in the Global Economy*. Oxford: Hart.

Meknassi, F. (2006). Extending Social Security in the Developing Countries: Between Universal Entitlement and the Selectiveness of International Standards. *Comparative labor law & policy journal*, 27, pp. 202–233.

Routh, S. (2014). *Enhancing Capabilities through Labour Law*. New York: Routledge.

Seidman, G. (2007). *Beyond the Boycott*. New York: Sage Foundation.

Sharma, A. (2004). *Child Labour in Carpet Industry*. New Delhi: IHD.

Somavia, J. (2008). *Accountability and Transparency*. Geneva: ILO.

Stirton, L., Lodge, M. (2001). Transparency Mechanisms: Building Publicness into Public Services. *Journal of law and society*, 28, pp. 471–489.

Tanner, C., Medin, D.L., and Iliev, R. (2008). Influence of Deontological versus Consequentialist Orientations on Act Choices and Framing Effects: When Principles Are More Important than Consequences. *European journal of social psychology*, 38, pp. 757–769.

Weiner, M. (1991). *The Child and the State in India: Child Labour and Education Policy in Comparative Perspective*. Princeton: Princeton University Press.

Weiner, M. (1998). *Born to Work* (foreword). New Delhi: Oxford University Press.

World Bank. (2004). *Reaching Out to the Child*. New Delhi: Oxford University Press.

Zamir, D. (1998). Consumer Preferences, Citizen Preferences, and the Provision of Public Goods. *Yale law journal*, 108, pp. 377–401.

Part III

Informal workers and their multidimensional interactions

8 Informal employment and precariousness

Where social inequality begins, and where it leads to; society and policies in Argentina, 2003–2014

Claudia Danani and Javier Lindenboim

Introduction

Latin American scholars agree that from the end of the nineteenth century through the 1970s, Argentine society stood out from the majority of Latin American countries because of its greater internal homogeneity and reduced structural heterogeneity. Comparatively, Argentina recorded greater upward social mobility (with increasing middle classes, particularly in urban areas) and a "modern" and strong labour market, and developed a system of social protection with coverage and guarantees that were superior to the average for the region (Salvatore, 2006; Danani, 2013). An early urbanisation process and the greater weight of union activity partly offset the trends of what is today known as *economic and social informality*, which is quite widespread in Latin America. All this led to a lesser level of socio-economic inequality, supported in and at the same time nourishing a shared national worldview close to that of "modern" social rights, from both the paradigm of citizenship and that of labour rights.

This path and outlook were dramatically altered towards the end of the 1970s. First came the military dictatorship (1976–1983), which launched a direct attack on institutions and on those foundations we have described; the traces left behind by state terrorism have been indelible. Subsequently, in the 1990s, although in a democratic context, neo-liberalism built up a hegemony that included an even more drastic transformation. In effect, in those years, Argentina was noted for the adoption of "Washington Consensus" policies, and the result was that labour and social institutions and policies lost their most democratic content, living conditions became more unequal and precarious for the working classes, and social life underwent a radical de-collectivisation process. In short, Argentine society lost that characteristic of relative social integration. Scholars adopting different standpoints agree with this judgement (Grassi, 2003; Salvia, 2011).

In addition, from the end of the 1990s, the gravest socio-economic and institutional crisis of "modern Argentina" (from 1870 onwards) was gestating, and it burst forth between 2001 and 2002. In these circumstances, personal and social life fell into crisis, and even the most elementary notions of "social order" were called into question. As was the case in other Latin American nations, strong criticism was levelled at the neo-liberal supremacy. Since then, a new government has changed the direction of earlier institutions and policies, beginning a process that has led policies on employment, social protection (and, in some cases, economic activity) in a contrary direction.

In view of the fact that the overall purpose of this book is to analyse the link between neo-liberalism and informality, placing workers at the centre of the debate, we propose to discuss the relationship between living and employment conditions in Argentina at the start of the second decade of the twenty-first century. In the following two paragraphs, we explain the path we have marked out in order to make a contribution to the debate proposed by the editors.

We understand that workers "shape" and simultaneously "are shaped by" social conditions. We will therefore analyse how informality has become an important feature of Argentine labour relations, connecting those social conditions with individual experiences and visions. We seek an improved understanding of the neo-liberal inheritance, dealing with the "marks" it has left on society, not just on "policies" or "institutions".

We add one more definition: although we agree with the editors' broad concept of informality, we will focus on waged workers, not on informal workers in their different kinds of activities and relationships. Our hypothesis is that in the context of "Argentine history of labour", the neo-liberal changes in the meaning and content of salaried work have prompted the rest of the transformations, mainly by attacking social rights, as an idea and in reality. We will stress the situation of workers involved in *informal labour relationships*; we mean waged workers classified as *precarious*. We define them as waged workers not included within current legal conditions, *implying their being deprived of social protection and of labour security in general.*[1]

We advance our principal corollary of the analysis: one inheritance of the era left behind by neo-liberalism in Argentina is the "institutionalisation"/naturalisation of the space occupied by labour precariousness,[2] over and above what took place with the increase in informality from low-productivity self-employment and low income. This has been due to a particular conjunction between the historical domestic situation of labour and the specific forms assumed by the transformation process of neo-liberalism. In order to advance our reasoning, we would indicate that Argentine society became urban both very early and very quickly. In fact, already in 1914, 53 per cent of Argentina's population were living in urban areas (this situation did not happen until 1950 in Uruguay and Chile; Lattes, 2000; Torre, Pastoriza, 2002). Currently, the figure for Latin America is 80 per cent, with the urban population of Argentina rising to 90 per cent (United Nations, 2014); however, it is not the current level of urban development that matters, but the fact that it took place at such an early point in history. This is a great background for our analysis.

As to the importance we assign to labour precariousness as the topic for this chapter, we understand that its growth makes evident a structural transformation in Argentine capitalism at the end of the twentieth century, with the "new normality" including a level for precarious job rates of one-third of all waged workers. It is true that this estimate of the global magnitude includes areas that have historically contained high rates of precariousness, and that these tend to be seen in most countries.[3] It must be pointed out, however, that in Argentina various forms of informal labour have continued to exist and grow, particularly in the case of precarious labour, *even in a context of economic growth and rising employment* (Bertranou, Casanovas, 2013). This makes it necessary to analyse the "new" forms of capital–labour relationships and the forms of state intervention; it involves economic, legal and political as well as cultural aspects. What kind of subjectivity is being moulded under these conditions? We strongly affirm that the existence of labour precariousness exceeds the limits of this field ("labour aspects") and moulds life experiences so that *they become normalised in "precarious lives".*

The structure of the chapter is as follows. In the following section, we describe the overall characteristics of the Argentine labour market between the end of the nineteenth century and the 1970s. This brief description serves to justify the special nature of the "Argentine case" as regards social and labour conditions.[4] In particular, we highlight: 1) the historically lower relative weight in Argentina of informality from subsistence self-employment,[5] 2) the role played by a social and labour institutionality directed at waged employment. Despite its oscillations, this institutionality was a powerful force in regulating and ensuring compliance, and a factor of universalisation beyond the waged population.

The second section presents the principal aspects of "the great neo-liberal transformation", which began to be set in motion in the 1970s and reached its supremacy during the 1990s. We will argue that the crucial transformations of the cycle are those directed to labour conditions, under unequal orientations, at a time when a battle was being waged for *the political and cultural naturalisation of that inequality.* For reasons of space, these two sections contain only a brief presentation of the topics and the major lines of historical interpretation.

The third section focuses on social and labour market conditions since 2001–2002. In it we show that despite immediate improvement in working and living conditions, a regime based on precariousness has grown in strength and has found ways of interacting with social structural functioning as well as sheltering in the cracks of political and cultural meanings.

About the origins: work in Argentina from the end of the nineteenth century until the 1970s

The origins of the labour market, the construction of the national state and the establishment of the working classes are three factors of a single process which took shape at the end of the nineteenth century. Their understanding requires awareness of the specific characteristics of both foreign immigration and the proletarianisation of the native population, in the context of what Sábato has described as "a chronic workforce scarcity" (1985). We will not develop these topics, but we take note of them.

The initial period of labour absorption by agricultural production was followed at the beginning of the twentieth century by early industrial activity, which in turn generated new demand for labour. We do not uphold economist theories, but, nevertheless, we would indicate that the relative scarcity of labour persisted and probably explains part of the lower level of social inequality, because it provided workers with more and better employment opportunities and living conditions. They were able to claim for themselves some degree of choice, seeking the most advisable positions on each occasion, and this enabled them to experience a certain upward mobility. This was the peculiar Argentine labour matrix, which had a favourable impact on both waged work and self-employment.[6] This should be borne in mind when considering the following points.

The 1940s saw the rise of the Peronist phenomenon, a real watershed as regards social and labour conditions. A protective labour legislation, referring to unionisation and conditions for ensuring formal waged labour, and an expansive wage policy were the central measures to consider during this phase. All this resulted in the extension of citizenship and the incorporation of workers into the national political community by means of the *broadening and institutionalisation of social rights*. Labour policy also included systematic inspections designed to impose penalties for the concealment of waged relations and the consequent failure to fulfil employer obligations, as well as the regulation of workforce groups with a strong influence on the total (such as rural workers).

By 1947, urbanisation had progressed, and the urban population accounted for almost 63 per cent of the total population (two-thirds were concentrated in the largest cities). This increasingly urban Argentina demanded support for *life in the cities*: transport and communication, services for homes and businesses, a commercial network, and so on. At the beginning of the 1960s, the self-employment that performed these activities was fully engaged in social life; it fulfilled two conditions: 1) as the population grew and income distribution improved, there was an expanding social demand; and 2) the service sector was highly decentralised and was able to absorb a dense network of small units (stores, household and vehicle repairs, etc.). Beccaria *et al.* (2000) indicate that those activities satisfied recognised social needs, and therefore they were not embedded as a "refuge" but in the structures. In fact, these activities became means for upward social mobility.

Although there are differences between this period and the initial one, these characteristics provided continuity to the relatively positive scenario for workers that we have described. It can be said that waged workers and the self-employed (whom some authors describe as "satisfaction" workers, as opposed to "subsistence" workers) reciprocally reinforced their advantages: first, and due to the possibility of "flight" to prosperous self-employment jobs, the former strongly defended the quality of employment and social protection. Second, the self-employed – who usually acted (for reasons that will be mentioned shortly) in semi-formal structures – recruited their customers from among waged workers, and consented to moderate income levels because they found sufficient satisfaction in their greater work freedom; they did not receive strong specific social protection, but public services (founded on citizenship) were more than "reasonable". This dynamic would explain the stability of these two segments – around 26 per cent of the urban economically active population (EAP) for the self-employed,

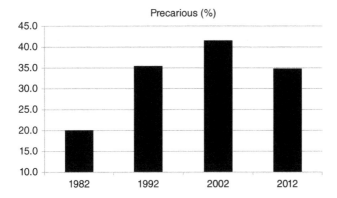

Figure 8.1 Evolution of labour precariousness as percentage of waged workers. Argentina, 1982–2012.

Source: Own estimates with data from EPH/INDEC figures. In all cases, social welfare programme beneficiaries are excluded.

and 68–69 per cent for waged workers[7] – as well as their similar levels of welfare, considered socially "satisfactory" (Torrado, 1992[8]) and adequate for social and cultural integration (on the notion of "satisfaction," see Beccaria *et al.*, 2000).

For these reasons, it would be a simplification to assimilate these conditions to those of the rest of Latin America: the non-waged jobs which characterised Argentina until the 1970s were different from the informal activities/occupations that were common in other countries in the region, and made a real contribution to the socio-economic welfare of the country.

With respect to labour precariousness, because of lack of information, little can be said. This indicates that the matter had still not been socially and politically problematised. Nevertheless, our data shows that by the early 1980s, precariousness already had a significant impact, at 20 per cent (see Figure 8.1).

Neo-liberalism, the radical change: new conditions, no rights, no protection

On both a "paradigmatic" and a "material" plane, the neo-liberal process in Argentina was comparatively acute, given that *the depth and speed of transformation were greater*. Two socio-economic areas, related to the favourable conditions for workers that we have described above, greatly changed: 1) the structure of commerce completely altered because of the spread of large retail chains in various sectors, with which small stores were unable to compete (Beccaria *et al.*, 2000); 2) manufacturing industry became more monopolistic, and there was a concentration of national income (Azpiazu, Nochteff, 1994). Simultaneously, all imaginable forms of precarious employment spread (Burchielli *et al.*, 2014). In short, the conditions that had ensured the viability of socio-economic continuity and primary social integration were completely changed. The deterioration in living conditions was evident (Lindenboim, Danani, 2003; Hintze, 2006).

This section and the next focus on the main lines of that process, and analyse what it meant for the personal and social quality of life of workers. We have been guided by two premises: 1) the neo-liberal transformation entirely altered the definition of work as a concept and as a social activity, so that workers tended to lose their recognition as valuable members of society; and 2) this new definition of work was successful because it mobilised society in that direction, achieving a natural status in the 1990s, and even today characterises the experiences of broad sectors of workers.

Furthermore, an extreme anti-statism dominated public discourse, and inefficiency, corruption and dependency were presented as intrinsic characteristics of the state. This worldview nourished the consensus in favour of the "shrinking" of the state and demands for "less state interventionism" and "rationalisation" (reduction) in public sector employment.

Elsewhere, we have stated that neo-liberalism constituted (as it still does) "an attack by capitalism on labour" (Lindenboim, Danani, 2003). This attack is not, however, the same as others, because it has generated an unprecedented concentration of global wealth[9] and new forms of commodification of labour. Here, we are interested in these forms because they sustain an "essentially private life": each individual alone is responsible for his or her life and welfare. In effect, *commodification of labour implies insecurity of livelihood.*

Regional studies show that in Latin America, neo-liberalism deepened what had traditionally been an extensive economic and labour informality, as it accentuated its function as a "refuge" (or "buffer"): a refuge against unemployment, privation and uncertainty. As we have already quoted, Monza has referred to this uncertainty as "the invention of the job" by workers themselves. However, the same author claims that during the neo-liberal hegemony, Argentina also presented differences relative to other countries: contrary to the dominant experience in Latin America, in the 1990s the rate of waged employment rose in Argentina. This means that while self-employment (mainly low-productivity self-employment) increased in the region at the expense of dependent employment, in Argentina, waged workers increased their share of the total.[10]

This process did not emerge from a "choice of alternatives", a sociological equivalent to the historical experience that has been described previously. On the contrary: alternatives declined, since self-employed activities lost part of their ability to offer improved work and living conditions. This fact encouraged the search for dependent employment, even if inferior and *precarious*. The collective memory of experience of protected waged work (requiring no investment or expense) contributed to such a strategy ... but the circumstances were very different, and dependent work became precarious, while self-employment became informal, and no longer provided the satisfaction (particularly, the acceptable level of stability) for which it had been noted.[11]. This historical process contradicts what theory indicates, leading to a worrying conclusion about the Argentine labour market: surprisingly, in the 1990s, *salaried employment acted as a "refuge" because of the reduction in and deteriorating opportunities for self-employment.* Bearing in mind this Argentine peculiarity, we will now consider the "other thread" of the "social integration" labour fabric: *waged labour.*

As we have stated, changes in the nature and conditions of waged work have been the core of neo-liberal transformation, and Argentina was noted for an increase in precariousness. We add that this process, so-called *labour flexibilisation*, was the way in which the neo-liberal concept of work became the state policy par excellence in relation to waged work. The argument is well known: rules hinder the hiring of workers because they introduce "rigidities" that threaten competitiveness.[12] *That is why the incorporation of workers into the economic process is weakened*, it is asserted.

The conclusion: legal requirements should be reduced to a minimum, the very definition of "flexibilisation". Clearly, this view coincided with the analysis by the World Bank and Peruvian economist De Soto. We, on the other hand, consider that it is always necessary to examine the content of legislation … to improve it, not to eliminate it. The proposal to reduce all regulation sends relations, conflicts and decisions into the market, which in turn is defined as a natural, impersonal and neutral space.

We are convinced that "in the market" there is but one law: *the law of the strongest.* We would add that, paradoxically, flexibilisation in Argentina took place in part along regulatory paths, since new laws were also passed: *flexibilisation became law*, even though there were already various *de facto* formats (seasonal or fixed period contracts, etc.; Marshall, 2014).

Because of both what is said in theory and the facts, we believe that all this labour remodelling prompted a strategic, long-term transformation. Why? Because, while concern and public debate spoke of "the jobs that were needed" (against unemployment) and "the needy" (against poverty), *existing work was being transformed, and flexibilisation led to precarious labour. In fact, the rise in waged work was, in effect, that type of work.*

A few figures are enough to support this interpretation: the rate of growth in precarious employment was several times higher than that of protected jobs, to such an extent that total waged jobs rose by 7 per cent as a consequence of a drop of 3 per cent in protected jobs and a rise of 10 per cent in precarious jobs. The outlook by sector was bleak: manufacturing industry lost one out of three salaried workers, almost all of them jobs with protection; waged employment in construction fell by 12 per cent, due to a 16 per cent fall in protected employment and a 4 per cent rise in precarious employment; and state sector employment increased by almost 25 per cent, based on 1.5 per cent growth in protected employment and 23 per cent growth in precarious employment. In short, employment fell by a larger proportion in the sector that traditionally accounted for most protected employment (manufacturing); it was mainly protected employment that was lost (manufacturing, construction), but, when jobs were created, there was an overwhelming predominance of precarious employment (the case of state employment; Lindenboim, 2008).[13]

These transformations were the labour side of a process of strong social polarisation, within the framework of which the middle classes (both waged and those performing "satisfaction self-employment") experienced widespread impoverishment. Kessler and Di Virgilio (2008) state that there was no return to the social integration vectors known previously: where there had been upward social mobility, channels of downward mobility multiplied; where there had been social continuity, distance was established; the aim of "halting the decline" displaced expectations of progress. The conviction grew that it would be impossible to successfully re-establish professional or commercial activity, or rise materially and symbolically in a worthy salaried position.

"Don't be a loser" was an instruction that pertained to the state's social protection systems, because neo-liberalism enshrined the notion that demand for protection was a sign of failure. The new rule was that "the successful manage on their own". As a result, social and labour life became distant, *and precariousness became culture.* Grassi has said that the decade was guided by the idea that people needed work "at any price, and in any condition" (2003). This statement became common sense and was *embodied in social practices that meant a lack of protection and an extended ignoring of rights.*

Indeed, the state was an essential actor of this process, since it issued rules leading to precariousness, and led the way in their application to its own personnel. Any reader can recognise how similar this process is to others around the world, although different paths can be seen: from the "typical" Russian case analysed by Bizyukov in this book, to the labour reform in Spain, or the so-called co-co-co (*Contratti di Collaborazione Coordinata e Continuative*) in Italy (for Latin America, see Marshall, 2014). In the next section, we will deal with the process of "normalisation" of labour precariousness and its consequences for the quality/inequality of life in these years.

Lights and shadows in the 2000s: a rare mix between "new" and "old"

It is well known that Argentina entered the new century in the midst of a crisis that was both deep and widespread, which paralysed democratic institutions and caused a collapse in economic and social life. More than 20 per cent of the EAP were unemployed, and almost half the population were below the income poverty level. Two years later (2003), official figures indicated that unemployment had fallen to 17 per cent. The same sources inform us that this rate was under 10 per cent of the EAP in 2013–2014, years in which it can be assumed that poverty declined significantly from those high levels.[14] Although it is difficult to determine an exact figure, it can be estimated that between 2003 and 2007 over two million jobs were created, mainly for waged workers; even more importantly, other private sources calculate that up to 2010, 81 per cent of the growth in employment was accounted for by registered waged workers (Damill *et al.*, 2011). Nevertheless, this process is facing major limitations, the most significant of which is the fact that labour precariousness, although down by 11 percentage points, still affects one-third of all waged workers (28 per cent of the workforce). Another figure that points in the same direction is that in 2012, 61 per cent of poor homes recorded a head of household in employment, an indication that this alone is insufficient to escape from poverty (Barrera *et al.*, 2013).

Below, we briefly describe some of the policies carried out to date; our proposal is to analyse how they contributed to creating jobs that have both adequate conditions of quality and protection, and social recognition. In doing so, we follow the premise that the role of "economic policies" in the reduction or increase in employment may be controversial, but the reduction or increase in precarious employment cannot be understood unless specific policies on labour are analysed. The reason for this is that in every period, regulatory and institutional measures and public action in general actively make conditions feasible for protected or precarious work. From this viewpoint, we consider that the creation of jobs that are largely protected during these first years expresses the efficacy of labour policies as opposed to the previous flexibilisation. This idea is compatible with what international literature indicates: sustained growth processes generate conditions that favour a reduction in precarious employment, but they are not sufficient, since specific policies are required to address this point (Marshall, 2014).

Regarding the relationship between labour and living conditions, we consider that precarious labour is the greatest threat to workers as a general and broad social category that includes different kinds of positions and relations (not only, but mainly, in Argentina). When we observe specific conditions, we see that the process becomes nuanced.

As indicated, the proportion of precarious work dropped from 43.8 per cent of waged workers in 2003 to 33 per cent in 2014 (the abovementioned 11 points; Figure 8.2). Nevertheless, when we observe the number of persons in that condition, the improvement is relative: at the beginning of the period there were 4,200,000, and in 2014 there were 4,300,000 (Figure 8.3), so the number has continued to increase. Even more disquieting is the fact that the undoubted social and labour improvement was halted in 2007: from then on, job creation has been weak, with almost no variation in precariousness or poverty levels.

How to explain that evolution? The first point of this history is that three presidents followed in quick succession between December 2001 and February 2002. The situation stabilised one year later (April 2003) with the holding of national elections, won by the Peronist candidate Néstor Kirchner. Observing the first condition of our premise (that is, the object of the economic conditions and policies), we underline that already in 2002 a series of policies, with a different orientation from those that had been carried out during the 1990s, had begun to be implemented in various areas. Combined with a favourable international context, these measures showed positive results: an asymmetric devaluation halted indiscriminate imports, encouraging the rebirth of the manufacturing structure, followed by firm growth of employment. This economic and employment growth prompted improvements in domestic demand (Lindenboim *et al.*, 2011).

When considering the second point of the abovementioned premise, we have to focus on social and labour policies. As the new social policies covered more of the population and expanded benefits, and the latter tended to regain a content of social rights, elsewhere we have defined this process as a counterreformation

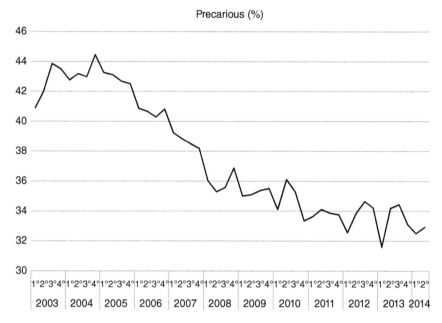

Figure 8.2 Evolution of labour precariousness as percentage of waged workers. Argentina, 2003–2014.

Source: Own estimates with data from EPH/INDEC figures. In all cases, social welfare programme beneficiaries are excluded.

("contra-reforma"; Beccaria, Danani, 2014)[15]. In the case of labour policies, flexibilisation was abandoned and the "normality" of registered and termless employment with employer obligations was re-established. In addition, new rules and mechanisms were introduced to combat labour fraud, and legislation was passed to protect worker groups that had historically been affected by high precariousness (domestic and rural workers). All this was backed by a public discourse that was full of explicit criticism of neo-liberal policies.

These policies are very advanced in their specific areas and represent a substantial change in relation to neo-liberalism, but if our premise is conceptually correct, as is the historical reconstruction, how can we interpret the continuing existence of one-third of waged workers in a precarious condition?

There are several explanations, and some of them may coexist. The first is that economic and fiscal policies have retained, rather than challenged, certain neo-liberal traits. These policies have boosted domestic demand and consumption, but the structural transformation from the neo-liberal era has not been removed (e.g. economic concentration, finance capital predominance). This implies that social and labour institutions and policies that renew their content in terms of rights coexist with previous (neo-liberal) economic orientations. How do they interact? Which prevail? In reply, we can state that a new public discourse – even new legislation – is insufficient to reverse individualisation,

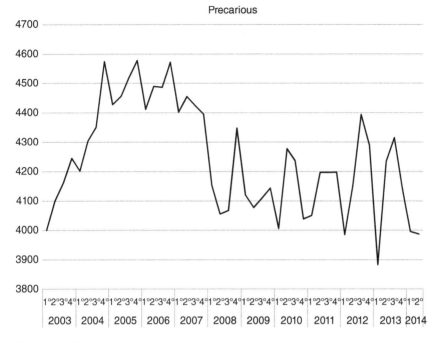

Figure 8.3 Evolution of labour precariousness, number of urban waged workers. Argentina, 2003–2014.

Source: Own estimates with data from EPH/INDEC figures. In all cases, social welfare programme beneficiaries are excluded.

inequality and precariousness. As we have said, these neo-liberal characteristics have become "normal".

Furthermore, in our opinion, at the heart of the process of transformation experienced by Argentine workers is a new configuration of social practices and values. Rubén Lo Vuolo has proposed a worrying hypothesis referring to the whole of Latin America, asserting that egalitarian policies fail in this region because they are not credible, and are therefore unable to gain the support of the population. According to his analysis, this situation derives from a long period of inequality that has become naturalised over time, to which has been added the recent neo-liberal experience that swept away even the most modest pretence of equality (Lo Vuolo, 2005). It can be said that we are facing a "self-fulfilled prophecy": societies mistrust egalitarian policies because they do not consider them to be capable of ensuring order. This mistrust has, in turn, become a source of "egalitarian inefficacy" that reinforces inequality. If this is the case, egalitarian initiatives must begin by overcoming this belief, a condition for gaining a genuinely democratic legitimacy in a substantive manner.

Our premise opens up other conjectures as we re-read the charts: are we facing a new threshold for precariousness on which Argentine capitalism will have based itself in the post-1990s? Can this case be interpreted as part of the global transformation of capitalism, as the editors and Bizyukov point out in this volume? If so, is it reversible? Or are we facing a society with high levels of tolerance or *accord* in relation to such precariousness and the inequality it represents? We strongly adhere to the idea that registering 32 per cent of labour precariousness over a long period without some tolerance by society is impossible. In Argentina, precariousness has become a culture that circulates by routes that remain almost invisible. The population, as well as institutions and policies, celebrate the reduction that has been achieved, but dismiss the idea of going forward, considering it to be impossible. We follow Routh and Fassi in not excluding any approach or any answer: dealing satisfactorily with our preoccupation with the neo-liberal legacy demands inclusion of factors both structural[16] and sociocultural. Moreover, they reinforce each other, since persistent precariousness shapes the subjectivity of workers, basing their experiences and strategies on a weak expectation of stability and protection, a factor that undoubtedly feeds the predominance of global concentrated capital and the most regressive social practices. The following analysis helps to observe the current structure and forms of work as well as providing a better understanding of the process analysed so far, which shows some important records.

On the one hand, the activity rate rose significantly in the early 1990s and showed little variation during the next decade. On the other, employment and unemployment rates behave in a complementary way: falls (recoveries) of the former are offset with increases (decreases) in the latter. As can be seen in Figure 8.4,

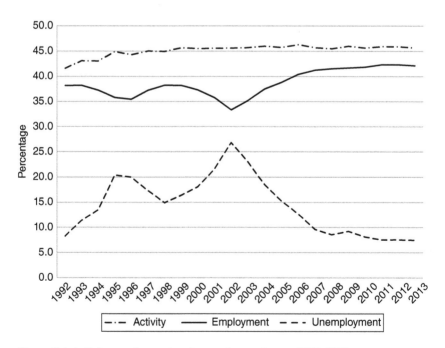

Figure 8.4 Activity, employment and unemployment rates, 1992–2013.

Source: Jaccoud *et al.*, 2015.

the drop in the unemployment rate and the growth in waged (protected) work cannot be attributed to a fall in the employment rate.

During the same period, the evolution of employed workers, especially waged workers, has been peculiar. Waged workers slightly increased their participation in the labour force, but the numbers of protected and precarious workers evolved in different ways, as is shown in Figure 8.5.

On the one hand, the number of protected waged workers varied negatively in the 1990s, and after the 2002 economic crisis, a percentage of them became precarious workers. On the other hand, precarious workers took an active role in the 1990s, but after 1998, they also reduced their number. After 2003, the increasing number of precarious workers resulted from the rise in GDP and labour demand, until it achieved definitive absolute and relative values some years later.

So far, we have attempted to present a general view of the process of deterioration, underlining the articulation and co-determination between structural and cultural processes (the constructions of meanings and values, because identities and subjectivity are forged in their folds). We now complete this analysis stage by considering the current scenario, which we will, for the moment, take to be the arrival point of the process we have analysed. See the composition of the labour force in 2003 and 2013 (Figure 6a and b).

In fact, the composition of the employed workers, as shown in Figure 8.6a and b, shows some changes, but none of them is definitive. First, the heads of household plan beneficiaries (*Plan jefas y jefes de hogar desocupados*) who were considered as employed workers are not included. Some of these beneficiaries could have become precarious workers (and many of the precarious workers could

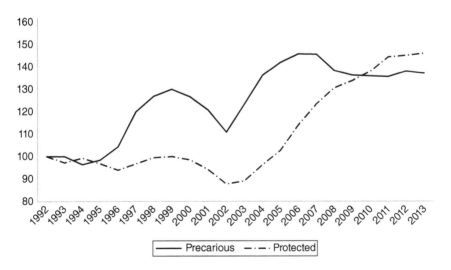

Figure 8.5 Evolution of protected waged workers and precarious waged workers.

Source: Jaccoud *et al.*, 2015.

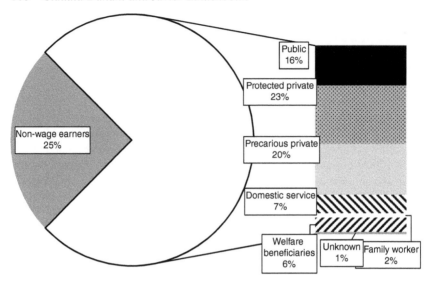

Figure 8.6a Workforce composition. Argentina, 2003.

Source: Own estimates with data from EPH/INDEC figures.

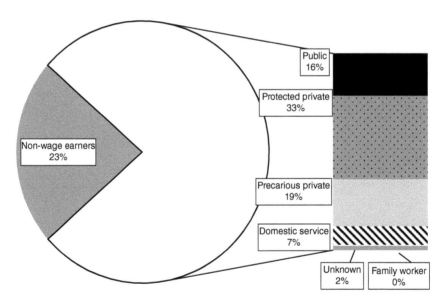

Figure 8.6b Workforce composition. Argentina, 2013.

Source: Own estimates with data from EPH/INDEC figures.

have become protected). Moreover, the weight of the self-employed and public employees has not changed substantially.

The most significant aspect to be underlined is that for approximately five years (2003–2007) Argentina experienced a recovery with high growth (6–8 per cent of cumulative GDP), and its labour structure has not changed substantially. Clearly, that growth enabled the largest drop in unemployment, reduced the precariousness index and created employment, but the main aggregates are quite similar, and precariousness has stabilised around 30 per cent. This deserves some reflection.

First, a significant number of small and medium-sized enterprises (SMEs) were successful in exiting the crisis dynamic, and they have provided the main demand for workers. Nevertheless, this stratum also hosts the largest proportion of labour precariousness; it is well known that there is an infallible inverse relationship between the size of the establishment and the proportion of "precarious employment". The Argentine case is no exception.[17]

But we also assert that we face two extreme processes: on the one hand, the social and economic crisis of 2001–2002 (an experience that was profoundly destructuring) and on the other, the rising social and economic cycle from 2002 onward, which ensured that in barely five years numerous groups reorganised basic aspects of their lives (jobs, incomes, etc.). In our view, these two extreme circumstances, which were very close in time from the perspective of personal life, collaborated with a relaxation of the willingness and collective capacity of co-responsibility to ensure correct social functioning and "sound practices". Conditions are, therefore, very different from those of the 1990s, but the memory of that dislocation made it vitally "reasonable" to accept work "at any price and on any terms". *The point is having a job.*

In short, "crises are opportunities" … for inequality, as only a few can take advantage of them. Indeed, the opportunities are quite different, and that is why, when life depends on the possibility of obtaining employment, earlier aspirations and demands tend to get left by the wayside.[18] Our information shows that the income gaps between protected and precarious workers are not only persisting but still increasing during the post-crisis years: in fact, in 2014, protected workers receive double the salary of precarious workers. This suggests that conditions favouring structural heterogeneity and social distance continue and strongly and negatively affect living conditions. This matter reinforces our concern regarding increasing inequalities.

As a result, our premise remits us to the socio-political and cultural contents that we have already mentioned and that has enabled us to speculate on the political and cultural path we have just outlined. On this path, labour precariousness is the complex result of economic, institutional and social conditions, broadly considered. In that regard, in some sense we agree with Kessler and Di Virgilio's idea of a "point of no return" for the old vectors of Argentine social integration. We believe that the current institutional and political reconstruction of social rights do not automatically recover a more democratic sociability. Both our idea and the analysis of Kessler and Di Virgilio contradict the government's view and discourse.

We therefore believe it is necessary to debate and explicitly and publicly problematise collective life. At the core of this debate should be strong recognition of work as a public issue. This recognition means that society should accept responsibility for the existence, distribution and quality of employment. Certainly, in modern societies, this requires the mediation of state institutions and policies that reinforce compliance with protective rules; breaking them should be considered the most serious of faults.

The weak public status currently assigned to labour is at the basis of behaviour that has become increasingly widespread in recent years and justifies failure to comply with regulations if there is a risk of company failure. In the context of the "recovery", these arguments have acquired a certain legitimacy by pointing out that small business owners "provide employment" to those who otherwise would lack a livelihood. Worse still, it is disturbing to find that often the precarious workers themselves express the desire to gain stable employment with contributions to social security; but they consider this desire is unlikely to be fulfilled because their employers, "despite their own efforts", will not meet their obligations. The building of the public nature of work, on the other hand, implies exposing these worker experiences to collective and public vigilance, because the more the idea of work is confined to that of "the market", face-to-face relations and the "needs of the subjects", the more workers tend to consider their own labour relations as "private". Accepting this kind of practice implies internalising the trickle-down theory in the labour field.

Certainly, large firms have a leading role in the strengthening of the public condition of the social and labour field. According to the data we have indicated, open and direct precariousness is not a feature of this segment. Nevertheless, they have great responsibility for this problem, because they transfer to small and medium-sized businesses not only part of the costs, but also the risk (economic and labour risk) and social conflict. Undoubtedly, this is the core of the transformations that lead to outsourcing, productive decentralisation and externalising, and these are processes that have made precariousness a permanent feature of the age (Basualdo, Morales, 2014). As Marshall has frequently stated, Argentine trade unionism has a debt because of its passivity in relation to small companies;[19] it has also been indifferent to the diversified outsourcing strategies of big business. No other sector possesses the means of the powerful Argentine unionism and its ability to perform systematic inspections. Nevertheless, this has not happened.

The active (justified and justifying) acceptance of failure by employers to comply with rules; the resigned acceptance of instability and lack of job protection of workers; and, in many cases, the passivity or acquiescence (even complicity) of union organisers: these are the three social practices that demand to be reversed. This calls for criticism and genuine alternatives "from within and from below" and long-term commitments, capable of giving way to a new, more desirable and ethically complete labour normality.

Conclusions

In the Argentine case, new socio-economic conditions at global level, added to a new political and cultural environment and worldview, have broken up the mutually reinforcing interaction between the various categories of workers (waged workers, the self-employed and even informal workers). The result has been a situation of increased competition in order to obtain a better job. It has weakened the position of all categories of workers: precarious waged work persists (and grows), and self-employment loses its ability to provide satisfaction. Both paths favour the rise and growth of various categories of vulnerable informal workers.

This occurs even when policies are implemented that extend protection to precarious waged workers and workers in the informal sector. These policies are insufficient: contexts in which the social recognition of workers has deteriorated require complex interventions that simultaneously address legal, redistributive, political and cultural aspects. This implies building a new social commitment and renewing the sociability pact, mainly around waged work and compliance with labour laws, understood not as bureaucratic mechanisms but as basic agreements of respect for coexistence and social protection. In this chapter, we have attempted to show that in Argentina the basis for the existence of a reasonably cohesive and less unequal society has been seriously harmed. That is the most negative legacy of neo-liberalism.

Notes

1 See Bizyukov about the ambiguity that reigns between precarious and informal employment.
2 By "space of precariousness" we refer to *the structure of social relations that serves as a framework for such precariousness, which is itself a social relationship.*
3 For example, domestic work and construction represent one-sixth of waged employment; nevertheless, together they account for one-third of all unprotected waged workers.
4 Standing (2011) contributes in clarifying the concept itself and also the general historical process of increasing precariousness.
5 Monza (2000) indicates that one of the traits of "informal subsistence labour" is that the worker generates the occupation. We will repeatedly return to this concept.
6 We believe that the "refuge employment" for self-employed workers or self-employment is not suitable for this period.
7 These dates correspond to population census years.
8 The percentage missing to complete 100 per cent corresponds to the "upper class", without differentiation between self-employed and waged, and the "unknown" remainder.
9 In January 2015, Oxfam International published figures prior to the Davos Summit: in 2014, 1 per cent of the population accounted for 48 per cent of global wealth.
10 Between 1992 and 2001, the percentage of waged employment rose from 72 to 74 per cent (Graña, Lavopa, 2008).
11 Qualitative surveys show that labour transitions from self-employment to waged employment were experienced as declining social mobility (see Belvedere *et al.*, 2000).
12 Williams and Martínez deal with this viewpoint and discourse carefully and deeply. See also La Hovary's chapter: she analyses how World Bank and diverse authors argue in the sense of "protecting competitiveness".
13 Precarious employment indicator: "unregistered labour" (waged workers from whom no pension contributions are deducted). Source: EPH/INDEC databases, excluding social plan beneficiaries.
14 The National Institute for Statistics (INDEC) was subjected to intervention in January 2007. Since then, methodological and institutional changes of all kinds have been introduced, causing deterioration in the quality of public statistics, so we make selective use of them here. Since 2013, INDEC has no longer provided information on poverty indexes, as a result of which calculations range between 5 per cent (official) and 15 per cent (private estimates). See Lindenboim (2011).

15 Routh and Fassi describe the most important social and labour policies related to this process.
16 One of the factors could be the model provided by SMEs: we will show below that, being subordinated to concentrated capital, they work with a negative impact on the labour sector as regards quality of employment.
17 La Hovary analyses legal and socio-economic conditions of informal labour according to company strata. Our focus is more specific (precarious waged work).
18 Esping-Andersen (1990) gives a suggestive example by comparing people to washing machines.
19 The author refers to the "traditional" unions (representing formal waged workers). Excluded are organisations of informal workers, dealt with by Routh and Fassi.

References

Azpiazu, D., Nochteff, H. (1994). *El desarrollo ausente*. Argentina: FLACSO/Tesis Norma.
Barrera, C., Fernández, A., Manzanelli, P. (2013). *Trabajo y pobreza: virtudes y desafíos de la posconvertibilidad*. CIFRA. Mimeo.
Basualdo, V., Morales, L. (Eds). (2014). *La tercerización laboral: orígenes y claves en América Latina*. Argentina: Siglo XXI.
Beccaria, A., Danani, C. (2014). El sistema previsional entre la transformación y la normalización, 2003-2013. In C. Danani, S. Hintze (Eds), *Protecciones y desprotecciones (II): la seguridad social argentina, 2010-2012*. Buenos Aires: Universidad Nacional de General Sarmiento.
Beccaria, L., Carpio, J., Orsatti, A. (2000). Argentina: informalidad laboral en el nuevo modelo económico. In J. Carpio, E. Klein, I. Novacovsky (Eds). *Informalidad y exclusión social*. Argentina: FCE/SIEMPRO/OIT.
Belvedere, C., Carpio, J., Kessler, G. (2000). Trayectorias laborales en tiempos de crisis. In J. Carpio, E. Klein, I. Novacovsky (Eds). *Informalidad y exclusión social*. Argentina: FCE/SIEMPRO/OIT.
Bertranou, F., Casanovas, L. (2013). *Informalidad laboral en Argentina*. Argentina: OIT.
Burchielli, R., Delaney, A., Goren, N. (2014). Garment Homework in Argentina: Informal and Precarious Work. *The economic and labour relations review*, pp. 1–18.
Damill, M., Frenkel, R., Maurizio, R. (2011). *Macroeconomic Policy for Full and Productive Employment: Argentine Experience*. Argentina: OIT.
Danani, C. (2013). El Sistema de protección social argentino 2002-2013: el modelo que nunca tuvo. *Revista Uruguaya de Ciencia Política*, 22, December, pp. 145–170.
Esping-Andersen, G. (1990). *The Three Worlds of Welfare Capitalism*. Cambridge: Polity Press-Basil Blackwell.
Graña, J., Lavopa, A. (2008). 15 años de Encuesta Permanente de Hogares, 1992-2006. *Documento de Trabajo CEPED N° 11*. August.
Grassi, E. (2003). *Problemas y políticas sociales en la sociedad neoliberal*. Argentina: Espacio Editorial.
Grassi, E., Alayón, N. (2004). Neo-liberalism in Argentine. In I. Ferguson, M. Lavalette, E. Whietmore (Eds). *Globalisation and Social Work: Perspectives from the Left*. London: Routledge.
Hintze, S. (2006). *Políticas Sociales argentinas en el cambio de siglo*. Argentina: Espacio Editorial.
Jaccoud, F., Monteforte, E., Pacífico, L. (2015). Evolución del mercado de trabajo en la posconvertibilidad. In J. Lindenboim, A. Salvia (Eds). *Hora de balance. Argentina, 2002-2014*. Buenos Aires: Eudeba.

Kessler, G., Di Virgilio, M. (2008). The New Urban Poverty: Argentine Dynamics during the Last Decades. *CEPAL Review*, 95, pp. 31–50.

Lattes, A. (2000) Población urbana y urbanización en América Latina. *II° Jornadas Iberoamericanas de Urbanismo*, Quito.

Lindenboim, J. (2008). *Trabajo, ingresos y políticas en Argentina.* Buenos Aires: Eudeba.

Lindenboim, J. (2011). Las estadísticas oficiales en Argentina. ¿Herramientas u obstáculos para las ciencias sociales? *Trabajo y Sociedad*, 16, pp. 19–38.

Lindenboim, J., Danani, C. (2003). *Entre el trabajo y la política. Las políticas sociales argentinas en perspectiva comparada.* Buenos Aires: Eudeba.

Lindenboim, J., Kennedy, D., Graña, J. (2011). *Share of Labour Compensation and Aggregate Demand. Discussions towards a Growth Strategy.* Paper 203. UNCTAD.

Lo Vuolo, R. (2005). *La credibilidad de la política económica.* Argentina: Miño y Dávila.

Marshall, A. (2014). *The Incidence and Structure of Flexible Employment in Latin American Countries.* 35th Annual Meeting of the International Working Party on Labour Market Segmentation. Manchester: EWERC.

Monza, A. (2000). La evolución de la informalidad en el área metropolitana en los noventa. In J. Carpio, E. Klein, I. Novacovsky (Eds). *Informalidad y exclusión social.* Argentina: FCE/SIEMPRO/OIT.

Sábato, H. (1985). El mercado de trabajo en Buenos Aires, 1850–1880. *Desarrollo Económico*, 24 (96), pp. 561–592.

Salvatore, R. (2006) Stature Growth in Industrializing Argentina, 1916-1950. *XIV International Economic History Congress.* Helsinki.

Salvia, A. (2011). De marginalidades sociales en transición a marginalidades asistidas. In C. Barba, N. Cohen (Eds.). *Perspectivas críticas sobre la cohesión social.* Argentina: CLACSO/CROP.

Standing, G. (2011). *The Precariat. The New Dangerous Class.* New York: Bloomsbury Academic.

Torrado, S. (1992). *Estructura social de la Argentina: 1945–1983.* Buenos Aires: De la Flor.

Torre, J., Pastoriza, L. (2002). La democratización del bienestar. In J. Torre (Ed.) *Los años peronistas (1943-1955).* Buenos Aires: Sudamericana.

United Nations. (2014). *World Urbanization Prospects. The 2014 Revision.* New York: United Nations.

9 Precarious employment in Russia

A form of degradation in labour relations

Petr Bizyukov

Introduction: informal employment in Russia?

This chapter explores the phenomenon of *precarious employment* in the Russian economy and its implications for the system of labour relations in Russia. As the different chapters in this volume show, this phenomenon is global; experts articulate it across the world. In Russia, this problem has particular resonance due to the manner in which labour relations evolved historically. In Soviet times there was only one form of employment – state-controlled formal employment. Informal employment, i.e. work outside the framework of an employment contract, was perceived as criminal. Several generations developed their ideas about labour during this period, and many of these people continue to be active today. Even after the collapse of the Soviet Union and the transition to a market economy, employment in the formal sector was considered to be the norm.

Discourse about employment has been very slow to change, and the Soviet understanding of employment lingers on, even though the Soviet economy with its full employment disappeared over 25 years ago. In Soviet times, it was impossible to lay off workers because of an enterprise's bankruptcy or because of the need to downsize personnel – that would have been deemed illegal and unfair. At that time, dismissal of a worker was limited to two situations – either he/she had violated a law or he/she decided to quit.

The market reforms introduced in 1991 shocked most Russians. Workers were thrown into a new environment characterised by unemployment, non-payment of wages, plant closures, and the absence of opportunities to work in the formal economy. This new reality was largely a consequence of the hasty neo-liberal reforms. The authors of the market reforms, led by Russian President Boris Yeltsin and Prime Minister Yegor Gaidar, had hoped that "the invisible hand of the market" would quickly establish order and put everything in its place.

Instead, the Russian economy experienced a huge downturn, and the population faced falling living standards. People did not simply lose their jobs; they lost all means of survival. Even those who retained their jobs went without pay for months, forcing them to seek additional work or a new job that provided at least some income for survival. In such circumstances, if someone was lucky enough to find a job that paid anything, he/she was very unlikely to worry about whether or not the work was legal or whether or not the labour contract corresponded with the law.

At this time, workers developed a new attitude towards working "without papers". Working off the books came to be seen as unavoidable and a way of avoiding unjust taxes. But people retained the idea that in a normal situation, employment should be executed according to the law, labour contracts should be signed, salaries paid on time, and so on. However, by this time, employers refused to return to the former system of labour relations as defined by law. They understood the economic benefits of using informal labour and refused to relinquish it. Neo-liberal ideas about "flexible labour" fell onto well-prepared ground. Formalised labour relations were seen as excessively rigid and inconsistent with the spirit of the market, hampering business and unreasonably increasing labour costs. "The more persistently the state tries to tire out the labour relations in the Procrustean bed of standard employment, ... the lower is the competitiveness of the economy" (Gimpelson, Kapeliushnikov, 2006).

Today, informal employment is a large-scale phenomenon that characterises the work of millions of Russians. As was true previously, there is no exact data on the number of people working without a formal employment contract. Experts cite various statistics about the number of informal workers. In 2013, Russian Deputy Prime Minister O. Golodets said that the government has no information concerning the work of 38 million of the 86 million people of working age.[1] Later, she explained that according to the state statistics agencies, 20 million people are employed in the informal economy. Other experts give more conservative estimates (Gimpelson, Kapeliushnikov, 2014); they claim that 7.6 million people worked in the informal sector in 2012. But regardless of their quantitative estimates, all the experts note the sharp increase in the number of informal workers after 2000. Against the backdrop of this huge amount of informal employment in Russia, the following section reflects on the theoretical issues involved in the debate.

Theoretical discussion: not standard employment?

Recently, Russian experts have been actively discussing employment issues. Obviously, the attributes of formal labour relations – open employment contracts, fixed time schedules, predetermined salaries, and employee participation in labour relations through collective agreements – are no longer universal. Such a question implies that in addition to "standard employment", there are other forms of employment that have come to be known as "non-standard employment".

The simplest approach is to consider anything outside of standard labour relations to be non-standard employment. That was the approach followed a few years ago by the best-known Russian authors in this area, V. Gimpelson and R. Kapeliushnikov. They defined standard employment as "full-time employment on the basis of a termless contract at an enterprise or organization under the direct management of the employer or a manager appointed by it. In most countries this 'standard' is reflected in legislation in some manner". Then, moving from this definition, the authors define non-standard employment thus: "All forms of employment (and labour relations) deviating from the above standard, can be considered as non-standard" (Gimpelson, Kapeliushnikov, 2006).

Thus, non-standard employment is presented as a negation of the norms of labour law. The inadequacy of this approach is demonstrated by the following example. One of the characteristics of non-standard employment is employment on fixed-term labour contracts or civil contracts (so-called contractual agreements). But these forms of employment are stipulated in Russian legislation. They are completely legitimate, although their application requires a number of conditions.[2] Moreover, considering the situation as it evolved over time clarifies the shortcomings of a definition based on a negation of legal standards. For example, in 2006, the Labour Code was amended to expand the scope of fixed-term contracts. After these changes, what had previously been illegal became legal, and therefore forms that had belonged in the sphere of non-standard employment became legitimate, standard employment.

"Informal employment" would, in this context, seem to be a more appropriate term. It is used widely by state statisticians, government authorities and many experts, who consider the evolution of this term in detail (Gimpelson, Zudina, 2011) and note a plurality in its usage. But even a detailed analysis based on multiple sources does not provide a clear definition. The authors come to consider not only "informal employment" but also another concept – "sources of informality". Using this approach, they identify several sources that influence employment and one of its forms, which is called informal employment.

One source is simple self-employment, which occurs when the state cannot guarantee work to those who need it. A second is the emergence of the informal business sector, which is a reaction to the over-regulation of the economy and corruption. As a rule, small, private, unregistered companies operate in this sector, and all personnel work informally. A third source is an overabundance of rules, prompting entrepreneurs to cease to comply with them and begin to operate informally.

However, research requires precise definitions, which identify the subject matter of the study exactly. In the best-known and largest-scale Russian study on employment[3] (Household Survey on Employment (LFS), which is held on a monthly basis by official statistical agencies), informal employment is defined as follows: the informally employed include "persons who, during the survey period were employed in at least one production unit of the informal sector, regardless of their employment status and of whether or not this was their main job or secondary employment".[4] The informally employed include:

- "people engaged in entrepreneurial activities without having formed a legal entity or on an individual basis, regardless of whether they have registered with the state as an entrepreneur;
- people working in rural (farming) holdings that are not registered as legal entities;
- people providing professional or technical services (doctors, notaries, auditors, and others), irrespective of whether they have registered with the state as an entrepreneur without a legal entity;

- people providing paid services in the home (maids, guards, drivers, governesses, babysitters, cooks, secretaries, etc.);
- people who are employed by individuals or individual entrepreneurs;
- people employed in the household production of goods or services, including agricultural, forestry, hunting, fishing and fish processing, if the product will be sold."[5]

The publication emphasises that "workers involved in informal relations in production facilities that are legal entities are not included in the informal sector and are considered separately".[6]

The above definition illustrates that the use of the concept of informal employment is associated with a number of methodological difficulties, primarily due to the criteria selected to determine informality. According to this definition, the absence of official registration of the employer would make all employees informal. But, those working without a contract for a registered employer would not be classified as informal. Consideration of those who "work on the basis of a verbal agreement without paperwork" shows another aspect of this problem – "informality" is not only a question of where a person works; it is also a question of the manner in which the employment is processed or documented. Strictly speaking, these two criteria – (1) work in informal enterprises, and (2) undocumented work in formal official enterprises – have become the main justification for considering employees to be informally employed. But, as always happens when a complex and multidimensional phenomenon is described using simple criteria, the resulting simplification does not enable one to describe the totality of the object of the study.

Evidently this difficulty caused R. Kapeliushnikov to propose an alternative approach to quantitative estimates of informal employment (Kapeliushnikov, 2012). He suggested identifying several groups of criteria and analysing these groups separately. For example, one group might include those who do not have a formal contract, and another those receiving wages "under the table" with no taxes being paid.[7] Subsequently, an attempt is made to identify the manner in which these groups of workers who "differ in their informality" relate to one another.

O. Sinyavskaya takes a different approach to defining informal employment (Sinyavskaya, 2005). She tries to depart from the definition of informal employment in the manner of documenting employment in one or another sector of the economy. She bases her approach to the study of informal employment on the definition provided by E. Feige, a well-known American researcher on the informal economy. He wrote that "the informal economy comprises those economic activities that circumvent the costs and are excluded from the benefits and rights incorporated in the laws and administrative rules covering property relationships, commercial licensing, labour contracts, torts, financial credit and social security systems" (Feige, 1990).

In other words, here the informal economy is defined as economic activity outside the institutional framework, with the departure from institutional regulation explained by a desire to avoid paying the costs required for operations within the institutional system. However, this approach does not provide an easy path to a definition of informal employment either. Informal employment here is defined as follows: it "covers all forms of paid work, employed and self-employed, that are not formally registered and, therefore, not included in the enterprises' statistics by tax agencies, not subject to regulation and not protected by existing legal or regulatory structures" (Sinyavskaya, 2005). In this definition, little remains of the idea underlying E. Feige's approach – that this is not just an activity that has not been formalised. More importantly, the informality is a means to save money. Against the backdrop of these different definitions, the following section discusses the nature of the relation that exists between informality and precariousness.

Informality and precariousness

There are still a number of phenomena that are difficult to assess unambiguously in terms of formalisation (or informalisation) of relations. An example is the phenomenon of partial under-the-table wages, i.e. when an employee is officially employed and receives part of his/her wages in compliance with the rules and regulations. But at the same time he/she receives some wages unofficially with no payment of taxes or contributions to state social benefit funds. These unofficial wages can account for as much as 90 per cent of an employee's earnings. How does one characterise this worker's employment? On the one hand, he/she is formally employed and has a documented salary; on the other hand, a large part of his/her salary and, consequently, the volume of his work, working hours, relations with superiors, etc. will be determined by an informal arrangement. Such an arrangement is made primarily to avoid taxation, i.e. to evade the institutional system of regulation.

Preoccupied with untangling the system of standard labour relations, labour unions take a different approach to the issue of informal employment. They define it by listing characteristics associated with informal forms of employment. For example, informal or *precarious* employment is associated with fixed-term, sequential or informal contracts covering activities outside the normal hours of work, when workers are paid less. And sometimes unions simply enumerate the labour conditions that they consider to be precarious. For example, these conditions include the following (ILO, 2011):

- low wage;
- low level of protection from termination of employment;
- direct recruitment on temporary contracts – for a particular job or for a fixed term;
- lack of access to the mechanisms of social protection, benefits and allowances, traditionally associated with full-time employment;
- lack or limitation of opportunities for workers to realise their rights in the workplace.

The listing of these multiple forms illustrates that here, too, there are no clear and unambiguous criteria to distinguish those who work in standard employment from those in informal or precarious employment. As a result, the effects of deviations from standard employment relationships started to appear as an additional important characteristic of non-standard employment. (Lyapin *et al.*, 2007; Bizyukov *et al.*, 2012). It was not just about the lack of permanent employment and hiring without guarantees of continuous work; nor was it just about low pay. It was about the worst hiring conditions and discriminatory pay levels, putting such workers in conditions far worse than those of workers employed in standard conditions. In other words, *precarious employment began to be considered as employment that worsens the position of the worker*.

However, not all forms of informal employment worsen the situation of workers. For example, many freelancers are working on the basis of sequential agreements, or even on the basis of oral agreements. But not only do they not perceive any hardship in such arrangements; they see any attempt to bring their activities into conformity with standard employment practices as a clear worsening of their situation. And it is not only highly paid freelancers who do not want to work within the frameworks of labour standards – there are other categories of workers who have no desire to become highly skilled and land high-paying jobs. They want to work a little bit for low wages, just to maintain their status as working people. Therefore, it is accurate to say that *not all informal labour relations are perceived by workers as worsening their position.*

Once again, the issue is where to draw the line. How does one categorise, for example, a situation in which an employee is hired on the basis of a verbal agreement and works unregulated hours, but receives a high or very high salary? Looking at the parameters used to define precarious employment, only one condition of precariousness or informality is not met here – i.e. low wages. Does the correlation of the job's characteristics with those listed in the definition give sufficient cause to classify this work as precarious employment? I will explore this through my case study.

Research description

The present review of definitions demonstrates that the answer to the question of the precarious plight of workers will not be found in the formal characteristics of the workers. It will be found in what determines the nature of the worker's employment, in what makes an employment standard, non-standard or precarious. We are talking about *labour relations, i.e. the system of relations between workers and employers concerning inclusion in the labour force, the conditions in which work will be carried out, terms of dismissal, as well as opportunities for mutual regulation of these relations*. In this context, the basis upon which labour relations are built is of fundamental importance. It is obvious that the standard employment relationship is founded on labour law, and the interactions of workers and employers are based in a framework of social partnership. Non-standard – especially precarious – labour relations are arranged differently and must have some other foundation.

The research "Studying the practices of regulation of labour relations in the conditions of precarious employment" attempted to determine the specific configuration of labour relations that makes the system of labour relations, and consequently the employment of workers, precarious.[8] The purpose of the study necessitated the undertaking of the following details in order to address the research problems.

First, it was necessary to obtain information about the system of non-standard employment relationships, which includes workers in various industries and sectors of employment. Second, it was necessary to identify both differing and consistent practices of recruitment, methods of remuneration, hours, including overtime, regular paid holidays and vacation time, disability payments and other benefits. Third, it was necessary to determine the reasons for the inclusion of workers in labour relations that deviate from the standard, to determine the features of the social position of employees participating in such a system of relations. This set of tasks could only be undertaken within the framework of a qualitative methodology, which presupposes a broad study of the entire context of labour relations in which employees are involved.

Since the object of this study was employees who are directly involved in labour relations of this kind, i.e. *who do not have an official, indefinite employment contract*, the people interviewed work on the basis of:

- official fixed-term employment contracts;
- official civil contracts covering a certain scope of work (contractual agreement);
- unofficial, including verbal, agreements.

Additionally, experts were interviewed, i.e. people who are not in non-standard employment relations but have information about how they arise and are regulated. First of all, these experts were *union representatives* – leaders of local organisations and heads of regional, sectoral and federal structures. In addition, interviews were conducted with *employers* who are experienced in organising and managing workers working under non-standard conditions and with *representatives of regional authorities* responsible for the regulation of labour relations. In total, 45 people were interviewed (33 employees, 12 experts).

The main method used was that of free focused and expert interviews. During the research, a series of in-depth focused interviews of workers were carried out. Workers were divided into two groups. In the first group were workers with *low and medium job potential, working in conditions that are associated with precarious employment* – migrant workers, agency workers, temporary workers, etc. The second group consisted of employees with medium and high job potential who work outside the sphere of standard employment – creative professionals, freelancers, specialists, etc.

In the study, it was important to ensure regional and sectoral diversity. The surveys were conducted in the following regions: Chuvash Republic, Kemerovo oblast, Omsk oblast, Samara oblast, Moscow, St Petersburg, Leningrad oblast

(Kingisepp) and Krasnodar kray (Yeisk). Interviewed employees worked in the machine-building and metallurgical industries, the food industry, services, culture, journalism, construction, education and research.

Hiring

In exploring this issue, it is necessary to understand how the living employment "contract" between an employee and an employer relates to its formal reflection in a document called an "employment contract". An understanding of the existence of the two agreements – one on paper, and the other verbal – was provided by those interviewees who had a formal, written agreement. Some of the respondents had no contract and worked only on the basis of verbal agreements. The role of formal employment contracts for workers surveyed was insignificant: at best they only know of its existence, and its content has no meaning for them. Official employment contracts act *as screens* that hide the real agreement.

From the interviews, it became clear that there are two forms for real agreements on employment: the *established order* and *arbitrary agreements*. *The established order* means a certain consistency in conditions. Workers receive the same wages and work under the same conditions. A radio journalist says: "… I was hired on the radio. Fixed salary, worked for seven hours per day, five days a week. But I had no employment contract; it was only an author's contract [type of contractual arrangement]. Some shifts started at five o'clock in the morning until noon. But I had no additional pay for night work, on weekends or holidays. I had no sick leave, no vacation. It was not just me, everyone who does not have a permanent contract …."[9]

When an employee leaves, another will take his/her place, under the same conditions as defined in the framework of the "order". In fact, these are *standard labour relations, but the standards are not taken from the law, they are designed by the employer, in accordance with his interests, and applied*. Of course, these standards allow the employer to avoid "costs" dictated by law (taxes and state benefit contributions) and to manipulate workers and their labour.

The second type of non-standard arrangements can be called *arbitrary agreements*. In such agreements, unique conditions and parameters are specified for each employee, for each stage of work, and for each project. Sometimes *arbitrary agreements* are *negotiated* and sometimes they are *dictated by the employer unilaterally*. This is the most flexible form of work contract, and the manner in which they are concluded is very important.

Arbitrary agreements that are *negotiated* between employees and employers are executed *between economic agents or economic partners*, who are not allowed to infringe upon each other's interests. As a rule, the workers are desirable because of the high or very sought-after special qualifications. The greater the potential of an employee, the more he/she is involved in the formation of working conditions. For example, "freelancers" almost completely control their work conditions, defining the most important parameters themselves. A freelance designer talks about his work: "At the same time I realize two or three projects.

Usually I have a stock of orders for the future. If the project is unprofitable or not interesting to me, I refuse it."[10]

The second kind of arbitrary agreements differs sharply from that described above. There is no possibility of coordinating interests; the employer dictates whatever conditions he/she considers beneficial for him/herself. This "here and now" agreement is based on whatever resources the contracting parties do or do not possess. This practice is based on *complete domination by the employer*. Such an arrangement can only be called an agreement because the employee, for whatever reasons, agrees to abide by it. His/her active role ends there; subsequently he/she only obeys. Such practices are especially effective in relation to socially weak categories of workers – migrants, the disabled, low-skilled workers, those desperate for work of any kind. These practices do not differ significantly from forced labour. Under these agreements, conditions may change "as needed"; the employer may fully or partially abandon its obligations, and a worker cannot influence either his/her position or the situation as a whole.

These agreements are short-term in nature. Through the interviews, it became clear that even weak workers in desperate need are not always able and/or willing to work in such conditions. Foreign migrant workers said in an interview: "I've been looking for a job. Friends said there is a job in a warehouse. Chief hired me without any documents. I worked how many will say, and at the end of the day the salary was paid. Three months we worked, then came a new head and lowered salaries. But I normally despise this situation ...."[11] Unable to defend their interests, they have only one option – to leave at the first opportunity (when they have found another job, even if it has very few attractions) or as conditions demand (when the situation becomes threatening).

Labour paths of precarious workers

As part of the study, workers were asked to describe the path that had led them to the system of precarious labour relations. Most people followed one of two paths. *The first – descending labour mobility –* forces the person to accept any job. They do this in order *to stop the "slide" into poverty*. As a rule, these are experienced workers with a history of long-term employment who are victims of external structural changes in the economy or adverse changes in their personal lives. These people include external and internal migrants; people who have received specific but no longer needed qualifications; and people who have had a serious illness, become disabled, have sick relatives, etc. Their decision to enter into precarious labour relations, with which they are well acquainted, looks like a responsible economic decision. Their main goal is to begin work on any terms, gradually try to improve the situation and, eventually, get a "normal" job, one that has standard conditions. Such a path could look like this: *a military officer, communications specialist with high qualifications – low-ranking supervisor (foreman) in a commercial company – employee of a municipal utility company – handyman – junior partner electrician – self-employed electrician on call.*[12]

The second type of path can be described as *adaptation*. It involves finding places that, in the employee's opinion, allow success and, above all, provide money. These are young and middle-aged workers with little history of employment. They have never worked in standard labour relations; they participate in precarious labour relations because they do not know any others. Some of them – those who have adapted to the conditions of precarious employment – may express satisfaction with their situation and may have some savings. However, they are well aware of the instability of their position: a clerk strikes out your name, tariffs change, or a new boss decides that your job or you personally are no longer needed. Normal life disappears into a catastrophe without any hope of protecting your job, your income or your position. An adaptive path could look like this: *locksmith – master at the plant – rolling mill operator – massage therapist – small businessman (food trade) – a specialist in recycling of non-ferrous metal scrap – small businessman (metal trade) – electrical installer.*[13]

Almost all employees believe that work within a standard employment relationship is better. However, there is one feature that allows employees to evaluate precarious labour relations as normal. This feature is social myopia, i.e. the unwillingness or inability to look to the future. The absence of taxes and state benefit contributions from wages will eventually turn these workers into poor retirees, and lack of vacation, sick leave and regulated overtime work inevitably leads to health problems. Since they are constantly at work, people lose the ability to participate fully in the lives of their families, and young people lose their chances to create families. People basically are pushed out of the system of social relations. They cease to lead a life with culture, do not participate in the local community, and are apolitical. Existing within the labour standards set by the employer becomes the most important aspect of their lives.

Regulation of working hours

The study of regulatory practices of work and rest time provides information about several variants of the organisation of work time. The first variant is *the employer's complete refusal to determine the work time of employees*, i.e. a regime of "unlimited work time". Instead, workers are controlled through the results of their labour. In this case, the employer is freed from the need to control the amount of effort required of workers, including the time required to achieve the necessary result. In the framework of standard employment conditions, the situation is different, with the value of the "result" negated by the cost of unlimited labour time. By refusing to control time, and controlling through results, employers shift responsibility for success from themselves to the worker. More precisely, the employer removes his/her responsibility for determining optimum methods of work. If the number of hours worked is of no concern, then the employer does not need to determine the optimal technological basis – equipment – for the work. The less an employer is responsible for the workers, the greater the opportunity for relinquishing control over working hours and relying on control through results.

The other extreme is an employer's introduction of *maximally rigid regimes*. The interviews point to several variants of the manner in which a rigid schedule of working hours is implemented in precarious labour relations. First of all, this *schedule exceeds the norm of working hours established by law*. For example, a shift extends for 12 hours with infrequent and short breaks. A Russian worker who found a job in another town (an internal migrant) describes his work schedule: "We work from 7.30 am to 8.00 pm. On Saturdays and Sundays, we are working for 6 hours, up to 2 pm. We have only one break for lunch at noon, for 45 minutes."[14] A second variant of the rigid schedule is *work specifying normal working hours, but with mandatory overtime*. Needless to say, this overtime does not involve additional wages, and it is impossible to refuse.

Another variant involves the use of *flexible work schedules*. Flexible schedules do not have fixed start and stop times for the working day, but they maintain its overall duration. Or employees may be required to choose a more convenient regime of fixed working hours; for example, they might work only in the morning or in the afternoon. Flexible schedules contain an element of negotiation with an employee and may seem like compensation for low wages. The option of regulating work time in a flexible schedule is available only to employees with high qualifications.

The issue of work time should not be considered separately from the *regulation of rest time* and, above all, of paid vacation. In some cases, this relational consideration simply does not make sense, for example in the case of day labourers. But the more common situation is that in which an employee receives approval to take time off work but does not receive any money for that time, i.e. the employee takes a vacation at his/her own expense.

Wage system

The wage system used in precarious labour relations is very simple, almost primitive. It is determined within the framework of a verbal agreement, dominated by simple, sometimes primitive time rates – hourly, daily or monthly. Such a system is primitive because there is no clear means of accounting for working hours. The standard monthly rate includes a fixed number of days in the month, and each day has a fixed number of hours. In precarious relations, it is unclear how many hours one is required to work in a day – eight or twelve – and the daily calculation of pay will be the same regardless of the length of the work day. The same situation applies to the monthly rate. The daily or monthly rates are more symbols of an approximate period of time, rather than a quantitative measure of labour, as is the case in standard relations. If work is evaluated by the final result, payment is stipulated as a *fixed sum of money receivable upon completion of the work*. This system does not take into account the number of people working, what they actually did or how long they worked.

The primitive approaches to payment are defined by the manner in which people are hired. In the case of verbal agreements, without a written text, it is difficult to detail a complex system that reflects an employee's qualifications and the duration and quality of his/her work. Wage levels are determined by the parties' capacity, their ability to bargain, and competition on the job market. But in the absence of rules and institutions necessary to evaluate the activities of both workers and employers, bargaining is often spontaneous. Employees may try *pulling wool over the employer's eyes* by claiming qualifications that they do not have. An employer may assign tasks that would normally require resources and capacity that do not exist. Mutual dishonesty generates payment *with a squint*, i.e. approximate, leading to competition between those who *pretend to pay* and those who *pretend to work*.

Avoiding *approximate* wages can be achieved in only one manner – standardisation of payment terms. The task should take into account the availability of materials and equipment, the workers' qualifications, etc. Adequate and fair payment for work should be determined by the duration, complexity, functionality, quality and timing of the work, i.e. on the basis of standards that require carefully designed wage and bonus systems that specify a value for quantitative and qualitative work. But it is not enough to develop the payment system; it must be negotiated with the workers, and this implies a dialogue between the employer and employees.

Within the framework of precarious and unilaterally defined labour relations, job evaluation is made not on the basis of the quantity and quality of expended labour, but on the basis of a spontaneous and situational determination of the parties' market potential. In this situation, the employer – as the holder of financial resources, as the party with decisive influence on the formation of labour relations – is interested in minimising the social potential of workers and seeks to render them incapable of advancing their interests. The employer's position is characterised by intolerance towards any activity by workers to defend their labour rights.

As a result, employers aspire to a maximum lowering of wages. The advantages of employing poor people are not limited to their preparedness to work here and now for any fee in any conditions. Poor employees are a strategic advantage – continuous poverty restricts access to education, to training, and to civil and legal culture. This guarantees that there will always be socially weak people who are ready to work for mere peanuts and upon whom it is possible to impose unfavourable conditions of employment.

Benefits package and sick leave

Modern labour relations cannot be reduced to an economic interaction between workers and employers involving a simple exchange of labour for money. They must include an element of "humanism"; they should have the imprint of "human relations". This is especially true in Russia, where workers have traditionally received large bonuses from companies in non-monetary forms. This practice led to so-called economically unjustifiable things such as regular paid holidays, paid sick leave and the existence of a social package, i.e. a system of benefits and privileges granted by employers to their employees in addition to salary.

Although paid vacations and sick leave continue to be required by law, the social packages are not, and these require the voluntary consent of both parties. These social packages are very popular at those enterprises and organisations that adhere to standard employment relations. They are a sign of the humanisation of labour relations.

Precarious labour relations are completely dehumanised. Benefits packages, as a form of caring for workers, are completely absent. Moreover, within a single enterprise there may be some staff members with benefits packages, but their colleagues, excluded from the standard system of labour relations, do not have access to these packages. This unequal access once again emphasises the discriminatory nature of precarious employment.

The situation is no better in regard to sick leave. In many cases, there simply is no sick leave. If a day labourer falls ill, he/she may lose his/her job in addition to missed wages. There is no provision for such leave. If a worker is employed on a continuous basis and falls ill, he/she may be able to take sick leave, but it will not be paid. Within the framework of precarious employment, the right to sick leave and rest is provided in its most minimum form. Employees may be able to take time off work, but they will not be paid for this time. And they are allowed very little sick leave. It is not possible to avoid illness, but a long convalescence is impossible, as you may lose your job.

Regulation of labour relations

Russian employers are in a very uncertain situation too. Economic instability, legislative chaos, corruption and many other external factors require that entrepreneurs exhibit maximum adaptability, honing their ability to change/adapt to external conditions. It is understandable that employers try to require their employees to exhibit the same adaptability. But, in the absence of constraints such as legal standards and strong trade union movements that are able to ensure compliance with established rules, ideal conditions for despotism arise. Many employers delay or cut salaries not only because they are in a difficult financial situation, but also because they believe workers have no effective mechanisms for control and counteraction. Moreover, the law provides workers with no tools for exercising control when employment is structured in a form other than formal labour relations. In the case of precarious labour relations, dissatisfied employees have only one option for action – leaving that place of employment. They do not have the option of working to normalise the situation. The logic that flows from an employer's diktat does not lead to any normalisation. If one side of the relationship (the employer) has the right to arbitrarily set standards in their own interests, those standards are *normal*. Any attempt to change them is perceived as a destructive activity – a riot – aimed at destroying the entire system.

Therefore, employers who create their own labour standards in the place of legal standards respond to disagreements with employees with a universal principle of conflict resolution – *if you don't like it, leave!* This principle may seem rude, but it is the only reasonable principle for settling disputes in a unilaterally regulated system of relations. Our study results show that workers agree with the value of such a system. Conflicts between workers and employers in precarious labour relations do not happen. Understanding all the shortcomings of their position, workers see that they have only one way to resolve a conflict – they endure as long as possible and leave when the situation becomes unbearable. Employees have accepted the "if you don't like it, leave!" principle as normal. It is the only means by which they can regulate labour relations in precarious employment. The clerk of a small trading company notes: "I can't have a conflict because it means a rupture of relationship with the employer. In that case, I will be unemployed. I will keep the main thing – my job. And if I can find another job, I immediately turn around and leave."[15]

Conclusion

Consideration of the above-cited practices highlights the main feature of precarious labour relations in Russia. Precarious labour relations are those that are unilaterally generated by the employer. The employer's main goal is to use any means available to minimise labour costs. This is achieved in two ways: first, they ignore the requirements of labour legislation and other institutional controls that limit employers' ability to be arbitrary; second, the situation supports the employer's dominant position in relation to the worker and excludes the possibility of workers' participation in forming and regulating labour relations.

The degree to which precarious labour relations and, consequently, precarious employment can be considered in any way better than non-standard employment depends upon the level of agreement sought by the employer with his/her employees when forming the parameters of labour relations. The more dialogue used in relations between employers and employees, the less precarious are the employment and relations.

Many experts in Russia highly value labour relations that reject norms and standards and are free from institutional regulations. These experts propose that labour standards hinder employee initiative, prevent the real emancipation of labour, and limit economic freedom. Rejecting standards and moving towards informality are considered to be breakthroughs towards a new, more progressive reality.[16] However, our study of actual non-standard and precarious labour relations suggests that there has been no breakthrough towards freedom.

A similar position is taken by C. Williams, J. Round and P. Rodgers. In their study of the informal economy in the post-Soviet world, they suggest that the emergence of informal economy and informal work is a natural process, breaking the Soviet monopoly on formal employment (Williams *et al.*, 2013). They do not assess the informal economy as a marginal option, but accept it, and see it as an alternative to the rigid formal system, which will make the situation more diverse and variable. It would be possible to agree with this. But our research shows that the framework of precarious labour relations has not prompted a shift in favour of new principles that ensure development, help employees realise their potential and improve the efficiency of their labour. The practices currently being used hark backwards in time to those used in the pre-industrial era, i.e. in the late nineteenth and early twentieth centuries.

Precarious employment is far from a harmless phenomenon that affects only direct participants in labour relations. The spread of unilaterally regulated labour relations leads to *withholding many socio-economic values*, such as the importance of labour-free time for a decent life, the need for remuneration that corresponds to the quantity and quality of labour expended, and the need to humanise labour relations. The denial of these values and attempts to "soften" established labour standards weaken and dismantle social institutes that not only regulate employment relations, but also form the basis for the socio-economic life of society.

Unfortunately, currently in Russia precarious employment is expanding. As yet, nothing has effectively counteracted this trend. Trade unions are not involved in this problem; they are focused instead on regulating standard employment relations. Authorities resemble outside observers, unable or unwilling to limit the spread of precarious labour practices. G. Standing labelled those people who participate in precarious labour relations the "precariat". He considers such people to constitute a new, dangerous class (Standing, 2011). Precarious labour relations are spreading rapidly in Russia, and the number of workers affected is growing accordingly. The Russian precariat are people who, living in the twenty-first century, have been transported back in time over 100 years. For them, this period is not a transition from socialism to modern capitalism; it is a return to the pre-socialist era.

Notes

1 Labour Market Doesn't Leave the Shadows (Rynok truda ne vyhodit is teni), *Nezavisimaya Gazeta*, 068(5832), 4 April 2013.
2 Trudovoy Kodeks Rossiyskoy Federatsii [Labour Code of the Russian Federation], 2001. Sobranie Zakonodatelstva RF, 7 January 2002, No. 1, Art. 59.
3 Federalnaya slujba gosudarstvennoy statistiky. Obsledovaniye po problemam zaniatosty. (Federal State Statistics Service. Household Survey on Employment). http://www.gks.ru/wps/wcm/connect/rosstat_main/rosstat/ru/statistics/publications/catalog/doc_1140097038766 (Accessed 31 August 2015).
4 Metologicheskiye polojeniya po provedeniyu obsledovaniya naseleniya po problemam zaniatosty (Methodological Guidelines for Conducting Population Surveys on Employment). http://www.gks.ru/bgd/free/B99_10/IssWWW.exe/Stg/d030/i030110r.htm (Accessed 31 August 2015).
5 Ibid.
6 Ibid.
7 In accordance with Russian legislation, employers are required to pay the state taxes from the wages of workers, in particular income tax.
8 This research was carried out by the NGO "Center of Social and Labour Rights" CSLR (Moscow) by order of the Moscow branch of the Friedrich Ebert Foundation in 2012–2013.
9 Interview conducted in July 2012, in Moscow, Russia.
10 Interview conducted July 2012, in Cheboksary, Russia.
11 Interview conducted September 2012, in St Petersburg, Russia.
12 Interview conducted August 2012, in Eysk, Russia.
13 Interview conducted September 2012, in Samara, Russia.

14 Interview conducted September 2012, in Omsk, Russia.
15 Interview conducted August 2012, in Samara, Russia.
16 In 2010, representatives of the main employers' association of the Russian Union of Industrialists and Entrepreneurs (RUIE) proposed to overturn a number of limitations in the Labour Code. It was proposed to increase the working week to 60 hours, arbitrarily change the conditions of the employment contract and eliminate restrictions on temporary contracts, among others. Discussion of this initiative can be seen in the article by E. Gerasimova, "Order revolution" (Zakaz na revolutsiyu) / Gazeta.ru, 18 November 2010. http://www.gazeta.ru/comments/2010/11/18_a_3439245.shtml (Accessed 31 August 2015).

References

Bizyukov, P., Gerasimova, E., Saurin, S. (2012). *Agency Labour: The Consequences for Employees*. Moscow: CSLR.

Feige, E. (1990). Defining and Estimating Underground and Informal Economies: The New Institutional Economics Approach. *World development*, 18(7), pp. 989–1002.

Gimpelson, V., Kapeliushnikov, R. (Eds). (2006). *Non-Standard Employment in the Russian Economy (Nestandartnaya zanyatost v Rossiyskoy economike)*. Moscow: HSE Publishing House.

Gimpelson, V.E., Zudina A.A. (2011). *"Informal" in the Russian Economy: How Many and Who They Are? ("Neformaly" v Rossiyskoy ekonomike: skolko ih I kto oni?)*: preprint WP3/2011/06, National Research University Higher School of Economics. Moscow: HSE Publishing House.

Gimpelson, V., Kapeliushnikov, R. (Eds). (2014). *In the Shadow of Regulation: Informal Employment in the Russian Labor Market (V teni regulirovaniya: neformalnaya zanyatost na rynke truda)* Moscow: HSE Publishing House.

ILO (2011). *From Precarious to Decent Work. Policies and Regulation to Combat Precarious Employment*. Geneva: ILO.

Kapeliushnikov, R.I. (2012). *Informal Employment in Russia: What Tell Alternative Definitions? (Neformalnaya zaniatost v Rossii: chto govoryat alternativnyie opredeleniya?)*: preprint WP3/2012/04, National Research University Higher School of Economics. Moscow: HSE Publishing House.

Labor Market Doesn't Leave the Shadows (Rynok truda ne vyhodit is teni). (2013). *Nezavisimaya Gazeta*, 068(5832), 4 April 2013.

Lyapin, A., Noinhoffer, G., Shershukova, L., Bizyukov, P. (2007). *Precarious Employment and Its Consequences for Workers (Neustoychivaya zanyatost I posledstviya dlya rabotnikov)*. Moscow: CSLR.

Metologicheskiye polojeniya po provedeniyu obsledovaniya naseleniya po problemam zaniatosty (Methodological Guidelines for Conducting Population Surveys on Employment): http://www.gks.ru/bgd/free/B99_10/IssWWW.exe/Stg/d030/i030110r.htm (Accessed 8 October 2015).

Sinyavskaya, O.V. (2005). *Informal Employment in Modern Russia: Measurement, Scale, Dynamics (Neformalnaya zanyatost v sovremennoy Rossii: izmereniye, mashtaby, dinamika)*. Moscow: Pomatur.

Standing, G. (2011). *The Precariat. The New Dangerous Class*. London: Bloomsbury Academic.

Williams, Colin C., Round, J., Rodgers, P. (2013). *The Role of Informal Economies in the Post-Soviet World: The End of Transition?* London: Routledge.

10 The urban informal sector in Africa

New players, solidarity economy and socio-aesthetic transformations in Cameroon

Alioum Idrissou

Introduction

Studying the informal sector in Africa – and in Cameroon – is tantamount to outlining its importance and impacts, both on the economy and on society at large. It is also important to determine the prerequisites on which our discourse would be based with regard to definitions, operational concepts, and other related notions in the domain. In this chapter, from an empirical point of view, the aim is to explain, on the one hand, the context of the emergence and interactions of new players in the informal sector in Yaounde, the political capital of Cameroon, and on the other, the issue of Cameroon's alignment with globalisation, through the implementation of private strategies and other innovative alternatives deployed by these actors to adapt to this new reality, in a bid to achieve permanent resilience.

Several studies and surveys have focused on the informal sector in Africa. However, out of this plethora of relevant publications, the collective work by Nancy Benjamin and Ahmadou Aly Mbaye titled *The Informal Sector in Francophone Africa: From Size, Productivity and Institutions* has served as a compass for this chapter, for two reasons. First, the mentioned book chooses to base its empirical approach on three West African urban cities, Dakar, Cotonou and Ouagadougou, political capitals of the Francophone countries of Senegal, Benin and Burkina-Faso, respectively. Second, apart from being political capitals, these towns share similar economic characteristics and behaviours to those of Yaounde, which is the geographical focus of this study (Benjamin, Mbaye, 2001).

From a statistical point of view, studies carried out in about ten Sub-Saharan countries (excluding South Africa with 50 per cent) in the 1990s show that the informal sector accounts for between 70 and 90 per cent of non-agricultural jobs (Charmes in ILO, 2002). Less than a decade later, it was established that in Cameroon, about 90 per cent of jobs are in the informal sector (NIS, 2005, 2011a), thus corroborating the major role played by the informal sector in the national economy. Furthermore, the first survey conducted in 1993 that focused exclusively on Yaounde concluded that 60 per cent of informal activities were carried out in Yaounde and Douala, a figure that was scaled down to 49 per cent by the 2005 survey (Fouoking, 2009, pp. 240–241). This is, therefore, a study targeting a city that produces at least one-fourth of all informal activities in Cameroon.

So far as the existing literature is concerned, studies and surveys have been undertaken in various domains of the informal sector in Cameroon (Fouoking, 2009, pp. 237–261; Amougou *et al.*, 2009, pp. 130–200; Backiny-Yetna, 2009, pp. 91–108; Cogneau *et al.*, 1996, pp. 27–63; NIS, 2006, 2005, 2011a, 2013). However, these works have not often paid attention to the atypical players who operate in this field, especially on the strategies deployed by these players to address or adapt to difficulties encountered. While focusing on the non-agricultural informal sector and more specifically on services in an urban area, this study also aims at assessing the level of organisation and the resultant empowerment of targeted actors, in a bid to modify the existing socio-urban relationships.

With regard to the methodology, specifically in the research field, the survey has targeted 10 activities performed by actors of the urban and non-agricultural informal sector: barbers, food sellers, car washers, book sellers, tailors, street vendors, cobblers, photocopying machine operators, call boxers or airtime retailers, and commercial motorbike riders. The aim is to broaden our scope in furtherance of making relevant comparisons. Concerning the technique used to collect data, the choice of a simplified questionnaire was obvious, since the idea is to make a descriptive mapping of these activities and actors. So, this simplified questionnaire was structured around items such as age, gender, marital status, years of study, property, number of years spent in the activity, number of working days per week, number of working hours per day, salaries, membership in one or more intra-professional solidarity groups, payment of taxes, and registration with the social insurance. The total number of respondents stands at 540 actors, including more than 50 *commercial motorbike riders* and *call boxers*, who are the main targets of this study. In addition to this purely quantitative approach, I also adopted a qualitative approach that consisted of interviews with officials in the administration and in the formal private sector, as well as civil society leaders. These data have naturally been compared with those contained in available literature on this topic, namely, studies carried out by the Cameroon National Institute of Statistics. Participant observation was also used, and it has enabled me to refine the findings and analyses made. The details follow.

Descriptive and analytical mapping of informal sector actors in Cameroon

Informal sector, informal activity, informal economy, and informal employment are words and expressions used to generally refer to activities which are complex to codify. To avoid this difficulty, some authors talk of the *informal sector* as an active entity that can be defined in a unique way. Historically, in its terminology and significance in Africa, the concept of the informal sector was characterised in the early 1970s, especially depending on the size of activity and lack of official declaration (Hart, 1972). This understanding was also adopted by the International Labour Organization in 1993 and in 2002 (Benjamin, Mbaye, 2012, p. 2). In the 2005 employment and informal sector (EESI) survey in Cameroon, "any company without a taxpayer number or that is subject only to the basic tax system or fixed rate income tax, but lacking a bookkeeping compliant with the OHADA system is said to be informal" (Amougou *et al.*, 2009, p. 132).

According to Nancy Benjamin and Ahmadou Aly Mbaye, the informal sector can be characterised using six criteria: "size, registration, honesty of accounts, fixity of workplace, access to credit and tax status" (Benjamin, Mbaye, 2012, p. 28). Therefore, the same authors declare that "informality is better described as a continuum defined by a combination of criteria" (Benjamin, Mbaye, 2012, p. 25) showing the limitations of using each of the criteria defined above in isolation. In the same light, the choice of multiple criteria to define the informal sector has also been preferred by Guha-Khasnobis and Kanbur, according to whom "defining informal employment, give prominence to the absence of social security coverage, rights to vacation, written contracts, low levels of revenue, lack of affiliation to workers organization, unstable work conditions, and the illegal or quasi-illegal nature of the firms" (Guha-Khasnobis, Kanbur, 2006, p. 26). Furthermore, this remark is equally true to various degrees of the formal sector "in terms of different characteristics such as nature of registration, payment of taxes, management structure, contractual arrangements with employees, market orientation etc." (Benjamin, Mbaye, 2012, p. 25). When we combine the different approaches, it goes without saying that the informal sector in Cameroon can only be characterised and operationalised by taking into account a mix of criteria. Specifically, for the urban and non-agricultural informal sector – activities which are our focus here – the following criteria could be applied: non-compliant bookkeeping, lack of contracts, absence of registration with a social security institution, and the absence of liability to fixed rate income tax. In fact, they are small individual production units.

The institutional distribution of jobs in Cameroon is represented schematically in Table 10.1.

We can derive at least four trends from the above employment patterns in Cameroon. The first one points to the weak or atrophic nature of the formal sector, which accounts for only 9.6 per cent of jobs and is mostly visible in urban areas. Second, the informal sector represents about 90.4 per cent of employment. Third, the informal sector is dominated by the agricultural sector, thus the primary

Table 10.1 Structure of jobs as per the institutional sector by place of residence in Cameroon

Place of residence	Urban	Rural	Cameroon
Institutional sector			
Public sector	10.5	2.6	4.9
Formal private sector	11.8	2.0	4.7
Non-agricultural informal sector	67.4	22.5	35.2
Agricultural informal sector	10.3	72.9	55.2
Total	100	100	100

Source: NIS, *The Employment and Informal Sector Survey*, 2005, phase 1 (working document) in Walthier (2006, p. 10).

sector, which makes up 55.2 per cent of informal GDP. Fourth, and this is very significant for our purposes, the non-agricultural sector covering the urban area accounts for 67.4 per cent of informal jobs.

Once again, the rise of the informal sector in Cameroon is the result of a combination of both exogenous and endogenous factors. The exogenous factors can be classified into three categories: the economic crisis of the 1980s, structural adjustment plans, and the *scramble* of Asian countries, including the focus of China towards Africa, and consequently Cameroon.

The deterioration of terms of trade and the drop in commodity prices in the mid-1980s resulted in reduced purchasing power of the rural population, especially the farmers, and the exodus of the rural population to urban areas. Yaounde, which is located at a crossroads of areas with high agricultural potential, growing cocoa and rubber, which are the main export crops, after the economic crisis of the 1980s[1] could not escape the influx of people fleeing the countryside, especially as farmers' management structures such the National Fund for Rural Development (FONADER) had been closed. The management of the mass influx of countryside workers, without technical training, could only result in an increase of activities that are less demanding in terms of qualification.

Structural adjustment programmes (SAPs) of the 1990s, imposed by the International Monetary Fund (IMF) and the World Bank (WB) to curb the effects of the economic crisis of the 1980s, proved to be counterproductive in many African countries. Cameroon, for its part, experienced negative impacts at the social level with the mass layoffs following the privatisation, and even liquidation of state or parastatal companies such as the Régie Nationale des Chemins de Fer du Cameroun (REGIFERCAM)/The Cameroon National Railway Company, Société des Transports Urbains du Cameroun (SOTUC)/The Cameroon Urban Transport Company, Cameroon Airlines (CAMAIR), Société Nationale des Eaux du Cameroun (SNEC)/The Cameroon National Water Company, and also the Société Nationale d'Electricité (SONEL)/The Cameroon National Electricity Company. The non-payment of workers' social benefits to workers in privatised or liquidated structures pushed large sections of workers into insecurity. Thus, on a purely economic level, the crisis of the 1980s and the SAPs of the 1990s had direct impacts on the boom of informal sector activities in Cameroon.

The liberalisation of all sectors of national life in the 1990s favoured the rise of new actors, especially in the economic domain in Africa. Cameroon witnessed the arrival of the Chinese, specialising in major construction works, such as roads and hydroelectric dams, and manufactured products and other means of transport. So, as far as means of transport are concerned, following the collapse of the public intra-urban transport systems, alternatives emerged, especially in major towns such as Yaounde and Douala, with the advent of commercial motorbikes. These vehicles, which were once very costly, flooded the streets of these two towns with a specific market value. The commercial motorbike business now appears to be indispensable for many city dwellers, in the absence of any other alternative. I would like to emphasise that this phenomenon of commercial motorbikes has been supported by preferential rates granted to importers of these two-wheeled vehicles.

Another exogenous factor that contributed to the development of the informal sector in Cameroon is the advent of mobile telephony, which has given rise to subcontractors such as "call boxers", also known as airtime credit retailers. This business also experienced a boom in Yaounde, where it seems to be structuring the landscape of street businesses.

Among endogenous factors, we can mention stringent public policies such as the freezing of recruitment into the public service concurrently with mass-scale layoffs, mentioned above, and the flexibility of work regime. The impact of both measures, which are closely linked to SAPs, increased the number of unemployed people and thus broadened the pool of informal stakeholders in Cameroon and especially in Yaounde, headquarters of many state and parastatal companies, and nerve centre of university education.

As a direct effect of globalisation, flexibility, which aims at reducing the cost of production by informalising jobs through subcontracting, for instance, has led to a new perception and role of the informal sector in the economy (Nana Djomo *et al.*, 2014, p. 2). An overview of the mapping of non-agricultural informal sector workers in Yaounde outlines many players. Findings derived from data collected edify us on the following aggregates.

Report from the field: informal workers in Yaounde, Cameroon

Table 10.2 offers an overview of the distribution by ages of targeted actors.

It appears clearly that the age range 26–30 years is strongly represented, making up more than one-third of all targeted actors. This observation can be corroborated by the fact that unemployment in Cameroon is essentially an urban phenomenon, with an average age of 27 years. More precisely, in Yaounde, the average age of unemployed persons is estimated to be 28 and 27 years for men and women, respectively (INS, 2011b, pp. 63, 69), while the gender distribution is 74 per cent and 26 per cent of men and women, respectively, or in absolute statistical terms, 370 and 129 actors, respectively, from the total number of persons interviewed, as shown in Table 10.3. It is clear that by their nature, some activities could tend to be considered as *reserved* for a particular gender, such as commercial motorbike riders, car washers or cobblers, in a context where taboos and other socio-anthropological considerations strongly determine or influence the socio-economic environment.

Also, a basic review of the data shows us that about one-third of actors (29 per cent) interviewed are holders of at least the First School Leaving Certificate

Table 10.2 Distribution by age of informal sector actors in Yaounde

Age range	16–20 years	21–25 years	26–30 years	31–35 years	36–40 years	41–45 years	46–50 years	51–55 years	Total
Number of actors	26	97	157	72	54	23	04	03	436

Source: Data collected by the author.

(FSLC), while half of that number hold the Brevet d'Etudes du Premier Cycle (Secondary School) certificate in addition to the FSLC (33 per cent), or a total of 62 per cent. Moreover, 58 per cent of the actors interviewed work six days out of seven per week, for an average of 60 hours. The time spent in terms of seniority, or the maximum time spent in a job, is 21 years on average for the targeted activities. Other information derived from the data collected is shown in Table 10.4.

Some useful elements should be highlighted with regard to Table 10.4. Under the headings "owners" and "wage workers", the percentages of 62 per cent and 29 per cent, respectively, are justified by the fact that the survey targeted individual activities and as such, the notion of a wage is not taken into account in the case of owners. It also appears that 68 per cent of the targeted actors pay taxes, namely, the fixed rate income tax, for which the annual turnover threshold is estimated at 15 million CFAF.[2] At the same time, I would like to indicate that the remaining actors that evade tax very often belong to stakeholders whose activities are difficult to "locate" or even "volatile". Lastly, as regards the notion of solidarity, this can be appreciated by the fact that 57 per cent of the actors declare that they belong to self-help groups. In the following section, I describe one of the specific informal activities – commercial motorbike operators – that I study.

Table 10.3 Distribution by gender of informal actors in Yaounde

Actors	Men	Women	Total
Commercial motor riders	143	–	143
Barbers	10	30	40
Call boxers or air time retailers	25	15	40
Food sellers	14	14	28
Car washers	32	02	34
Book sellers	28	03	31
Tailors	10	30	40
Street vendors	23	12	35
Cobblers	37	01	38
Photocopying machine operators	48	22	70
Total	370	129	499

Source: Data collected by the author.

Table 10.4 Distribution of indicators of non-agricultural informal sector in Yaounde

Indicators	Owners	Wage workers	Taxes	Solidarity networks
Answers				
Yes	308	143	336	242
No	188	349	160	179

Source: Data collected by the author.

Commercial motorbike operators

In addition to the traditional informal sector actors in urban areas in Cameroon, two new players have been targeted in this study: the "okada riders", or commercial motorbike riders, and the "call boxers", or airtime credit retailers. The phenomenon of commercial motorbike riders in Yaounde is relatively new compared with the northern towns of the country, which undertook lucrative experimentation with two-wheeled vehicles as early as the 1980s. One reason may justify the early popularity of these vehicles in that part of the country: the proximity to northern Nigerian towns where motorcycle assembly plants were created, which facilitated their acquisition, not forgetting the fact that they are a practical means of transport.

Two decades later, towns in the south of Cameroon, notably Douala, Bafoussam and Yaounde, experienced this activity thanks to exemptions granted to operators of this sector, especially the Chinese. It should be noted that the establishment of commercial motorbikes in Yaounde follows an increasing demand by inhabitants for urban mobility and a total lack of viable alternatives from the government or private stakeholders. It is against this backdrop that the okada rider or commercial motorbike rider emerged: in the eyes of the lower- and middle-class citizens of Yaounde, these are akin to medical personnel at the side of an abandoned patient (Figure 10.1).

In Cameroon, there are 350,000 commercial motorbike riders, according to figures given in 2008 by the national trade union of motorbike owners and riders.[3] The commercial motorbike riders business in Cameroon is regulated by the Decree of 31 December 2008 that lays down the conditions and modalities for the commercial motorcycle business. In order to better organise the *trade* of commercial motorbike riders, another 15-article Decree of 30 July 2013 was adopted in order to amend and supplement the previous instrument. This latter Decree specifies that nine items are required to enter the business of commercial motorbike operation, including the special Category S2 transport licence, a public road transportation card per motorbike, a taxpayer's card, a valid insurance policy and motorcycle registration with territorially competent offices of the Ministry of Transport, before taking to the road. Besides these regulatory requirements, 11 pieces of equipment and accessories should be employed by the operator, including yellow paint on the fuel tank, a protection helmet for the driver, a helmet for the passenger, a repairs tool kit, and front and rear bumpers.

In the case of Yaounde, an order of the government delegate dated 12 January 2012 regulates traffic areas for commercial motorbikes. This instrument specifies that commercial motorbikes are allowed to ply the roads in the outskirts of Yaounde, and also lists the main roads banned from the business of commercial motorbikes, such as Place Awae, Boulevard de la réunification, Place Melen, Place Elig effa, Rond Point Bastos and Avenue Nsimeyong, Rue Noah Tsogo (Rue Manguiers), Boulevard OUA, Rue Kondengui and Avenue de Biyem Assi. In addition to this normative framework, traffic areas have also been demarcated by subdivision. The colour of the jacket where the name of the competent council

Figure 10.1 A view of "okada riders" or "commercial motorbike riders" in Yaounde.
Source: Author's collection.

and registration of the driver will be printed indicates the subdivision: Yaounde I (yellow colour); Yaounde II (fluorescent orange); Yaounde III (purple); Yaounde IV (pink); Yaounde V (green); Yaounde VI (blue); and Yaounde VII (red). In view of the number of regulatory requirements, it is no surprise that these measures are not all respected, and defaulters run the risk of having their motorcycles impounded and paying CFAF 25,000 as removal fees and CFAF 5,000 per day/per motorcycle as impoundment fees.

This description of the business of commercial motorbike riders would not be exhaustive if we did not mention their involvement – possibly against their own will – in the political sphere in recent years. In Cameroonian towns, commercial motorbike riders, indeed, represent a political asset over which politicians across all political divides fight. In this respect, Cameroon's head of state, during an official address to youth on 10 February 2013, lent his support to commercial motorbike riders by advocating for their official recognition. But, these actors did not wait until this surprise speech to organise and develop strategies towards strengthening their presence both in the social sphere and in political debates.

As a general rule, the scholarly attention received by these actors is relatively low, compared with that of other actors targeted in this study. We also find soldiers and policemen working as "commercial motorbike riders" without any clear justification for their presence in the business. I briefly discuss the nature of the other category of informal workers – the call boxers – in the following section.

Call boxers

On the contrary, with regard to "call boxers" or airtime credit retailers, there are two types: those who very often settle along the streets or near public buildings or shops, and those who are essentially mobile. Mobility is a major characteristic of this business, and as such, it appears to be a criterion for the characterisation of the informal sector, as shown by Nancy Benjamin and Ahmadou Aly Mbaye (Benjamin, Mbaye, 2012, pp. 23–24). Figures 10.2 and 10.3 give a visual overview of patterns of "call box" business.

In terms of basic tools required for entry into the business, four items will do the trick: a table, a chair, an umbrella to protect the seller from sun and rain, but also to serve as advertisement material, where communication costs are displayed

Figure 10.2 A female sedentary "call boxer".

Source: Author's collection.

Figure 10.3 A male mobile "call boxer" or airtime credit retailer in Yaounde.

Source: Author's collection.

on white sheets of paper, and a telephone, the main working tool. Mobile call boxers do not even need the first two items. It should be noted that the working conditions of call boxers can have negative effects on both their health, due especially to very long standing or sitting positions, and physical and even economic security, since their working tools can be seized by council workers. They are involved, through no fault of their own, in situations such as scams or verbal and physical threats via telephone calls by unscrupulous users. In any case, the general framework for the performance of this business shows inadequate legal supervision and lack of organisation. There is clearly a regulatory gap, therefore, between the motorcycle riders and the call boxers – one gets legislative attention and the other does not. The next section looks at the role of solidarity action in the lives of the informal workers in Cameroon.

The importance of solidarity networks among urban informal sector actors

An aspect that has been established in studies on the informal sector in Africa is the "lack of institutionalised social security systems" (Charmes in ILO, 2002). This finding is corroborated by the data collected, which do not indicate any individual or collective affiliation of one or more actors of the targeted informal sector to any of the social insurance organisations. This issue is, indeed, a challenge. In this situation, which is deemed unacceptable, actors of the informal sector have developed strategies aimed at addressing not only social contingencies, but also difficulties relating to the sustainability of their activities, through microfinance institutions, as well as through trade unions.

About 57 per cent of targeted actors say that they are members of a solidarity association. These groups play an important role in facilitating collective cohesion by developing self-help strategies through *tontines*, a kind of traditional mechanism that enables its members to save for themselves and the group on either a weekly or a monthly basis with the aim of securing a rapid response in the case of misfortune that may befall a member of the group. This practice is widespread in Cameroon, following the disengagement of the state during the economic crisis of the 1980s. This strategy is, however, not typical of informal workers.

In fact, absence of membership-based organisations is the main challenge of informal sector actors. Based on the data collected, it appears that the commercial motorbike riders are better organised than the call boxers. They have created the national trade union of Cameroon commercial motorbike riders. Like other trade unions, their association is very active when issues related to their business are raised. Besides this organisation at the national level, other associations have also been established, such as the association of commercial motorbike riders of the Yaounde-V subdivision.

Moreover, in Yaounde, the solidarity existing among the commercial motorbike riders is amazing: when one of them is in difficulties with a third party, his colleagues immediately mobilise. This *active* solidarity, which is seen as "blind" by their competitors, namely, cab drivers, enables commercial motorbike riders to position themselves in an environment where there is stiff competition among competing services.

Besides membership of collective groupings, other initiatives have been developed by urban informal sector actors, such as affiliation to formal banking institutions. It is in this light that microfinance institutions located in the town of Yaounde appear as preferred partners for these actors with regard to savings and loans. Marc Labie defines microfinance as "the granting of financial services (generally loans and/or savings), to people who are developing a productive activity, more often handicraft or trade and who do not have access to commercial financial institutions because of their socio-economic profile" (Labie, 1999, p. 23). In its contemporary orientation, microfinance in its formal structuring has witnessed a boom in Cameroon, thanks to the laws of 19 December 1990 on the freedom of association and 14 August 1992 on cooperative societies and common initiative groups (Ngafi Djomo, 2006). This boom is also a result of the crisis of the banking sector in the late 1980s and the involvement of donors in public economic policies.

In Yaounde, one microfinance institution particularly stands out in its relationship with the informal sector: the Credit Communautaire d'Afrique (CCA). In its deployment strategy, its branch in the Ngoa-Ekelle neighbourhood in Yaounde, which was established in 1997, has a significant representation of informal sector actors among its members within one of its two components, that is, savings (loans being the other component) (Temomo, 2015). Under the *savings* category, two products are offered: the private savings account and the association savings account. The strategy to collect savings, especially private and daily savings, is simple: teams made up of staff of the microfinance institution go to meet targeted actors and carry out operations in the latter's workplace. Each potential saver holds a savings account booklet from the savings institution in which the signature of the "collecting" agent and deposited amounts are reported. The money is later deposited by the worker in the saver's account. This activity is seen by targeted actors as a form of solidarity and recognition of their trade and, consequently, of their membership.

Another issue with the informal sector in the urban area in Cameroon relates to taxation. Innovations introduced in Cameroon since 1996, notably the creation of the new fixed rate income tax, resulted in a relative decrease of the mistrust of informal sector actors towards public authority. There are three forms of taxation in Cameroon: the real tax system for a turnover in excess of CFAF 50,000,000, the non-presumptive tax regime for a turnover between CFAF 15,000,000 and CFAF 50,000,000, and the fixed rate income tax for a turnover below CFAF 15,000,000. Given the number of actors who reported that they have paid the fixed rate income tax (68 per cent), one is right to think that actors of this business do not seem to evade tax, as was feared by De Soto in the case of Latin America (De Soto, 1989). It is true that the tax scheme in Cameroon is declarative, and as such, potential taxpayers should get their tax affairs properly sorted out once the legal framework includes them in a specific business activity. Therefore, except for some actors such as illegal car washers or street vendors, all the other players, by virtue of the nature of their business, comply with the regulations in force.

The informal sector and the face of urban cohabitation

In the framework of the deployment of their activities, targeted actors are characterised by a noticeable presence in the urban area. In Yaounde, it is almost impossible to escape the services of commercial motorbike riders, call boxers, and other occasional food sellers or tailors. From large distribution centres to streets in town, the slogan of users seems to be "accommodation".

Two aspects relating to the obstruction of roadways, movement of both car drivers and pedestrians, and the overall aesthetics of the town highlight issues that are increasingly visible in relation to urban informal sector activities. In Yaounde, many actors, such as garment vendors or even "call boxers", occupy pavements reserved for pedestrians on main roads, with the resulting obstruction of these roads. It is well known that sedentary call boxers set up their working tools on roads meant for pedestrians, thereby obliging the latter to walk on the roadway while exposing themselves to the risks of road accidents. Commercial motorbike riders are no exception in this regard. It is common for these vehicles, in a bid to avoid traffic jams, to take to pavements reserved for pedestrians, with the ensuing consequence of risk of accidents. It also appears that commercial motorbikes are increasingly occupying roadways reserved for road traffic, particularly access routes towards neighbourhoods, thereby compelling car drivers and pedestrians to take dangerous deviations.

In the same light, car drivers and commercial motorbike riders, to name just two, very often exhibit aggressiveness, worsened by a rivalry which is, in a way, understandable. Ninety per cent of commercial motorbike riders do not wear helmets, and only 2.2 per cent of them hold a driving licence.[4]

With regard to the aesthetics of the town, the aim is to understand the changes attributable to informal sector actors. Thus, the settlement of call boxers in front of public buildings or housing complexes can have a three-fold consequence: change in the initial architectural landscape of the areas occupied, narrowing of access roads or roadways, and obstruction of areas reserved for the parking of cars. In many public places, the image of the overcrowding of these areas by actors of the informal sector is glaring: in Yaounde, the Avenue Kennedy is a symbol of the obstruction by urban informal sector activities, and in this respect, it is no different from other cities, such as Dakar, Cotonou and Ouagadougou (Benjamin, Mbaye, 2012).

Conclusion

This panoramic view on new informal sector actors in Cameroon, especially in the capital Yaounde, calls for at least four concluding comments. The informal sector boomed in Cameroon within a context marked both by the economic crisis of the 1980s and by the advent of SAPs imposed by international financial institutions. As a result of these, many public and parastatal companies were compelled to lay off their workers. People working in the public service suffered a similar fate, if they were unfortunate, or saw their wage divided by three, if they were among the most fortunate. Obvious consequences for their families followed, which could only push thousands of Cameroonians, both rural and urban, into activities of the informal sector. It should be noted that social and transport facilities also collapsed abruptly. The transport sector, for example, witnessed the rise of new actors, especially commercial motorbike riders. Even today, there is still no alternative proposed by public authorities or private operators with regard to public means of transport. This shows that this alternative solution, which obviously meets the actual needs for urban mobility, but is also an opportunity for job seekers, is fast becoming a rule, especially on difficult or poorly maintained roads. This rise of commercial motorbikes cannot be dissociated from the insufficient provision of urban transport facilities. On the contrary, the rise of call boxers is linked to far-reaching changes at world level with the development of information and communication technologies. The sedentary or mobile airtime credit retailers appear like peripheral players or relays of main international telephone groups.

Though the working conditions of informal sector actors are difficult, they stoically resist, and even develop protection strategies. In terms of organisation, trade unions to fight for the interests of informal sector actors are established, as are self-help groups to pool their actions together, as is the case with the Yaounde-V association of commercial motorbike riders. The importance of informal sector activities is emphasised by the increased interest from microfinance institutions, whose clients belong almost entirely to the group of actors targeted in this study.

However, in general, stunted development, lack of organisation and an inadequate legal framework appear to be dominant features of urban informal sector activities in Cameroon, especially in Yaounde, even though these actors are indispensable to economic development and urban sociability.

Notes

1 Since the years 1985–1986, Cameroon has been going through a severe economic crisis due to the drop in the international prices of main exports commodities (coffee, cotton, timber, oil …), combined with the depreciation by 40 per cent of the US dollar (benchmark currency) against the CFA Franc, in which commodity prices, and in particular oil prices, are denominated.
2 FCFA (in English, CFA Franc) is an acronym in French that has historically meant "Franc des Colonies Françaises d'Afrique" and is now called "Franc de la Communuaté Financière d'Afrique", which is a common currency used by former west and central French colonies in Africa (1 euro = 655.957 FCFA). In fact, 15,000,000 FCFA = 22,867 euros.
3 *Cameroon Tribune*, 13 August 2013.
4 *Cameroon Tribune*, 13 August 2013.

References

Amougou, R.A.B., Dzossa, A.D., Fouoking, J., Nepetsoun, S., et Tédou, J. (2009). Opérationnaliser des concepts d'informalité et élaboration des comptes des unités de production informelles: l'expérience de l'enquête nationale sur l'emploi et le secteur informel au Cameroun (EESI 2005): 130–147/Operationalization of concepts of Informality production units: the experience of the Cameroon National Employment and Informal Sector Survey (EESI 2005): 148–164.

Backiny-Yetna, P. (2009). Secteur informel, fiscalité et équité: l'exemple du Cameroun. *STATECO*, 104, pp. 91–108.

Benjamin, N., Mbaye, A.A. (2012). *The Informal Sector in Francophone Africa: From Size, Productivity and Institutions.* Washington: A co-publication of The Agence Française de Développement and the World Bank.

Cogneau, D., Razafindrakoto, M., Roubaud, F. (1996). Le secteur informel urbain et l'ajustement au Cameroun. *Revue d'économie du développement* (ed. PUF), 3, pp. 27–63.

De Soto, H. (1989). *The Other Path. The Invisible Revolution in the Third World.* New York: Harper and Row.

Fouoking, J. (2009). L'intégration de l'informel rural non agricole dans les comptes nationaux: l'expérience camerounaise / Integration of the Informal Rural Non-Agricultural Sector into National Accounts: The Cameroon Experience. *African statistical journal/ Journal statistique africain.* 9 (November), pp. 237–249/250–288.

Guha-Kasnobis, B., Kanbur, R. (Eds). (2006). *Informal Labour Markets and Development Studies in Development Economics and Policy,* New York: Palgrave Macmillan.

Hart, K. (1972). *Employment, Income and Inequality: A Strategy for Increasing Productivity and Employment in Kenya.* Geneva: ILO.

ILO. (2002). *Women and Men in the Informal Economy: A Statistical Picture.* Geneva: Employment sector, International Labour Office.

INS. (2011a). *Intégration des enquêtes sur l'emploi et le secteur informel (EESI) dans les concepts nationaux.* Yaoundé: Département des Synthèses et des Analyses Economiques.

INS. (2011b). *Jeunes et marchés du travail au Cameroun en 2010.* Yaoundé: Juin.

Labie, M. (1999). La micro finance en questions, limites et choix organisationnels. Bruxelles: Editions Luc Pire.

Nana Djomo, Jules Médard, *et al.* (2014). *L'analyse socio-économique du secteur et de l'emploi informel au Cameroun*, Projet de recherche, mars.

Ngafi Djomo, O.B. (2006). *Etat des lieux de la microfinance et du système bancaire camerounais*. Master en sciences de gestion (option: finance). Facultés universitaires catholiques de Mons, Belgique.

Talom Kamga, A. (2013). *Intégration de l'Informel dans les comptes nationaux du Cameroun*. Cameroon: National Statistics Institute (NSI).

Temomo, M. (2015). *Interview*. Yaoundé.

Walthier, R. (2006). *La formation professionnelle en secteur informel*. Rapport sur l'enquête de terrain au Cameroun. AFD, Direction de la Stratégie, Département de la Recherche.

11 Informal workers' organising strategies in India and Argentina

Supriya Routh and Marisa N. Fassi

Introduction

In this chapter, we aim to contribute to the legal and policy debate over strategies for improving informal workers' labour conditions through collective action. We do so by focusing on two case studies of the concerned actors' agency, organising mechanisms and partnership-building strategies in Kolkata, India and Córdoba, Argentina. This debate is currently relevant for labour studies scholarship, because informal work significantly shapes the productive forces in the Global South, and is increasingly doing so in the Global North as well. Regardless of the challenge informal economic activities pose to statistical measurement, the available statistical indications offer us a hint of the enormity of informality and, accordingly, indicates the relevance of collective action we want to discuss in this chapter. The International Labour Organization (ILO) Report *Statistical Update on Employment in the Informal Economy* (2012)[1] shows that in 2009, 49.7 per cent of Argentina's workers were engaged in informal employment and 32.1 per cent were employed in the informal sector; it also shows that, in that same year, 83.6 per cent of India's workers were in informal employment and 67.5 per cent were employed in the informal sector.

A comparative evaluation of the Indian and the Argentinian situations is particularly apt because of the similarities in the constitutional goal and extent of informality between the two countries in the Global South, irrespective of their geographical distance. The constitutions of both the countries envisage a dignified life for workers. In spite of such constitutional guarantees, conditions necessary for the furtherance of the realisation of such a dignified life are divided between the enforceable civil-political rights and the unenforceable social-economic rights in India, even though it is the unenforceable rights that are more important in the context of informal workers. As it happens, in spite of their exclusion from the law and policy of the state, informal workers (waste pickers for our chapter) are becoming active agents of change in their own lives through strategically organising themselves. The strategies of this organisation, in both countries, offer important lessons to be learned.

In spite of the constitutional similarities, in the context of each country, informal workers face their own contextual particularities and obstacles.

Nevertheless, the resistance mechanisms and strategies developed in both country contexts are worth exploring as possible guidance for workers' collective action. One of the fundamental commonalities between the two countries under discussion that we have been able to observe is the engagement with a *broader collective approach involving networking and multidimensional action*. The argument we pursue in this chapter is that neither a purely constitutional rights-based approach from above nor a purely worker-based collective approach from below can be seen as a sufficient response for struggling against the marginalisation, deprivation and vulnerability that informal workers face in their everyday lives.

On the one hand, purely rights-based approaches from above tend to perceive informal workers as voiceless beneficiaries. They suggest that states must reinforce their efforts to incorporate the informal workforce into the formal economy. Notwithstanding this effort, in countries where informal employment is the reality of half or almost the entire workforce, the struggle for accessing labour rights becomes a complex scenario. In this complexity, the relationship that the state has with informal workers is, at least, two-fold. First, at one level, the state (advertently or otherwise) fails to realise workers' constitutional rights by excluding informal workers from law and policy, thereby making them face major obstacles to accessing justice. Second, at another level, the state interferes in informal workers' lives by systematically targeting informal workers with state policies that indirectly refer to them but directly affect their lives; for instance, security and urban policies that determine where and by whom particular work can be performed influence the livelihoods of such workers in very concrete terms.

On the other hand, purely worker-based approaches from below in groups that suffer perennial and systematic marginality, illiteracy and other sorts of vulnerability may result in a perpetual struggle against the bureaucratic labyrinth of the state, as we will particularly note in the Argentinian context. The broad collective approach we propose indicates that setting one approach against the other is a false dilemma. By studying urban waste recyclers' organising initiatives in India and Argentina through our qualitative empirical study in the two cities – Kolkata and Córdoba – we emphasise experiences in which informal workers deploy a number of strategic organising mechanisms through a variety of legal forms and partnerships. We argue that this collective approach of informal waste pickers is strategically effective in enhancing their power of bargaining with the state and other institutions.

The second section discusses the gap between constitutional labour rights and their realisation by informal workers in both countries. The third section offers a brief overview of informal workers' organisation initiatives in India and Argentina. This section is followed by case studies on informal waste pickers' organisations reported from Kolkata, India and Córdoba, Argentina (fourth section). Drawing on the lessons from the case studies, the fifth section concludes by offering some reflections on possible successful broad-based collective strategies by informal workers.

A rights-based strategy from above and the unrealised constitutional promise

In both the jurisdictions under discussion, informal workers have been systematically excluded from the constitutional right to a dignified life. This exclusion takes place in two stages: first, they are excluded from the benefits of labour regulations, and second, even when there are legislative protections, they are left out during the enforcement of those rights. The constitutions of India and Argentina provide for the right to unionisation, the right to freedom of speech and expression, the right against forced labour, the right against child labour, the right to worthy livelihood, the right to equal pay for equal work, the right to decent work, and the right to appropriate conditions of work, among others.[2]

During 2004–2009, the National Commission for Enterprises in the Unorganised Sector (NCEUS) conducted comprehensive reviews of Indian labour welfare and social protection laws in order to ascertain the coverage of informal workers under those laws. The Commission surveyed labour welfare legislation having a bearing on informal workers, and notes that these laws afford protection to only a small section of informal workers in the country (NCEUS, 2007, pp. 163–164, 284–287; Hensman, 2010, pp. 193–196). It also notes that the lack of representative voices for informal workers is one of the reasons for the "abysmally poor" enforcement of labour laws (NCEUS, 2007, pp. 164–171, 2009, pp. 186–187).

Informal workers suffer from multiple deprivations compared with formal workers (Jha, 2005–2006). The exclusion of informal workers from legislative protection happens in two stages – in their coverage and their actual enforcement (NCEUS, 2009, p. 180; Hensman, 2010, pp. 193–196). In India, the NCEUS shows that labour laws are biased towards formal workers employed in an industry and that many of the laws have a numerical threshold for their applicability, that is, they apply to an industry where at least 20 workers are employed (10 workers if electricity is used, and 5 workers for the applicability of the Migrant Workmen Act and the Motor Transport Workers Act) (NCEUS, 2009, pp. 178–180). Once the legislative threshold is set for industries employing at least 10 or 20 workers, about 90 per cent of the total workforce remains outside such legislative protection (NCEUS, 2009, pp. 180).

On the other hand, after the deep labour flexibilisation implemented during the neo-liberal era, in 2004, Argentina expanded the Millennium Development Goals by incorporating a new goal called *decent work*; by doing so, the country identified decent work as an enduring agenda to overcome cyclic crises in the global economy. This inclusion prompted the active participation of the private sector in the elaboration of a public-private agenda for social responsibility and decent work. The coordinated programme,[3] implemented since 2006, has, by 2010, shown relevant improvement in the regularisation and access to labour rights for the enterprise-based concept of informality.[4] That is, it has shown substantial progress in relation to employees who were working for companies or productive units that had informal characteristics (i.e. so far as legal status, registration of the company or of the employees, bookkeeping practices, etc. were concerned).

Gradually, Argentina has adopted definite legislative policies towards historically relegated sectors: one is the Housekeeping Act, 2013 (n # 26.844) and the second is the Housewife Pension or Pension without Retirement Payment.[5] However, informality as a multifaceted concept also includes informal self-employed workers. In this regard, in 2004, Argentina adopted the system of the Small Taxpayer's Simplified Social Scheme,[6] by which informal self-employed workers have access to health insurance and retirement benefits. It also makes them eligible for direct contracts with the state. The impact of this system can only be fully acknowledged in the mid–long term, and only in so far as the consecutive governments continue the policies towards decent work.

The formal existence of constitutional rights and the inability to realise some of them by informal workers is a relevant problematic that affects major sections of the population in both India and Argentina. In both the scenarios, if we only focus on the duties of the states, we are left with an unpredictable future for informal workers. States must proactively engage with informal workers: they must be attentive to the everyday obstacles faced by informal workers, and work in furtherance of eliminating the obstacles that exclude informal workers from the right to a dignified life. However, a rights-based approach depending on the good will of the state does not always work, as is clear from the enormous number of informal workers in India and Argentina who are deprived of their rights. Informal workers cannot, therefore, remain merely passive recipients of the top-down policies – and they are not. As we show in the following section, informal workers have developed innovative collective strategies by organising and building networks to overcome their marginalisation.

A strategy from below: informal workers' organising mechanisms

Informal workers are increasingly organising themselves in order to change their position in law, in society, and in the economic structure of productive relations. There are both organisations working *for* informal workers and organisations *of* informal workers. In this section, we discuss a range of organisational experiences that show that these processes involve a variety of legal statuses (trade unions, registered societies, cooperatives, etc.), of networking processes (networks built among peers, with outside members, with non-governmental organisations (NGOs), etc.), and of degrees of participation that these networks may involve (i.e. some networks are fundamental in the formation process, some express solidarity in the functions, and some are involved in processes of a wider collective action).

The experiences discussed in this section have been chosen in order to show this variety. As we will see, despite the diverse legal statuses and networking processes, all organisational experiences are functionally similar. The organisations undertake a range of socio-economic-political activities with the active involvement of their members (Kapoor, 2007, pp. 561–565). These organisations also network with state institutions and other non-government entities. By providing services and promoting political action, these organisations envisage facilitating a well-rounded, dignified life for informal workers.

In India, there are several organisations of informal workers. These organisations provide comprehensive social, economic, political and cultural resources that are promised to workers under the Constitution of India. In India, even though certain categories of informal workers have been able to collectively negotiate with the government to avail themselves of some economic benefits (Agarwala, 2013), the majority of informal workers in India remain excluded from legislative and executive assistance (NCEUS, 2007, pp. 163–164, 284–287). This exclusionary backdrop creates a void, which informal workers' organisations seek to fill.

The Self Employed Women's Association (SEWA) is an important organisation in this respect. The SEWA is a trade union of women informal workers in India (Kapoor, 2007, pp. 555).[7] The SEWA offers banking services, health care, childcare, insurance services, legal services, housing aid and educational facilities to its members.[8] The SEWA also lobbies with the government and resorts to agitation in furtherance of its demands (Bhatt, 2006, pp. 70, 213).

While the SEWA is a trade union, the *Sramajibee Mahila Samiti* (SMS) is a registered society[9] of women agricultural workers in West Bengal (Antony, 2001, pp. 22, 32, 75). Through direct political action, the SMS has taken up issues such as women's employment, government corruption and minimum wages (Antony, 2001, pp. 75–80). The SMS has successfully organised rallies, agitations and picketing in order to pressure the government of West Bengal to implement government welfare schemes in a fair and transparent manner. Additionally, the SMS organises training of new members, imparts social education and promotes self-help groups. The SMS is part of a network of 40 women's organisations named *Maitri*.

Another organisation, the *Annapurna Mahila Mandal* (AMM), is more concerned with informal workers' socio-economic betterment than with their political empowerment. The AMM is a charitable trust and society registered in Maharashtra (Antony, 2001, pp. 91). The AMM undertakes a microcredit programme, offers medical and legal aid, maintains a crèche, mediates domestic disputes, offers housing aid, and imparts leadership and vocational training to its members (Antony, 2001, pp. 28, 91–95).

In Argentina, there are at least 147 informal workers' organisations that correspond to a variety of activities: housekeeping, street vending, arts and crafts work, cardboard picking and small self-employment (excluding professionals and technicians) (Busso, 2004). Some have an area of influence so restricted that it is limited to informal workers in a specific neighbourhood; others operate at a regional or national level. As in India, these initiatives are organised as unions, associations, cooperatives, federations, etc. These forms are not random, but depend on the legal requisites the government sets to accept an organisation as a valid social dialogue partner.

It is worth mentioning that the labour union *Central de Trabajadores Argentinos* (CTA) has undertaken a leading initiative in incorporating informal workers into the structure of the union.[10] This incorporation has increased political and rights awareness among the informal workers, and has opened up a whole network for collective political action. In the Latin American context, certain experiences, such as the *Força Sindical* union in Brazil and the Rerum Novarum Confederation in Costa Rica, which have undertaken concrete actions to include informal workers in the union's structure, stand out as examples of the growing prominence of informal workers' organisations.[11] By integrating informal workers, these traditional trade unions have undertaken relevant social and political functions and mainstreamed informal workers' voices into the overall political discourse.

At the global level, there are organisations working to link experiences, ideas and strategies, and information on informal workers. In this respect, we can mention the International Street Vendors Organization (StreetNet),[12] which is an alliance of street vendors that promotes the exchange of information and organising and advocacy strategies for street vendors, and Women in Informal Employment Globalizing and Organizing (WIEGO),[13] which is a global network that aims to promote the well-being of informal workers, particularly women.

Despite the diverse legal statuses and networking processes, all organisations undertake a range of socio-economic-political activities with the active involvement of their members (Kapoor, 2007, p. 561). These organisations also network with state institutions and NGOs. By providing services and promoting political action, these organisations envisage facilitating a well-rounded, dignified life for informal workers. In the next section, based on empirical study, we narrate specific organisation initiatives of informal waste pickers in India and Argentina.

Informal waste workers' organising strategies: examples from two countries

Against the backdrop of our discussion in the earlier sections, we locate our empirical study in Kolkata, India and Córdoba, Argentina. We adopted qualitative semi-structured interviewing and participant observation methods for our study. The case study in India was conducted during March to July 2011 (an earlier study with the same groups of workers was undertaken in 2009), and the study in Argentina was undertaken from 2011 to 2014.

Experiences in Kolkata, India[14]

Kolkata is the capital of the state of West Bengal in India. Waste pickers, as a specific category of informal workers, are excluded from legislative protections and executive schemes in the state of West Bengal.[15] The experience in West Bengal indicates that one of the prominent reasons for the exclusion of waste pickers from the purview of government welfare schemes is the absence of an association of waste pickers. The then minister-in-charge of labour of the government of West Bengal noted: "[Our] government cannot protect workers … workers have to compete in [an open] market … we could of course discuss the needs of specific categories of workers if they collectively submit a report to us."[16] His reflections percolated down well to his officials, one of whom observed: "If [workers] have a union they can apply to the government for the inclusion of their names in [government welfare schemes]."[17] These functionaries' views were corroborated by the ILO senior specialist of international labour standards (in New Delhi), Coen Kompier, who emphasised that "the first element would be organising … [it] creates some kind of a platform for them to raise their voice".[18]

Against this backdrop, waste pickers of the city of Kolkata organised themselves into a trade union. While it is early to analyse the significance of the unionisation initiative *in toto*, some early indications point to the advantages of the unionisation. We discuss how, through effective networking, within a very short span of time, the waste pickers' union in Kolkata has been able to attract attention from various quarters, which is useful in promoting the visibility of the waste pickers and drawing attention to their predicament.

During the course of an informal meeting between the members of an NGO (Calcutta Samaritans), waste pickers, some city intellectuals and other activists, a proposal on the formation of a trade union of waste pickers was mooted.[19] Strongly supporting the initiative, one Calcutta Samaritans organiser noted: "the [Calcutta] Samaritans has been engaging with multiple issues involving the waste pickers in Kolkata for a long time. But, our [i.e. the Calcutta Samaritans'] initiatives have been piecemeal on the basis of our program priorities. If together with the waste pickers we could establish a trade union of waste pickers, it would be a culmination of our previous initiatives."[20]

The Calcutta Samaritans' organisers reached out to waste pickers in the different locations of the city, proposing the formation of a trade union. The Calcutta Samaritans' organisers and some city intellectuals approached the Legal Aid Society of the West Bengal National University of Juridical Sciences (WB NUJS),[21] Kolkata, India, to become partners in the trade union initiative. Accordingly, a trade union of the informal waste pickers was formed with the active involvement of these several entities, including the WB NUJS.[22] The union members also elected the executive committee members, with Kalu Das, a waste picker himself, elected as its general secretary. In its first meeting, the executive committee of the union decided a name for the union: *Barjya Punarbyawaharikaran Shilpa Shramik Sangathan* (BPSSS), translated into English as Association of Workers engaged in Waste Recycling Industry (AWWRI).

The executive committee members identified five primary agendas for the new union: first, to provide their members with safety gear such as gumboots, gloves and aprons; second, to lobby the government of West Bengal in order to bring waste pickers within the purview of the existing legislative protection for informal workers; third, to lobby the Kolkata Municipal Corporation so that waste pickers could be integrated with the municipal solid waste management system; fourth, to prepare a Comment on their deprivations to be submitted to the ILO; and fifth, to generate funds in order to institute a group health insurance scheme for waste pickers.

During the first executive committee meeting, the WB NUJS Legal Aid Society expressed interest in providing legal and other assistance to BPSSS.[23]

The Legal Aid Society subsequently adopted BPSSS as one of their projects, thereby enabling students of the law university to work in furtherance of promoting BPSSS's interests.[24] Students engaged with the Legal Aid Society have undertaken to educate waste pickers' children.[25] Students have also undertaken a membership drive on behalf of the union through awareness campaigning among waste pickers in Kolkata.[26] The Legal Aid Society is also providing legal assistance to individual members of the union when they are arrested or are harassed by law enforcement officials.[27] In 2012, the WB NUJS Legal Aid Society devoted an open house discussion session to discussing their role in promoting BPSSS initiatives.[28] The Legal Aid Society prepared a petition to be filed with the Ministry of Urban Affairs, Government of India, the National Human Rights Commission and the Supreme Court of India, advocating the right to work and livelihood for homeless waste pickers in Kolkata.[29]

What is evident from the above description is that the waste pickers who were living on the margins of the society became significantly visible with their organisation initiative. Within days of formation of the union, the Legal Aid Society began collaborating with waste pickers on different issues. Within months of the formation of the union, the Legal Aid Society brought the waste pickers to the notice of academics and policy-makers through a national conference. The union also managed to generate funds from some sympathetic quarters. The union has decided to use the funds to establish a group health insurance for their members. What is prominent in this example is that their organisation works as an instrument of social dialogue. In the absence of an organisation, the government officials refused to interact with these informal workers. However, in addition to this fundamental advantage, the broader network-based organisation also generates other benefits – such as strategic petitioning and group health insurance – for the informal waste pickers. As we indicated earlier, the role of informal workers' organisations in promoting the overall improvement of informal workers is also evident from the other prominent organisation initiatives of informal workers in India.

Experiences in Córdoba, Argentina

Waste pickers in Argentina are called "carters" because they tend to use a horse and cart to collect the recyclable material. Among the urban waste pickers, there is a difference between the traditional carters, who have been doing the activity generation after generation, and the new ones, who are doing it as a consequence of the lack of employment opportunities (Bermúdez, 2009).

Urban waste pickers are a heterogeneous group who have been developing heterogeneous organisational strategies over the years. At a national level, we can mention the larger solidarity initiative called MoCaR (National Movement of Cardboard pickers and Recyclers) that started in 2006.[30] It was launched as an initiative by some political activists and some cardboard pickers to bring their political actions to prominence by gathering together members of different associations and cooperatives in the main cities of Argentina. Another example of a large collective initiative is the MTE (Excluded Workers Movement), which strongly identifies itself as an independent network of political parties that aims to safeguard urban waste pickers against politicians, the police, and corrupt practices of the recycling companies. In Buenos Aires, the labour union CTA has included cardboard pickers in its organisation, thereby helping to integrate their claims into the larger political agenda. Among their achievements is the incorporation of informal workers into the Urban Hygiene Social Management Public System in that city.

In Córdoba city, waste picking is not a recent economic phenomenon either. Our data[31] reveals that there are families whose members have been carters for four generations. Accordingly, their collective action, which took the shape of cooperative societies, also has a history. The first cooperative initiative of waste pickers began in San Vicente neighbourhood during the 1970s. Among the oldest cooperatives undertaking the business in a collective manner, which are still active, we find the Carters Cooperative of Villa Urquiza, which obtained legal status in 1993, and the Sangre y Sol cooperative, which obtained legal status in 2002. Both of these cooperatives started as a reaction to the municipal attempt to forbid carters in the city. There are currently over seven carters' cooperatives working in the city.

Over the years, more cooperatives were formed to facilitate the activity of waste picking, and these cooperatives have developed a variety of organising strategies and networking mechanisms among themselves and with other associations, NGOs or professionals. These strategies have had both a positive and a negative impact upon their socio-economic situation. Their experiences show that there are several obstacles and scepticisms that have inhibited positive social action. One of the founding members of Sangre y Sol cooperative stated that politicians and members of associations "take advantage of us, steal the money that was for us, for we are illiterate and we don't know about those things."[32] Another member of Carters Cooperative, while describing their multiple organising strategies, added: "I have started primary school again because we are tired of getting ripped-off for being illiterate … so many times they took advantage of us."[33]

A member of a different cooperative,[34] denouncing the cooperative, noted that "where I work, the leader take advantage of us, he continuously exploits us and everyone must stay quiet and do what he says or you don't have your job anymore … that is not a cooperative."[35] Similar grievance is vented by another carter, who observed: "I've changed cooperatives because I was tired, we were robbed all the time, the money that was supposed to be for us, the medicine for the horses …."[36]

Alongside these negative experiences, waste pickers have also been able to grasp and keep the best of their experiences. Like the experience of the waste pickers in Kolkata, these organising mechanisms helped them gain public visibility as well as political and communication skills. Particularly lawyers and accountants were important to get them through the tedious bureaucratic procedures necessary to become legal persons. In 2010, two cooperatives were included as part of the governmental recycling process after a hard bargain with the government representatives. Lawyers were, in the bargaining process, a nexus between the government and the carters. The role of this kind of nexus becomes extremely important, since the legal language is in itself an exclusionary mechanism that widens the gap between governmental bureaucratic arrangements and the most vulnerable of the population.

Waste pickers played an important role as a political powerhouse for the negotiations. Whenever the negotiation got into a blind spot, carters would develop active political strategies, such as demonstrations or road blockades. The comparison between Kolkata and Córdoba shows a particular dynamism in organising mechanisms that provide the bases for what we refer to as the broader collective approach. The following final remarks of this chapter point out the potentialities and pitfalls of these experiences for improving the conditions of informal workers in line with their right to a dignified life.

In conclusion: a broad-based collective approach for informal workers' organisation

The examples of organisations of informal waste pickers in Kolkata, India and Córdoba, Argentina show that in spite of social and political marginalisation, informal workers are increasingly using their collective agency in order to develop a countermovement against the dominant political discourse. Alioum Idrissou also reports a similar instance of an informal workers' countermovement from Cameroon in this volume. By looking at urban waste pickers' organising experiences – as trade unions and as cooperatives – in India and Argentina, we highlight the ways in which efficient collective action could be devised by informal workers to overcome their marginalisation. These experiences provide the bases for a possible broad-based collective approach to organising informal workers.

As we mention earlier, the rights-based approach pursued in isolation inherently brings the risk of increasing workers' marginalisation by excluding their voices, demands and proposals from state policies. This exclusion, in turn, diminishes their political position and does not acknowledge informal workers as proactive agents. Another objection to such strategies is that they tend to be promoted mainly by non-worker elites. NGOs have been particularly criticised for being democratically unaccountable organisations in this respect: their agenda may be determined by their funding bodies, and there is sometimes lack of transparency in the functioning of some NGOs (Ebrahim, 2005, pp. 1–3; Kilby, 2011, pp. 103–109; Meritus, 1999, p. 1340; Castells, 2000, pp, 5, 13).

However, as we have seen, an NGO has been central in the organisation strategy of waste pickers in Kolkata, India. Such integration might undermine the autonomy of the informal workers and their trade union movement, and such collaboration could also vitiate a trade union movement with suspicions related to transparency and accountability. Further, institutions such as the WB NUJS Legal Aid Society and the NGO might dominate and dictate the agenda of a workers' organisation. The workers' voice might also get lost in the process, and as a result, an organisation initiative might not become a truly grassroots movement, just like the rights-based approach. On the other hand, a purely worker-centric grassroots movement in groups that suffer from systematic marginalisation, illiteracy and other sorts of vulnerability would result in their entanglement in bureaucratic networks and officialdoms.

Informal workers need to bargain mainly (but not solely) with the state and not with employers (Agarwala, 2013). Accordingly, their priority is to enhance their bargaining power vis-à-vis the state – an entity characterised by obscure administrative forms, regulations, legal conditions, bookkeeping requirements, and skilful government representatives who manage the system from within and know that by changing one word or comma, or adding a particular requirement, substantial claims of the workers may be rendered unfeasible. These experiences suggest that the dilemma between a purely worker-based grassroots approach and a rights-based strategic approach needs to be superseded by a broad-based collective approach, which is able to bring together joint efforts of informal workers and other more privileged entities in the struggle for a dignified life.

Far from being a naïve proposal, the broad-based collective approach promotes strategic relations involving informal workers, the state and other institutions. Non-state entities such as NGOs, research institutions, activists, universities and professionals can all become coalition partners at different stages of the informal workers' organisation process. This coalition causes informal workers' organisations to be socially and politically broad-based. In this context, each organisation needs to ascertain which institutions and individuals might be important for its specific circumstances. Once these are identified, informal workers' organisations need to integrate them into their collective action.

Notwithstanding the significance of coalitions in furtherance of informal workers' collective action, coalitions should allow autonomy to informal workers in the decision-making process. Even though partnerships are fundamental, the fact that elite partners tend to be in a better position to bargain with the state presents a risk for workers' autonomy. In that sense, valuable partnerships in a broad-based collective approach are those which can work as facilitators of deeper debates, thereby inculcating political and communication skills in workers. The informal workers' organisations discussed earlier do not completely fit into the notion of a contributory, membership-based and autonomous trade union of workers. That notion of trade unionism is based on certain assumptions. The assumptions are: that the workers work together in an industry or establishment; that they are aware of the advantages of association; that they have reasonably sufficient information about the issues involving the stakeholders relating to their work; that they are aware of the social, economic and political context of their work; and that they have an employer with whom they are to bargain in order to promote their interests.

These assumptions, rooted in the industrial production process, do not hold true for informal workers engaged in varieties of informal economic activities, primarily in the Global South and increasingly in the Global North, as is discussed in the Introduction and other chapters in this volume. Since these assumptions do not hold true for informal economic activities and informal workers, there is a visible gap between the enormous number of informal workers engaged in different activities and the number of their membership-based organisations or trade unions (Haan, Sen, 2007; Chen *et al.*, 2007, pp. 3, 8, 12).

The primary difference between membership-based and beneficiary-centred organisations is that functionally membership-based organisations adopt a participatory method, while beneficiary-centred organisations adopt a benevolent method towards their functioning (even these two approaches have different variations). While a participatory method for autonomous decision-making and functioning through trade unions might be more effective and, indeed, the preferable form of organisation under most circumstances, in view of the contingencies surrounding informal work and the obstacles posed by governmental agencies, sometimes other alliances are vital in order to overcome restrictive conditions. Integration of different institutions and individuals makes organising initiatives a wider social phenomenon, not limited only to the perspective – both intellectual and strategic – of informal workers such as waste pickers.

In relation to the state, the broad-based collective approach proposes to overcome the adversarial approach that is generally associated with trade union activism and focuses on the possibilities that different institutions of the state may have to offer. The state consists of varieties of institutions: the parliament, the judiciary, the members of parliament, the opposition parties, the local administrators and local elected representatives. Each of these entities may open up room for a variety of possibilities for informal workers at different times. Even awareness of the plural and multidimensional possibilities that state institutions can offer would also necessitate strategic alliances.

The proposed organisation approach is fluid and works incrementally. Thus, the drawback of the proposed organisation model is that it is incapable of bringing in radical changes in socio-political structures, which might be necessary for significant changes in the lives of informal workers. Moreover, there are possibilities of external pressure and ulterior motives vitiating workers' collective action. Irrespective of these drawbacks, we need to be mindful that the incremental, wider social network-based, somewhat fluid, short-term agenda-centric organisation mechanism is only the initial stage in promoting informal workers' bargaining power. However, this organisation approach does not envisage a coalition of privileged and marginalised groups so that the privileged can espouse the marginalised groups' cause (Chen *et al.*, 2007, pp. 5–6). Any coalition with other entities should be initiated on the terms set by the organising informal workers in furtherance of their strategic agenda.

As we indicate in this chapter, informal workers in the Global South are already pushing back through their strategic organising mechanisms to pursue their right to a dignified life. At a time when the countries of the Global North are witnessing rapid erosion of labour rights, a systematic increase in unemployment rates, and the unpromising future that traditional resistance mechanisms used to offer, the North, too, might learn a lesson or two in strategic organising from the initiatives of some of the most vulnerable workers of the Global South. To sum up, the organising approach we are advocating in this chapter proposes to make use of plural opportunities and building wider social networks in furtherance of an organisation-mediated improvement in informal workers' lives.

Notes

1 Employment in the informal sector and informal employment refer to different aspects of informality. Employment in the informal sector is an enterprise-based concept and covers persons working in units that have "informal" characteristics in relation to the legal status, registration, size, the registration of the employees, their bookkeeping practices, etc. Informal employment is a job-based concept and encompasses those persons whose main jobs lack basic social or legal protections or employment benefits and may be found in the formal sector, the informal sector or households. See ILO, *Statistical Update on Employment in the Informal Economy*, June 2012. ILO – Department of Statistics. http://laborsta.ilo.org/applv8/data/INFORMAL_ECONOMY/2012-06-Statistical%20update%20-%20v2.pdf (Accessed 25 September 2014).

2 See the Constitution of India, 1949; also the National Constitution of Argentina, 1853 (1994).

3 The coordinated programme includes national and multinational companies that voluntarily joined the Corporate Social Responsibility and Decent Work Network and the UN Global Compact Network. Enterprises in both networks follow coordinated actions in the country designed to lead to labour standards good practices.

  Further information on the local policy can be found at Objectivos de Desarrollo del Milenio, available at http://www.politicassociales.gob.ar/odm/publicaciones.html (Accessed 30 September 2014).

  Further information on the country's reports to the coordination at United Nations Development Group on this issue is available at: http://undg.org/home/country-teams/latin-america-the-carribean/argentina/ (Accessed 22 January 2016).

4 Further information can be accessed in the report Decent Work and Social Responsibility in Argentina, available at http://www.trabajo.gov.ar/downloads/responsabilidad/trabajo_decente.pdf (Accessed 10 September 2014).

5 Integrated Retirement System, 2014 (n# 24.476).

6 Small Taxpayer's Simplified Social Scheme (*Monotributo Social*), 2003 (n# 25.865).

7 See, generally, Self Employed Women's Association (SEWA) at http://www.sewa.org/ (Accessed 5 January 2014).

8 Ibid. (Accessed 20 June 2014).

9 The *Sramajibee Mahila Samiti* (SMS) is a society registered under the Societies Registration Act, 1860.

10 See, generally, *Central de Trabajadores Argentinos*, available at http://www.cta.org.ar (Accessed 20 September 2014).

11 See, generally, *Força Sindical*, available at http://www.fsindical.org.br/new/ (Accessed 20 September 2014); also Rerum Novarum Confederation, available at http://rerumnovarum.or.cr/apps/ (Accessed 20 September 2014).

12 See StreetNet International, available at http://www.streetnet.org.za/index.php (Accessed 20 September 2014).

13 See Women in Informal Employment: Globalizing and Organizing, available at http://wiego.org (Accessed 20 September 2014).

14 This section of the chapter has been earlier published in Routh, S. (2014). *Enhancing Capabilities through Labour Law: Informal Workers in India*. New York: Routledge.

15 The study in Kolkata, India was undertaken by Supriya Routh as part of his doctoral research. He employed semi-structured interviewing and participant observation

methods for his study. He interviewed 75 waste pickers, six middle-persons (intermediaries), nine government officials, five elected representatives, and 11 trade union leaders and organisers. A more detailed version of the study can be found in Routh (2014).

16 Interview conducted on 29 June 2011 in Kolkata, India.

17 Interview conducted on 9 June 2011 in Kolkata, India.

18 Interview conducted on 22 June 2011 in New Delhi, India.

19 Meeting on 12 June 2011 at the Calcutta Samaritans Office at Ripon Street in Kolkata, India.

20 Interview conducted on 30 June 2011 at the Calcutta Samaritans Office at Ripon Street in Kolkata, India.

21 The West Bengal National University of Juridical Sciences (WB NUJS) is a premier law university in India, located in the city of Kolkata. See http://nujs.edu/index.html (Accessed 20 September 2014).

22 Inaugural convention of the trade union initiative, 6 July 2011 in Kolkata, India.

23 Meeting of the Executive Committee of BPSSS on 6 July 2011 at the West Bengal National University of Juridical Sciences, Kolkata, India.

24 Legal Aid Society – Brief Report of Activities Undertaken over the Period from July 2011 to January 2012; also e-mail conversation with Prof. Anirban Chakraborty, assistant professor and faculty advisor of the Legal Aid Society, the West Bengal National University of Juridical Sciences, Kolkata, India, on 8 February 2012.

25 e-mail conversation with Prof. Anirban Chakraborty, ibid., on 5 February 2012.

26 Ibid.

27 Ibid.

28 "Open House Discussion on Deemed Homeless", AWWRI Project of NUJS Legal Aid Society & Center for Human Rights, National Conference on Place of Deemed Homeless in Good Governance and Inclusive Growth in India, 27–29 January 2012, WB NUJS Campus (in file with author).

29 e-mail conversation with Prof. Anirban Chakraborty, ibid.

30 See, generally, National Movement of Cardboard pickers and Recyclers, available at http://www.mocar.org.ar (Accessed 30 September 2014).

31 This data was collected as part of PhD research titled "Living in the Legal Limbo: Sex Workers and Cardboard Pickers' Legal Struggles in Cordoba-Argentina", carried out by Marisa N. Fassi during 2011–2014. The data collection included primary sources such as in-depth interviews (19 cardboard pickers, five NGOs and professionals, and an interview with the civil servant in charge of dealing with urban recyclers' matters) as well as secondary sources (newspaper articles, official websites, reports, international agreements, contextual literature).

32 Interview conducted on 9 November 2013 in Cordoba, Argentina.

33 Interview conducted on 26 November 2013 in Cordoba, Argentina.

34 Ethical considerations do not allow the disclosure of this interviewed membership.

35 Interview conducted on 19 November 2013 in Cordoba, Argentina.

36 Interview conducted on 20 December 2013 in Cordoba, Argentina.

References

Agarwala, R. (2013). *Informal Labor, Formal Politics, and Dignified Discontent in India*. New York: Cambridge University Press.

Antony, P. (2001). *Towards Empowerment: Experiences of Organizing Women Workers*. New Delhi: ILO.

Bermúdez, N.V. (2009). Sueño de pibe...de oficios, clasificaciones y distinciones en Villa Sangre y Sol, Córdoba-Argentina, *Revista del Museo de Antropología*, 2, pp. 103–118.

Bhatt, E.R. (2006). *We Are Poor but So Many: The Story of Self-Employed Women in India*. New York, Oxford: University Press.

Busso, M. (2004). *Los Trabajadores Informales y sus Formas de Organizacion Colectiva – Un Estudio en Ferias de la Ciudad de la Plata (2001-2003)*. Maestría en Cs Sociales. Universidad de Buenos Aires, Buenos Aires.

Castells, M. (2000). *Globalización, Estado y sociedad civil: el nuevo contexto histórico de los derechos humanos. Isegoría*, 22, pp. 5–17.

Chen, M., Jhabvala, R., Kanbur, R., Richards, C. (2007). Membership-Based Organizations of the Poor – Concepts, Experience and Policy. In M. Chen, R. Jhabvala, R. Kanbur, C. Richards (Eds), *Membership-Based Organizations of the Poor* (pp. 3–20). New York: Routledge.

De Haan, A., Sen, S. (2007). Working Class Struggles, Labour Elites, and Closed Shops – The Lessons from India's Trade Unions and Experiences of Organisation. In M. Chen, R. Jhabvala, R. Kanbur, C. Richards (Eds), *Membership-Based Organizations of the Poor* (pp. 65–82). New York: Routledge.

Ebrahim, A. (2005). *NGOs and Organizational Change – Discourse, Reporting, and Learning*. Cambridge, UK: Cambridge University Press.

Hensman, R. (2010). Labour and Globalization: Union Responses in India. In P. Bowles and J. Harriss (Eds), *Globalization and Labour in China and India* (pp. 189–206). Hampshire: Palgrave Macmillan.

Hill, E. (2010). *Worker Identity, Agency and Economic Development: Women's Empowerment in the Indian Informal Economy*. New York: Routledge.

Jha, P. (2005–2006). *Globalization and Labour in India: The Emerging Challenges*. http://www.nottingham.ac.uk/shared/shared_scpolitics/documents/gwcprojectPapers/India.pdf (Accessed 16 June 2012).

Kapoor, A. (2007). The SEWA Way: Shaping Another Future for Informal Labour. *Futures*, 39, pp. 554–568.

Kilby, P. (2011). *NGOs in India – The Challenges of Women's Empowerment and Accountability*. London and New York: Routledge.

Meritus, J. (1999). From Legal Transplants to Transformative Justice: Human Rights and the Promise of Transnational Civil Society. *Am. U. Int'l L. Rev.* 14(5), pp. 1335–1389.

NCEUS (2007). *Report on Conditions of Work and Promotion of Livelihoods in the Unorganised Sector*. August 2007. New Delhi: NCEUS.

NCEUS (2009). *The Challenge of Employment in India – An Informal Economy Perspective*. Volume 1 Main Report. April 2009. New Delhi: NCEUS.

Routh, S. (2014). *Enhancing Capabilities through Labour Law: Informal Workers in India*. New York: Routledge.

Self Employed Women's Association (SEWA). http://www.sewa.org/ (Accessed 5 January 2014).

Workers and the global informal economy

Issues and perspectives

Vando Borghi

Informality, formality: going and return

Whatever definition of informality we decide to refer to, the literature about it presents a large convergence regarding its structural nature. Despite many (partially different) interpretations of the modernisation theory, according to which informality was a residual reminiscence of the past, and was expected to disappear as a society approaches modernity, informality remains a prominent phenomenon – one scholar says (Harris-White, 2010; see also Breman, van der Linden, 2014), a growing one – in both Northern and Southern countries. As already stressed in Routh and Borghi (see Introduction to this book), figures on informality show that it oscillates between 10 and 20 per cent of global output in developed countries and one-third of global output in the rest of the world. Whereas *undeclared work* constitutes a significant problem in Western European societies, even if variegated in its forms and motivations, ILO data suggest that informality constitutes 48 per cent of non-agricultural employment in North Africa, 51 per cent in Latin America, 65 per cent in Asia, and 72 per cent in sub-Saharan Africa. In particular, in the African continent, estimations report that the magnitude of informal economy ranges from 50 to 80 per cent of gross domestic product (GDP) and, more importantly, generates 90 per cent of new jobs.[1]

Moreover, not only does informality negate those visions insisting on its supposed unavoidable fate of progressive disappearance, but it also demonstrates a structural and dynamic relationship with what is conventionally identified as the formal economy. One of the main thrusts of our book is the connection of the neo-liberal global capitalist process of restructuring with informality, which is far from being an inverse correlation. According to some scholars, growth itself, far from formalising the informal, produces it (see, for instance, Harris-White, 2010). Both "the interstitial informal economy" – developed in and around formal businesses or state bureaucracies – and "small-scale informality" – a very heterogeneous field of work and firms not registered, under the threshold size for taxation, not easily distinguishable from the household producing it – finds opportunities for development where the economy in general is growing. "When it was recognized and named, the informal economy was expected to disappear. It is doing the opposite in every part of the world" (Harris-White, 2010, p. 178).

At the same time, when socio-economic decline and crisis are experienced, as they are currently, the informal economy negates (new) expectations and displaces mainstream representations as well. According to the latter, in the evaluations of economic journalists, policy-makers, and/or transnational agencies and organisations, informal economy should act as a second opportunity, a waiting or transit room for labour surplus pushed out from formal work, in which working men and women can arrange themselves through temporary income-sharing solutions until a new favourable economic wave. Nevertheless, looking at the insights of some of the experts, we "have never found any evidence that such a horizontal drift has taken place" (Breman, 2009, p. 33). On the contrary, under the impact of the global crisis, the informal economy is also registering a significant worsening of working conditions and earnings (ibid., p. 31), and the Self-Employed Women's Association reports that "incomes have declined, days of work decreased, prices have fallen and livelihoods disappeared".[2]

Nonetheless, benevolent interpretations of informality go beyond the *defensive* representation of it as the last safety net, and detect in the informal economy the sheer soul of the economy itself, which is compressed, bureaucratised and restrained in the regulated formal economy. In this perspective, informality is no longer a wreck of the past, or a second temporary opportunity; it becomes the model which the formal economy should adopt. In this context, a growing proportion of the global workforce is experiencing – within the formal economy (via outsourcing, subcontracting, the "dormitory labour regime,"[3] and so on) – quasi-informal working conditions: here, informality becomes "simply a way to reduce the price of labour, to reduce it to a pure commodity, with no provisions for security or sustainable working conditions, let alone for protection against adversity. You buy labour but only for as long as you need it; then you get rid of it again. That is very much the way of the informal economy" (Breman, 2015: 57–58).[4]

This does not mean that any border between formality and informality, or between free and unfree labour (Barrientos *et al.*, 2013), is breaking down, that there is no longer a difference between working in formal and informal conditions, and that finally a new, global, homogeneous and uniform (dangerous) class of (precarious, insecure and underrepresented) workers is rising.[5] On the contrary, multiplication of borders and frontiers is a crucial device through which capitalism reproduces and innovates its own logics of working (Mezzadra, Nielson, 2013). Rather, it means that any attempt to understand and research informality needs to look at it as a historical product of the structural relationship between formality and informality, which is at the very core of evolutionary development of capitalism.

Bringing informality back into capitalism

The other big question motivating our book has been the ways in which informal work affects workers' *human agency*. In order to answer that question, we need to specifically contextualise our agenda. The evolution and the changing dynamics of formality and informality have to be examined as a historical result of the development and metamorphosis of capitalism. In this sense, instead of insisting again, as happened for a long time in the international debate, on the "varieties of capitalism" (Peck, Theodore, 2007), we should respond to Wolfgang Streeck's invitation (2009, p. 1) about the fact that "the time has come to think, again, about the *commonalities* of capitalism". According to this perspective, we have to abandon any generic idea "of an abstract 'economy' as a distinct sphere of social life" and "the misunderstanding that economic action is about uncontested and incontestable common objectives [...] to be identified by scientific analysis and incorporated in specifically designed institutions" (Streeck, 2009, p. 232).

Streeck writes (2012, p. 3) that a capitalist society "or a society that is inhabited by a capitalist economy, is one that has on a current basis to work out how its *economic social relations*, its specific relations of production and exchange, are to connect to and interact with its *non-economic social relations.*" In such a society, economic social relations tend intrinsically to expand and to assume a dominant role, always attempting to subsume non-economic social relations into themselves.

Consequently, capitalism has to be studied in its different articulations (Streeck, 2012), which we can cover here only very briefly. First of all, capitalism as history has an endogenously unstable and dynamic nature, depending on its own expansion. Second, capitalism as culture is founded in a symbolic order arising within an imaginary of modern materialism (Mukerji, 1983) and shaping expectations, structure of needs, hierarchy of priorities, scientifically legitimated ideas (economy) of man, future, rationality (Appadurai, 2013, in particular Chapter 9), and so forth. Third, capitalism as polity is a field of conflict, to put it schematically, between two different principles of social organisation: one based on definitions of what is right and fair, the other inspired by logics of efficient allocation of resources based on marginal productivity. Finally, capitalism as a way of life is strictly interwoven with many and different ways of organising personal and intimate life, which are themselves affected by the process of expansion of marketisation and commodification. This often contrasted, ambiguous, ambivalent, and always incomplete subsumption of life into the global value chains (Tsing, 2009) affects daily individual and family life and many other social institutions, such as the concept of individualisation and self-realisation (Honneth, Hartmann, 2006; Honneth, 2004); the gendered "total social organization of labour" (Glucksmann, 2005; Nadin, Williams, 2012); the idea of the *social* as (also) a social and public policy responsibility (Borghi, 2011); the emotional structure of social relationships (Illouz, 2007); and so forth.

It should not be difficult to see in this framework that the formality/informality blending is systematically at stake in each of its dimensions. We can see, for example, that this blending immediately raises issues concerning ("capitalism as culture") the categories and the cultural schemes structuring actions and interventions: as Bhatt (2009) testifies, "when asked what the most difficult part of SEWA's journey has been, I can answer without hesitation: removing conceptual blocks. Some of our biggest battles have been over contesting pre-set ideas and attitudes of officials, bureaucrats, experts, and academics. Definitions are part of that battle." Again ("capitalism as a way of life"), informal employment (waged workers and self-employed), markets for labour, and arrangements between formal businesses and informal activities are all "persistently embedded in social institutions such as the state, language, caste, ethnicity, religion, gender, life cycle, space/locality, and – even in the non-farm economy – the needs of the local agroecology" (Harris-White, 2010, p. 172). For instance, gender "is used to reduce the costs of production, to reduce the probabilities of organization or unionization, to avoid the provision of the minimal standards of decency and safety at work required by the Labour Laws, to ignore the pay levels stipulated in Minimum Wages Laws, and to prevent access to social security" (ibid., p. 173). Informality ("capitalism as polity") is at stake also when issues of compromise between social justice principles and objectives of efficient resource allocation are raised, and the moral economy (Thompson, 1971) of people – their own judgement of the continuum of formality/informality – is questioned and mobilised. And, of course, the historical process of transformation and institutionalisation of the economy as a formal system is structurally interwoven with the historical evolution of its informal side.

This analytical perspective not only enables us to avoid any identification of informality as a residual part (or, worst, sector) of a modern (or modernising) capitalist economy; it also allows us to remove some of the misleading interpretive categories at work when informality is concerned. The North/South divide, for instance, still sometimes deployed (Roberts, 2014) for sketching "the geographical profile of global informality", is misleading if "taken to imply a distinction between a formal 'core' and an informal 'periphery'", because such a dualistic picture "does not capture the reach of informality and informalisation across all societies and economies" (Philips, 2011, p. 381). Moreover, what strongly emerges concerning our topics in the context of contemporary societies is the issues at the core of the first articulation mentioned above. The historically changing nature of formality/informality, which is part of the dynamic that Streeck summarises in the key dimension of "capitalism as history", is, indeed, particularly evident due to the profound changes and crisis that capitalism is undergoing. So, following the path outlined so far, we need to contextualise the connection between formality and informality in the contemporary historical framework.

Contextualising informalisation: the fading of the "société salariale"

The specific stage in which we have to understand the contemporary relation between formality and informality is the current crisis of what we can term *democratic capitalism*. The latter can be taken as a political economy produced by the already mentioned conflicting regimes of social organisation and resource allocation (Streeck, 2011). The first regime operates according to the idea of merit detected by the so-called "free play of market forces", whereas in the second, collective choices about social needs and relative entitlements are deliberated via "politics of need interpretation" (Fraser, 2013, pp. 53–82). The crisis of this political economy does not confine itself to only a political or an economic system: what is at stake here are the complex and multifaceted consequences of the fading of a (contingent) historical setting of the relationship between labour and society, which Robert Castel (1995) defined as "la société salariale" (the wage-earning society). Even if differentiated across space (full, partial, minimal or no application, not only along the North/South divide but also transversally) and time (from a relatively long period sometime after the Second World War, to a significantly shorter period, or only to a horizon of possibility elsewhere), this social, economic and political regime has played a crucial practical and symbolic role during the last century, giving a new shape to the relationship between labour and society (and, consequently, to the formality/informality blend).

The grammar of the relationship between labour and society characterising the "société salariale" was based on five great pillars (Castel, 1995 in particular Chapter 7), so that it could be schematically recalled. The first aspect concerns a clear and rigid distinction between those who are working regularly and stably according to standard arrangements and those outside of the labour market or who need to be integrated through specific measures (labour or welfare policies). The second concerns the workplace, to which any worker must be bound – the workplace resulting from a set of instructions, independent of the worker, to be strictly executed – and a labour process that is "scientifically" organised. A third pillar regards the relationship, now enabled by the wage itself, between workers and the mass production of goods and services: in this labour–society regime, the worker becomes a consumer of the goods who also contributes to produce. Then, according to the fourth pillar, the worker is inscribed in the condition of a subject who has the right to access social property (education, health, social protection, welfare; Castel, 2002), financed via a fiscal system to which he or she contributes. Finally, the worker is embedded in a framework of rights and labour laws, which configures him or her as a member of a collectivity: the social status enabled by this membership positions the worker above and beyond the solely individual dimension of the labour contract.

Even if this framework was the result of a historical, conflicting process of progressive institutionalisation of the relationship between labour and society, informality has always been present at the border of, in the interstices of, and together with, these pillars. Some of these pillars – for instance, the framework of rights and laws enabling the worker as a member of a collectivity – have increased the distance between formality and informality, whereas some other features of the "société salariale" – for instance, as far as the many duties of social reproduction are concerned – have also been reached through, or in combination with, the informal dimension. As we already said, if we consider the "total social organization of labour" (Glucksmann, 2005; Nadin, Williams, 2012), even the most formalised employment or activity always presupposes some informal, paid and unpaid, labour. The approach we are drawing here – a "structuralist" perspective, versus the dualistic and legalist perspectives – enables us to point out what really does make the difference to working life, either formal or informal, i.e. *power relations*. Informality and formality can, indeed, be understood "as referring to a set of conditions in which people work and the sets of power relations and practices (employment practices, regulation or its absence) that shape those conditions. The 'informal' thus exists within the 'formal', not simply alongside it, and *vice versa*" (Phillips, 2011, p. 389).

The turning point, as far as our interest in the continuum of formality and informality is concerned, consists in the fact that the regime of the "société salariale" has increasingly faded since the 1970s. The extent of decline of that labour–society relation has led some scholars to talk about the rise of a global regime of informalisation as a multi-sited strategy. The essence of this labour and work regime "is a type of waged employment thoroughly flexibilized and unregulated by public intervention. There is nothing to prevent the degradation of labour to a commodity, pure and simple, that is unprotected and can be bought at the lowest possible price and only for as long or as short as the labour power is required. 'Hire and fire' is the *modus operandi*" (Breman, van der Linden, 2014, p. 7). In this sense, the new global *social question* is emerging.

However, it is to be stressed as well that simply employing the same interpretive categories in the same way as they were employed for the *social question* in the past century would be misleading. For instance, the global context we are describing, of course, calls for the concept of "exploitation". Nonetheless, contemporary network capitalism presents many differences from the past context. One of the deepest analyses of the "new spirit of capitalism" has redefined the concept of exploitation in terms of "differentials of mobility", emphasising the asymmetries of mobility that characterise different possibilities to take advantage of the global networks and to appropriate the value produced along them (Boltanski, Chiapello, 1999, in particular Chapter 6). At the same time, commodification – as an experience concerning not only work, but also land, water, education, health, and many other spheres of common life – becomes "the key experience in our world today", whereas often "exploitation, while essential to any *analysis* of capitalism, is not *experienced* as such" (Burawoy, 2010, p. 307).[6] Struggles rooted in experiences of commodification, moreover, "are especially important in countries of the South where wage laborers are a shrinking elite, where informalization and dispossession define the experience of subalternity" (Burawoy, 2008, p. 384). The declining "société salariale" has not (yet) been substituted by another stable labour–society framework, and the contemporary social landscape presents many ambiguities, ambivalences and contradictions. For these reasons, the emerging new labour–society regime and the corresponding reshaping of the formality–informality continuum demand research to which our book can only partially, even if we hope usefully, contribute.

Notes on researching formality–informality: looking forward

This book is focused on a specific concern for individual autonomy and the relationship between autonomy and formality/informality. While conceptualising informal economic activities, one needs to be mindful of the experiences of workers themselves. One needs to inquire whether workers exercise choice over their work; how constrained such choices are; how social norms shape such choices; what are their own experiences of their work lives; whether their work opens up opportunities to them or restricts their well-being and agency; and what role culture plays in determining the contours of informality. Unless these aspects are brought centrally into the debates on informality, the idea associated with the term will remain obscure. Accordingly, we invited scholars from different countries and different disciplines – including law, anthropology, sociology, political sciences, economics and history – to explore these issues.

The different chapters collected here point out some relevant aspects for any further research effort. We can very briefly summarise here some key points resulting from our collective exploration, (partially) following the matrix of key variables elaborated by Vande Walle (2008). For a long time, informality has been understood according to specific disciplinary perspectives, and the discipline of economics has been largely hegemonic in these studies (Vande Walle, 2008, p. 653). More recently, since the 1980s, the importance of an interdisciplinary approach for defining, investigating and discussing formality–informality has been underlined. In our book, in particular, we emphasise the relevance of combining the analysis of the empirical characteristics and metamorphosis of the formal–informal relation (engaging sociology, economics, history) with inquiries reflecting the normative side of our issue, which is particularly crucial for legal scholars, and also for anyone attempting to contribute to public policy dealing with the formal–informal interaction (Fragale, La Hovary, Dumas, this book). Law is, therefore, at the centre of many chapters of the book (see also Routh, 2014), as it plays a delicate and complex role in the terrain in which the relationship between actors' freedom to pursue the life they have reason to value and the formality/informality continuum has to be formalised.

The state, in this regard, is a particularly important actor in the formality–informality interaction. Whereas the state is very often assumed to be a passive actor, merely responding to neo-liberal demands to loosen its control and avoid its responsibility, authors in this book clearly point out the active role of the state in conditioning the formal–informal relation. The state, through regulation, enforcement and control, is always simultaneously part of the problem and of the solution. It contributes to imposing formality as well as inducing informality; and it does so in many different ways, depending on the different contexts we concretely observe in the formal–informal evolution (Slavnic, Zheng, this book).

Confirming the most accurate research in this field, some chapters demonstrate that informality is not a residual factor of modern (or modernising) economies or something like an inheritance from the past. In these analyses, informality is studied as part of the general process of economic development, where economic development is constitutive of the combination of formality and informality (Williams, Martinez, Constantin, Danani, Lindenboim, Bizyukov, this book). Another way to investigate the complex (not merely residual) nature of informality has to do with some potentially positive aspects it accomplishes, that is, the functionality of informality. This can emerge in different forms, such as social cohesion (not only among ethnic minorities; Williams, 2006), strategic organisation, alternative networks for accessing services (for instance, borrowing money), enabling socio-economic opportunities for individual development of social actors otherwise marginalised or oppressed (for instance, Eastern European women going to work in Western European cities) (Idrissou, Routh, Fassi, this book).

More generally, the book insists (but much remains to be done, in this regard, in terms of research and analysis) on the crucial relevance of an approach to formality–informality interaction that takes seriously into account actors' capability and agency, that is, actors' freedom to pursue the life they have reason to value (Sen, 1999). This perspective has a specific importance for the way law, in general, and labour law, in particular – which are a terrain specifically at the centre of analysis of this book – have to be interpreted: as we emphasised already in our Introduction to the book's primary arguments (Routh, Borghi, in this book). The relationship between law and formality/informality blending has to be reframed by looking at the final objective, which is individuals' freedom to choose the essence of their lives.

From a theoretical point of view, not only does this approach offer a more correct perspective for studying the relationship between actor and structure – focusing on their reciprocal interplay, instead of assuming a determinist unidirectional relationship in which the second element conditions the first, or vice versa; it also offers a normative framework, according to which positive or negative consequences and effects of the formality–informality continuum may be evaluated from time to time. If formality and informality are structurally intertwined, as we have recalled several times, this means that we need a point of view, a normative angle, from which we can distinguish progressive or regressive changes of that combination. Let's try, finally, to consider this possible aspect more carefully.

(Re)considering formality and informality through the lens of emancipation

In our discussion of the formality–informality relationship, we have some starting points. The first one is the combination of formal and informal dimensions and its *structural* relation: for instance, even the most formal employment always presupposes informal caring (usually gendered) work in order to be efficiently performed. In this sense, we come to the conclusion that simply opposing formality to informality in a dichotomous relationship (labour or other) is unhelpful. A second element is directly linked to the first, and represents a step forward for constructing a more fruitful approach to the formality–informality interplay: that is, in order to avoid dead ends, a more convincing cognitive strategy for analysing any specific labour–society regime in reality consists of assuming the *total social labour organisation*. Not only scholars, but also policy-makers, need, as a starting point, an effective representation of the state-of-the-art knowledge, and taking into account the whole "total social labour organisation" can be particularly helpful as far as the "informational basis of judgement for justice" is concerned (Sen, 1991, p. 16, 1999, pp. 56–57), which will be the basis on which policies are based.

A third aspect involves the normative objective we recalled at the end of the preceding paragraph. At stake here is the terrain on which a *critical* appraisal of the formality–informality continuum can be established, where "critical" means the perspective enabling the distinction between positive and negative effects of the transformation of the "total social labour organisation". Here, social actors' "capability for voice" – a concept combining (Bifulco, 2013) the capability approach offered by Sen, its cultural translation in terms of "capacity to aspire" (Appadurai, 2013) and the concept of "voice" (Hirschman, 1970) – has a central role. Capability for voice is, indeed, very important in public policy issues, as a focus on capability for voice "implies the active involvement of the individual in the rule-setting process" (Bonvin, Favarque, 2005, p. 283); such an involvement would have significant effects on the policy-making process. In this sense, "policies would be designed, implemented, and assessed in very different ways if all citizens were really capable of participating effectively in the public policy processes" (ibid., p. 271).

So, our third pillar for constructing a fruitful approach to the formality–informality continuum involves the evaluation, in which social actors must have an active, deliberative role, of the extent to which their labour conditions, in the situated and contextualised conditions of the formality–informality continuum, give them more possibilities to pursue the life they have reason to value. In this sense, it is the relationship between emancipation and economy that needs to discussed. Accordingly, the two fields of tension should always be considered. On the one hand is the field in which the plan of the formality–informality combination interplays with that of working conditions (Figure C.1). Here, a crucial aspect of the possibility of pursuing the life actors have reason to value is at stake, manifesting itself in the form of those "power relations" (Phillips, 2011) we already stressed. An actor's reasons for engaging in informal work may be very different, ranging from motives of "poverty escape" to "moonlighting" solutions or practices of solidarity (Pfau-Effinger, 2009) or others. The differences in terms of "power relations" can be very significant. The point here is that any analysis should seriously take into account the "different motivations of the actors involved" (ibid., p. 80).

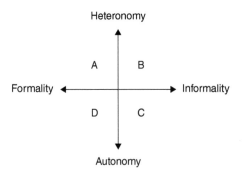

Figure C.1 Working conditions and power relations in formality–informality.

On the other hand, more generally, the structural blending of formality and informality has to be investigated in terms of its meaning for social ties. The economy always interacts with society (and vice versa), and this interaction can result in processes of disembedding[7] from or of (re-)embedding into social ties. What has to be addressed and analysed here (Figure C.2) is the social meaning that disembedding and embedding processes can have. In what circumstances can an economic activity transcending social ties enable an individual to better pursue the life she has reason to value? Or, on the contrary, can it impoverish individual autonomy? And in what circumstances do social ties play a role in social protection and, conversely, in limitation of individual freedom?

We owe to Karl Polanyi (2001) a fundamental discussion of the historical process that he defined as "great transformation", according to which, in the development of capitalism, the societal embeddedness of the economy was increasingly subject to a disembedding process resulting from a growing self-regulation of the economy. In his perspective, such a disembedding process would produce a societal reaction – the "countermovement"[8] – aiming at re-embedding the economy. In this scheme, disembedding has a negative meaning, whereas embeddedness is associated with a positive meaning, mainly in terms of social protection.

Polanyi's perspective is particularly valuable, as it enables critical analysis to avoid any economistic reductionism, taking into consideration social, cultural, political and institutional dynamics that do not merely function as economic principles of efficiency but are capable of producing social change. At the same time, our contemporary context asks for a reinterpretation of Polanyi's scheme. Polanyi's interpretation of the *great transformation* and the concept of *countermovement* opens up a space for emphasising the political dimension of the political economy, and emancipates the social aspects from being merely subsidiary to the economic ones (Streeck, 2009, p. 251). Moreover, and particularly important for our perspective on formality–informality-based analysis centred on actors' *capability for voice*, Polanyi's account of the great transformation brings to the foreground the projects of social actors. In this way, "the orthodox view of the crisis as an 'objective breakdown'" is rejected and it is conceived "instead as an *intersubjective* process" (Fraser, 2011, p. 144).

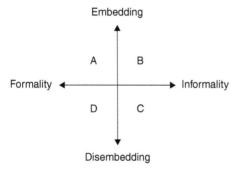

Figure C.2 Processes of disembedding/embedding and social condition.

However, at the same time, being systematically focused on harms caused by disembedded markets and commodification, Polanyi's analysis tends to neglect harms originating elsewhere, that is in the society itself, thus ignoring non-market (that is, embedded) forms of injustice – patriarchalism, for instance. We could find many examples in which informality in general, and informal work more specifically, have similar negative meaning (Harris-White, 2010); it is also a risk to overlook forms of social protection that are at the same time vehicles of domination (Fraser, 2011, p. 141). So, contemporary critical appraisal of the formality–informality continuum should resume and revise Polanyi's concept of countermovement, assuming as a key dimension of this revision a third social move (beyond the first one – disembedding as marketisation – and the second one – embedding as reaction in terms of social protection), that is, *emancipation.*

Emancipation introduces more complexity into an interpretative perspective otherwise based in a simplistic dualism between disembedding (as a bad move-ment due to the market dynamic) and (re-)embedding (as a positive movement of social protection). "Avoiding both wholesale condemnation of disembedding and wholesale approbation of reembedding" – as Nancy Fraser writes (ibid., p. 145) – "we must open both marketization and social protection to critical scrutiny. Exposing the normative deficits of society, as well as those of economy, we must validate struggles against domination *wherever* it roots"; in this sense, struggles for emancipation challenge "oppressive forms of social protection, while neither wholly condemning nor simply celebrating marketization" (ibid., p. 145).

What this emphasis on emancipation as a key normative factor for a criti-cal appraisal of the formality–informality regime and of the *total social labour organisation* enables us to introduce is a specific realm that a dualistic market/social protection scheme indistinctly conflates with society. This realm is the *public sphere.* This is the realm in which both society's *doxa* and the market's claims of efficient modernisation can be scrutinised, discussed, criticised and revised. Here lies the space in which the risks of *formalising the informality* (La Hovary, in this book), the cases of informalisation (via precariousness) of formal labour arrangements, or, in contrast, the situations in which informality (partially) enables social actors to approach, at least, the life they have reason to value, can be discussed and deliberated. The "informational bases" of this debate, the possibility of actors' voice to actively contribute to these informa-tional bases (capacity for voice; Bifulco, 2013; Bonvin, Favarque, 2005), and the role played by researchers in assuming actors' capacity for voice as an una-voidable dimension in the public debate about formality–informality are the key points we tried to draw attention to throughout our book.

Notes

1   Data and evaluations about the magnitude of the informal economy can be found in Schneider, Enste (2003), ILO (2002), Steel, Snodgrass (2008), Pfau-Effinger (2009), Benjamin *et al.* (2014).
2   See Self-Employed Women's Association newsletter, *We the Self-Employed*, no. 18, 15 May 2009.

3   Here, the border for differentiating workers is based on the condition of many workers in the Chinese factories being internal migrants: see Pun, Smith (2007).

4   "Another important reason why the informal economy is so popular among the employers and owners of capital—not to mention the Imf and World Bank—is because it makes collective action very difficult: the workforce is floating, so it's very hard to organize. If you sell your labour power standing in the morning market for the day, how can you engage in collective action with those around you, with your competitors?"

5   For critical discussions of the perspective of "the precariat" (Standing, 2011, 2014) see, among others, Breman (2013) and Munck (2013).

6   The relevance of the experience of commodification will lead us later to connect our analysis with the work of Karl Polanyi, who dedicated important parts of his work to its analysis.

7   "By disembedding" – Giddens (1991, p. 21) clarifies – "I mean the 'lifting out' of social relations from local contexts of interaction and their restructuring across indefinite spans of time-space."

8   Polanyi (2001, p. 138) defines the "countermovement" as "the principle of social protection aiming at the conservation of man and nature as well as productive organization, relying on the varying support of those most immediately affected by the deleterious action of the market – primarily, but not exclusively, the working and the landed classes – and using protective legislation, restrictive associations, and other instruments of intervention as its methods". This concept has recently received growing attention as an effective cognitive device for analysing social resistances to the contemporary "great transformation" and the last wave of commodification (see, for instance, Webster *et al.*, 2008; Streeck, 2014, pp. 56–57; for a critical discussion, see Burawoy, 2010).

References

Appadurai, A. (2013). *The Future as Cultural Fact.* London, New York: Verso.

Barrientos, S., Kothari, U., Phillips, N. (2013). Dynamics of Unfree Labour in the Contemporary Global Economy. *Journal of development studies*, 49(8), pp. 1037–1041.

Benjamin, N. Beegle, K., Recanatini, F., Santini, M. (2014). *Informal Economy and the World Bank.* World Bank, Policy Research Working Paper, 6888. http://econ.worldbank.org.

Bhatt, E.R. (2009). *Citizenship of Marginals.* Third R.K. Talwar Memorial Lecture, Indian Institute of Banking and Finance, Mumbai, 23 July, available at http://www.india-seminar.com/2010/605/605_ela_r_bhatt.htm (Accessed 20 January 2016).

Bifulco, L. (2013). Citizen Participation, Agency and Voice. *European journal of social theory*, 16(2), pp. 174–187.

Boltanski, L., Chiapello, È. (1999). *Le nouvel esprit du capitalism.* Paris: Gallimard (*The New Spirit of Capitalism.* London, New York: Verso, 2005).

Bonvin, J.-M., Favarque, N. (2005). What Informational Basis for Assessing Job-Seekers? Capabilities vs. Preferences. *Review of social economy*, 63(2), pp. 269–289.

Borghi, V. (2011). One-way Europe? Institutional Guidelines, Emerging Regimes of Justification and Paradoxical Turns in European Welfare Capitalism. *European journal of social theory*, 14(3), pp. 321–341.

Breman, J. (2009). Myth of the Global Safety Net. *New left review*, 59, pp. 29–36.

Breman, J. (2013). A Bogus Concept? *New left review*, 84, pp. 130–138.

Breman, J. (2015). A Footloose Scholar. Interview. *New left review*, 94, pp. 45–75.

Breman, J., van der Linden, M. (2014). Informalizing the Economy: The Return of the Social Question at a Global Level. *Development and change*, 45(5), pp. 920–940.

Burawoy, M. (2008). The Public Turn. From Labor Process to Labor Movement. *Work and occupations*, 35(4), pp. 371–387.

Burawoy, M. (2010). From Polanyi to Pollyanna: The False Optimism of Global Labor Studies. *Global labour studies*, 1(2), pp. 301–313.

Castel, R. (1995). *La métamorphose de la question sociale*. Paris: Fayard (*From Manual Workers to Wage Laborers: Transformation of the Social Question*. New Brunswick and London: Transaction Publishers, 2005).

Castel, R. (2002). Emergence and Transformations of Social Property. *Constellations*, 9(3), pp. 318–334.

Fraser, N. (2011). Marketization, Social Protection, Emancipation: Toward a Neo-Polanyian Conception of Capitalist Crisis. In C. Calhoun, G. Derluguian (Eds), *Business as Usual: The Roots of the Global Financial Meltdown*. New York: NYU Press.

Fraser, N. (2013). *Fortunes of Feminism*. London, New York: Verso.

Giddens, A. (1991). *The Consequences of Modernity*. Cambridge: Polity Press.

Glucksmann, M. (2005). Shifting Boundaries and Interconnections: Extending the "Total Social Organization of Labor". *The Sociological Review*, 53(2), pp. 19–36.

Harris-White, B. (2010). Work and Wellbeing in Informal Economies: The Regulative Roles of Institutions of Identity and the State. *World development*, 38(2), pp. 170–183.

Hartmann, M., Honneth, A. (2006). Paradoxes of Capitalism. *Constellations*, 13(1), pp. 41–58.

Hirschman, A. (1970). *Exit, Voice, Loyalty: Responses to the Decline in Firms, Organizations, and States*. Cambridge, MA: Harvard University Press.

Honneth, A. (2004). Organized Self-Realization. Some Paradoxes of Individualization. *European Journal of Social Theory*, 7(4), pp. 463–478.

Illouz, E. (2007). *Cold Intimacies. The Making of Emotional Capitalism*. London: Polity Press.

ILO (2002). *Decent Work and the Informal Economy: Sixth Item on the Agenda*. Report VI, 90th session of the International Labour Conference. Geneva, 20 June.

Mezzadra, S., Neilson, B. (2013). *Border as Method, or, the Multiplication of Labor*. Durham, London: Duke University Press.

Mukerji, C. (1983). *From Graven to Images. Patterns of Modern Materialism*. New York: Columbia University Press.

Munck, R. (2013). The Precariat: A View from the South. *Third world quarterly*, 34(5), pp. 747–762.

Nadin, S., Williams, C.C. (2012). Blurring the Formal/Informal Economy Divide: Beyond a Dual Economies Approach. *Journal of economy and its applications*, 2(2), pp. 1–19.

Peck, J., Theodore, N. (2007), Variegated Capitalism. *Progress in human geography*, 31(6), pp. 731–772.

Pfau-Effinger, B. (2009). Varieties of Undeclared Work in European Societies. *British journal of industrial relations*, 47(1), pp. 79–99.

Philips, N. (2011). Informality, Global Production Networks and the Dynamics of "Adverse Incorporation". *Global networks*, 11(3), pp. 380–397.

Polanyi, K. (2001). *The Great Transformation*. Boston: Beacon.

Pun, Ngai, Smith, C. (2007). Putting Transnational Labour Process in its Place: The Dormitory Labour Regime in Post-Socialist China. *Work employment society*, 21(1), pp. 27–45.

Roberts, A. (2014). Peripheral Accumulation in the World Economy: A Cross-National Analysis of the Informal Economy. *International journal of comparative sociology*, 54(5/6), pp. 420–444.

Routh, S. (2014). *Enhancing Capabilities through Labour Law*. New York: Routledge.

Schneider, F., Enste, D.H. (2003). *The Shadow Economy: An International Survey*. Cambridge: Cambridge University Press.

Sen, A.K. (1991). Welfare, Preferences and Freedom. *Journal of econometrics*, 50, pp. 15–29.

Sen, A.K. (1999). *Development as Freedom*. Oxford: Oxford University Press.

Standing, G. (2011). *The Precariat: The New Dangerous Class*. London: Bloomsbury Academic.

Standing, G. (2014). Understanding the Precariat through Labour and Work. *Development and change*, 45(5), pp. 963–980.

Steel, W., Snodgrass, D. (2008). *Raising Productivity and Reducing Risks of Household Enterprises*. Diagnostic Methodology Framework, World Bank.

Streeck, W. (2009). *Re-Forming Capitalism. Institutional Change in the German Political Economy*. Oxford: Oxford University Press.

Streeck, W. (2011). A Crisis of Democratic Capitalism. *New Left review*, 71, pp. 1–25.

Streeck, W. (2012). How to Study Contemporary Capitalism? *Archives Européennes de Sociologie*, 53(1), pp. 1–28.

Streeck, W. (2014). Taking Crisis Seriously: Capitalism on Its Way Out. *Stato e Mercato*, 100, pp. 45–67.

Thompson, E.P. (1971). The Moral Economy of the English Crowd in the Eighteenth Century. *Past and Present*, 50(1), pp. 76–136.

Tsing, A. (2019). Supply Chains and the Human Condition. *Rethinking Marxism*, 21(2), pp. 148–176.

Vande Walle, G. (2008). A Matrix Approach to Informal Markets: Towards a Dynamic Conceptualisation. *International journal of social economics*, 35(9), pp. 651–665.

Webster, E., Lambert, R., Bezuidenhout, A. (2008). *Grounding Globalization. Labour in the Age of Insecurity*. Oxford: Blackwell.

Index

For Product Safety Concerns and Information please contact our EU
representative GPSR@taylorandfrancis.com
Taylor & Francis Verlag GmbH, Kaufingerstraße 24, 80331 München, Germany

www.ingramcontent.com/pod-product-compliance
Ingram Content Group UK Ltd.
Pitfield, Milton Keynes, MK11 3LW, UK
UKHW021006180425
457613UK00019B/820